+5.4[...] FRA
IWK

£16.99 ✓

DESIGN UK 2

DESIGN UK 2 MAX FRASER

First published in 2003 by
Conran Octopus Limited
a part of Octopus Publishing Group
2–4 Heron Quays, London E14 4JP

To order please ring Conran Octopus Direct
on 01903 828503

British Library Cataloguing-in-Publication Data.
A catalogue record for this book is available
from the British Library.

ISBN: 1 84091 318 5

Publishing Director: Lorraine Dickey
Senior Editor: Katey Day
Assistant Editor: Sybella Marlow
Art Director: Chi Lam
Design: johnson banks
Picture Research: Max Fraser
Production Manager: Angela Couchman

Printed in Italy

p 2: Porca Miseria by Ingo Maurer

conran
OCTOPUS

CONTENTS

INTRODUCTION.6
SHOPS.8
DESIGNERS.250
DIRECTORY.298

INTRODUCTION

Who would have predicted that in only two years since the launch of the first edition of *Design UK* in 2001, Britain would witness such a significant growth in the number of design shops? Though some of the shops from the first book have ceased trading, almost fifty new shops have appeared. Once considered a London-centric industry, cities like Cardiff, Leicester, Sheffield, Birmingham, and Newcastle can now boast high quality contemporary design shops of their own.

So what has caused this nationwide expansion? While overall retail sales have remained inconsistent, the design industry has received previously unseen levels of media attention, in turn sparking the public's imagination. Encouragingly, institutions like the Crafts Council, the Design Museum, and the Victoria & Albert Museum have seen an increase in visitor numbers; there are more publicly-accessible awards recognising talented UK designers such as the annual OXO Peugeot Design Awards; and each year, more exhibitions and design events are introduced, culminating in September with 100% Design and Designersblock. More of the major Italian producers have realized that the UK accounts for a major percentage of their overall European sales and companies like B&B Italia, Artemide, Ligne Roset, and Poliform have opened dedicated own-brand showrooms. On the opposite extreme from the big boy brands, small, unique, independent stores also continue to crop up in unusual locations and collectively represent a trend towards individualism. That said, you will notice when reading through this book that there are many independent retailers who prefer the financial security conferred by selling big brands. I would urge them to search harder for new designs from lesser known producers and individuals, helping to differentiate their business from the rest.

The Designers chapter illustrates only a handful of the UK talents who can make this distinction possible. I have chosen these twenty designers from across the country, always searching for problem-solvers with an individual approach to a common goal. Each designer is different from the next – some are very brand orientated, others are concept driven, some are hands-on, while others strive for success in the mass market. Each one has responded to a common brief – simply to design a product of their choice for exclusive publication in *Design UK 2*. Such an open brief naturally yields a variety of results and this chapter helps to represent the diversity of talented individuals in Britain. I'm sure you'll agree that they shouldn't go unnoticed. And clearly they don't, as the designers from the first edition of this book have proved in a summary of their progress in the Where Are They Now? chapter.

The design industry is flourishing in the UK and that is thanks to you. May I encourage you to continue investing both your time and money in desirable interior products by using this guide to steer you around the UK's temples of contemporary living. Should you discover any new design shops or talented designers on your travels, please let me know.

Max Fraser
max@maxfraser.com
www.maxfraser.com

Icons

These icons will enable you to see the location of each store at a glance. They also show which products are stocked in each store.

 South-east England

 South-west England & Wales

 Midlands

 North England

 Scotland

 Northern Ireland

 Channel islands

 Nationwide

 Originals

 Furniture

 Lighting

 Glassware & Ceramics

 Textiles

 Tableware

 Jewellery

 Clothing

 Books

ALMA MORRIS & CO CHAPLI
MAC B&B ITALIA ROOST SC
THE CONRAN SHOP TONY WA
MINT BOWLES AND LINARES
DESIGNERS GUILD ATOMIC I
FLIN FLON THE DESIGN MUSE
PLANET BAZAAR SKANDIUM
LIVING SPACE VIADUCT SED
PURVES & PURVES UTILITY
LLOYD DAVIES CENTRAL FL
POP UK TWENTYTWENTYON
BUDGE + COWARD UNTO THI
OXO TOWER WHARF ISOKON

MASON LOUNGE CAPSULE
NG THE ROOM STORE BATIK
ER INTERIORS FUSION SARF
VERDOSE ON DESIGN PREGO
ERIORS MISSION **SHOPS** SCP
M SHOP LOUNGE HER HOUSE
LESSI EQUINOX INNERFORM
14 HOLLAND STREET MART
OFFREY DRAYTON ARTEMIDE
CHRISTOPHER FARR HEAL'S
FANDANGO TOM TOM VITRA
AST TEMPTER ARIA MOOCH
US CVO FIREVAULT LOFT XU

ABODE INTERIORS

DESIGNERS INCLUDE:
Cattelan
Dan Form
Fabbian
Heine Design
Innermost
Jesper Holm
Linie Design
Max Watt
Minotti
Naos
Verikon

SERVICES:
Bespoke Orders
Gift Vouchers
Interior Advice
Wedding List

CLOSE TO:
Capsule

Abode Interiors
7 – 9 Market Place
Leicester LE1 5GG
0116 262 9909
www.abode-interiors.co.uk
Open: Mon – Fri 10 – 5
Sat 9 – 6

Martin Coles opened Abode Interiors in the heart of Leicester in December 2002, at last contributing to the city's previously dry designscape. Occupying Leicester's oldest commercial building just a stone's throw from the rather ugly main market square, Martin and his family have returned this beautiful old property to its former glory. Stripping away any remnants of previous occupants, the new proprietors have transformed the merged 15th- and 18th-century buildings into a tantalising textural backdrop for modern European furniture and lighting. They have exposed the original features of the premises, such as the stunning oak floorboards, chunky wooden beams, and the earthy red brick walls, inserting modern touches only where necessary. The nature of the inherited layout means the shop space is split up into many different rooms at varying levels, giving a sense of discovery at every turn.

At Abode, they have opted for a contemporary style of product, with work from the likes of Minotti, Cattelan, Naos, Dan Form, Heine Design, Verikon, Jasper Holm, Fabbian, Max Watt, Linie Design, and Innermost. However, realising that high-end furniture can sometimes appear rather sterile when displayed on its own, they have opted for a few choice accessory items and artwork to soften their displays. Customers are greeted on entry, and then left alone to browse the various room sets, safe in the knowledge that efficient help and advice are on hand if required.

Serious effort and passion have been invested in the Coles' retail venture, and the project has also clearly received plenty of attention to detail – their slick brand packaging being one evident example of this. It is exciting to witness introductions like Abode Interiors to the city of Leicester, as it clearly illustrates that the appeal of contemporary design has continued to spread across the UK. Abode is a very welcome addition on the country's design map.

DESIGNERS INCLUDE:
Achille Castiglioni
Aldo Rossi
Alessandro Mendini
Alessi
Enzo Mari
Ettore Sottsass
Guido Venturini
Jasper Morrison
Marc Newson
Michael Graves
Philippe Starck
Richard Sapper
Stefano Giovannoni

SERVICES:
Gift Vouchers
Gift Wrapping
Wedding List

CLOSE TO:
Selfridges

Alessi
22 Brook Street
London W1K 5DF
020 7518 9091
www.alessi.com
Tube: Bond Street
Open: Mon – Sat 10:30 – 6:30
Thurs til 7:30

Concession in Selfridges, London (p 208)

In 1921, Giovanni Alessi founded his company Fratelli Alessi Omegna in Northern Italy, producing handmade metal tableware objects. Would he have ever imagined that his company would grow to the scale it can boast today, with a brand name that has widespread recognition and a growing global customer base? Producing an enviable catalogue of objects from various factories around Europe, the family-run business still operates its head office and metalwork factories from its original Italian base on Lake Orta, now headed by Alberto Alessi. From inception, quality has been a crucial attribute that the company has always maintained and the family has been careful to guard their brand to ensure that it is properly positioned in the market place.

With many authorized dealers throughout the UK, the largest display of the Alessi collection culminates at their showroom in London, off fashionable and expensive Bond Street. Opened in October 2000, here the consumer is at last able to experience the Alessi story within the three floors of a building that is a suitably colourful and quirky backdrop to demonstrate their philosophy. The company has worked with a plethora of fantastic talents over the years such as Ettore Sottsass, Richard Sapper, Achille Castiglioni, Alessandro Mendini, Aldo Rossi, Michael Graves, Enzo Mari, Philippe Starck, Stefano Giovannoni, Jasper Morrison, Marc Newson, and Guido Venturini, and its products are logically organized by designer within the shop to help bracket the diversity of styles across the collections. Perhaps the post-modern 9093 kettle from Michael Graves will attract your attention, the iconic Juicy Salif lemon squeezer from Philippe Starck, or the playful creations from Stefano Giovannoni. Whatever catches your eye, you will surely walk away with an object that performs everyday functions but, as Alberto Alessi puts it, 'somehow makes commonplace gestures more pleasing, more straightforward, and more personal'.

ALMA

DESIGNERS INCLUDE:
all own brand

SERVICES:
Bespoke Orders
Contract Division
Gift Vouchers
Interior Design

CLOSE TO:
The Conran Shop
(Conduit Street)

Alma
8 Vigo Street
London W1S 3HJ
Tel: 020 7439 0925
www.almahome.co.uk
Tube: Piccadilly Circus
Open: Mon – Sat 10 – 6

Few people realize that Alma was established in the East End of London in 1938 and, over the years, has grown into an internationally renowned producer of fine leather furniture, cushions and accessories. Working at the business helm is Saeed Khalique, whose vision and passion for his company have steered Alma in new directions over the past five years. Ambition and direction are certainly not lacking in the Alma entrepreneur – the company designs and manufactures everything from sofas, armchairs, pouffes, stools, floor and wall tiles, beds, shelving, cushions, beanbags, storage and rugs at the factory premises near Whitechapel.

Khalique's latest venture has got to be his most exciting to date: an Alma store selling bespoke leather interior products right in the heart of the traditional tailoring area of Savile Row. While parking there one morning, Saeed spotted a 'to let' sign on the front window of 8 Vigo Street. After rapidly negotiating the terms with the letting

agent, the property was soon in Saeed's hands, and the store fitted out and opened to the public in November 2002.

Entering this magnificent shop, with its high ceilings, old oak flooring, original cornicing and cosy fireplaces, is like stepping into someone's exuberant home. The difference here is that everything can be ordered, from the sofas in the living room, the leather wall and floor tiling in the study, to the punch bag in the gym and the leather-clad bathtub in the bathroom. The store is a unique showcase for the endless applications to which Alma can apply its signature material. Everything on display can be made to order to your exact specification and delivered to you within 72 hours. Larger and more complicated orders obviously take longer. All items are carefully produced by the efficient and highly skilled craftsmen in Alma's London factory. Leave the hard work to them – your role is simply to enjoy this new Alma experience. Explore the nooks and crannies of this intimate and welcoming showroom space, admiring the must-have collections as you go. With Gieves & Hawkes, Ozwald Boateng and Jil Sander all within spitting distance, surely the logical progression from a Savile Row tailor-made suit is a luxurious custom-made Alma study or leather-clad walk-in wardrobe.

APPLIED ARTS
AGENCY

DESIGNERS INCLUDE:
Andrew Davies
Amy Cushing
Claire O'Hea
David Design
DMD
Ella Doran
Fusion
Georg Baldele
Goods
Hive
Innermost
Julie Cockburn
Pia Wallen
Rainer Spehl
Snowcrash
Spaced Out
Tom Kirk
Tord Boontje

SERVICES:
Bespoke Orders
Gift Wrapping
Gift Vouchers
Interior Advice
Wedding List

CLOSE TO:
Inflate
Lowe Interiors
Mac London
Viaduct

Applied Arts Agency
30 Exmouth Market
London EC1R 4QE
020 7837 2632
www.appliedartsagency.co.uk
Tube: Farringdon
Open: Tues – Fri 11 – 6
Sat 11 – 5:30

Applied Arts Agency is situated among cafés, bars, restaurants, jewellery boutiques, independent music stores and funky hair salons on the vibrant semi-pedestrianized street that is increasingly becoming a destination hotspot in many discerning London address books. Contributing to the creative energy and community-like feeling in this street are the sister owners of AAA, Kate and Lulu Holmes. Since opening in November 2000, the ever-friendly duo have been introducing an eclectic selection of applied art product design to their growing number of new as well as regular customers.

As the shop occupies a very small space, the amount of furniture they are able to stock is limited. Instead, they place more emphasis on smaller items that they have sourced from individual designers, making sure that there is an interesting cross section of pieces available to suit all budgets. The AAA benefits from decent passing trade and caters to customers who are after something

that is perhaps a little more unusual. While Kate and Lulu deal in a lot of UK talents, they have started to introduce more Dutch design as they are particularly keen on its playful and experimental ethos.

Enter this mini design haven and let the cool background music guide you around pieces from the likes of Tord Boontje (pictured), Claire O'Hea, DMD, David Design, Rainer Spehl, Fusion, Pia Wallen, Spaced Out, Andrew Davies, Julie Cockburn, Amy Cushing, Innermost, Goods, Ella Doran, Snowcrash, Georg Baldele, Tom Kirk, and Hive to name but a few. Should you have difficulty making a decision, the owners are always on hand to recommend and advise. Because of their close relationship with a lot of designers, the sisters are able to work with you on unique commissions by acting as the link between client and creator.

An exciting element of AAA is the quarterly exhibition that they curate within the shop. Inviting only three artists or designers, they give them carte blanche to design to a particular theme for each show. The result is always an unusual fusion of creative responses that successfully pulls in the growing customer base at the private view. Personal service and customer care run high on their list of priorities, making each visit to this eclectic shop an inevitable pleasure.

DESIGNERS INCLUDE:
Alias
Artek
Cassina
Desalto
Edra
Eileen Gray Designs
Flexform
Fritz Hansen
Kagan
Knoll
Moroso
Porada
Porro
Tagliabue
Vitra

SERVICES:
Contract Division
Gift Vouchers
Interior Advice
Wedding List

Aram
110 Drury Lane
London WC2B 5SG
020 7557 7557
www.aram.co.uk
Tube: Covent Garden or Holborn
Open: Mon–Sat 10–6
Thurs til 7
Sun 12–6

Some might say that Aram has become a sort of institution at the Aldwych end of Covent Garden, the family-run business having sold contemporary furniture and lighting to the contract market since the 1960s, with Zeev Aram always firmly at the helm. Zeev's daughter and son, Ruth and Daniel, then joined the business, dealing with the buying and finance respectively. Ruth had her own shop in Hampstead for nearly 10 years until the family decided to amalgamate their talents and expand their Covent Garden operation into retail when the immense old fruit and vegetable warehouse next door went up for sale. Although the shop occupied a huge three-floor showroom, Ruth's architect husband David Walker of Walker & Martin knocked through into the adjoining building of equal proportions to create a five-floor emporium of more than 20,000 sq ft. The new store, with its wrap-around corner location, has maintained its raw industrial feel and was filled with a fantastic choice of modern furniture, lighting and accessories for the opening in spring 2002.

It is encouraging to see that people are buying into the fabulous high-quality creations from companies like Cassina, Edra, Moroso, Fritz Hansen, Eileen Gray Designs, Flexform, Vitra, Desalto, Tagliabue, Porada, Knoll, Kagan, Alias, Artek and Porro, as well as choosing innovative lighting solutions from the basement selection or smaller accessory items at ground level. Products are thankfully given plenty of room to breathe in the light and airy space, contributing to the calm shopping experience. Reach the top floor and you will encounter Zeev's gallery, dedicated to a changing display of work from new designers and where innovative concepts are given a forum to communicate.

It was a significant step forward to open this immense new design landmark in London, a bold confirmation that the public's perception of contemporary living is changing. Some shoppers might feel intimidated by the sheer size of this store but I can only encourage a visit to dispel this myth and introduce you to the design mecca that is Aram.

AREA SQUARED
DESIGN

DESIGNERS INCLUDE:
Apartment
Caré d'Art
De-ann Dale
Splat
Wendy Jung

SERVICES:
Bespoke Orders
Interior Design

CLOSE TO:
Aria
Crafts Council
Gallery Shop
Fandango
Living Space
Twentytwentyone

Area Squared Design
9 Camden Passage
London N1 8EA
020 7704 2734
Tube: Angel
Open: Tues – Fri 12 – 6
Sat 10 – 6

Interior designers Lyndall Fernie and Stuart Knock have been creating gorgeous domestic interiors together for several years but in 1999 had the bright idea of opening a shop to showcase their style and attract more customers in their word-of-mouth industry. Their first shop was located on a busy stretch of Islington's Upper Street but when the lease expired in 2001 the duo moved around the corner to a more permanent fixture on a quieter side street.

Surrounded by a number of antique dealers, Area Squared Design certainly stands out with a carefully styled, well-lit window display to lure you in. And once inside, you are likely to be greeted by either one of the owners, who are operating their interior design business from the basement. Browsing is one thing, but it is worth having a chat with them: this is when you will really uncover their passion for design, making it no surprise that their list of satisfied clients is growing all the time. Their design aesthetic is immediately communicated within the shop. The emphasis is on natural muted tones, textured materials and sheer beauty of form. While the dynamic duo create their own pieces of furniture, most of the items in the space are sourced from other designer makers, either locally or internationally. Lyndall and Stuart won't compromise on choice – they quite simply buy what they love instead of going for new seasonal stock. Catching the eye on my visit were serene white ceramic vases in unusual striking forms from London-based Splat ceramics, shown alongside textural vessels from Apartment, tea lights from Wendy Jung and flawless acrylic vases from Caré d'Art in Paris.

All contained in one small room, it is admirable that they have refrained from any clutter. On the contrary, this tiny shop feels deceptively spacious, which in turn creates a calm environment. Whether there to purchase or peruse, no one is ever in a hurry to leave Area Squared Design.

ARIA

DESIGNERS INCLUDE:
Alessi
Driade
Kartell
Magis
Philippe Starck
Ron Arad

SERVICES:
Contract Division
Gift Vouchers
Gift Wrapping
Wedding List

CLOSE TO:
Area Squared Design
Crafts Council
Gallery Shop
Fandango
Living Space
Twentytwentyone

Aria

295 – 297 Upper Street
London N1 2TU
020 7704 1999
Tube: Angel
Open: Mon – Fri 10 – 7
Sat 10 – 6:30
Sun 12 – 5

133 Upper Street
London N1 1QP
020 7226 1021
Tube: Angel
Open: Mon – Fri 10 – 7
Sat 10 – 6:30
Sun 12 – 5

www.ariashop.co.uk

Aria started trading in 1989 and has become almost an institution on Islington's busy Upper Street. Selling an accessible selection of furniture, lighting and accessories from initially small premises, the shop has witnessed the area's influx of cool bars, restaurants and boutiques, and prospered and grown alongside them. Increasing its space in 1999 and 2002 by expanding into the shops next door, has allowed Aria to increase its street presence and attract even more people to its contemporary design offerings.

The first expansion of space saw the introduction of one of London's largest Alessi concessions, the impressive range filling the back of the store and providing the Italian company with optimum branding exposure to the steady flow of customers.

Attracting a lot of passing trade, Aria has created a shopping environment that certainly isn't sparse or intimidating, with plenty of products on display at a generally accessible price point. Not pretending to be a store for the design elite, Aria has carved itself a niche in the sale of affordable items from the usual suspects – big-boy designers like Philippe Starck and Ron Arad. The buyers have always been fans of colourful plastic furniture from Italian giants like Driade, Kartell and Magis. These used to be stacked up around the shop, making the space rather cluttered, but with the shop's 2002 expansion, they were able to create a new, dedicated display space.

Aria stocks a huge quantity of items for all interior requirements between their two facing premises. The design savvy will already be familiar with most of the offerings, but Aria's success has lain in its ability to attract the everyday consumer in search of something more unusual than typical high-street pickings.

ARTEMIDE

DESIGNERS INCLUDE:
all own brand

SERVICES:
Contract Division

CLOSE TO:
Chaplins
(Berners Street)
CVO Firevault
Key London
Ligne Roset West End
Noel Hennessy
Furniture

Artemide
90 – 92 Great Portland Street
London W1W 7JY
020 7631 5200
www.artemide.com
Tube: Oxford Circus
Open: Mon – Fri 10 – 6:30
Thurs til 7:30
Sat 10 – 5

Of all of the endless lighting brands in the world, Artemide must be one of the most reputable and widely available companies producing contemporary lighting solutions and innovations for domestic use and public and private professional activities. Founded in 1959 by Ernesto Gismondi, the Artemide Group now has significant global reach with more than 35 exclusive distributors and endless authorized dealers. The group commands a catalogue of more than 9,000 products, making it impossible to showcase the entire collection in full. That said, the first London showroom provides an environment in which it can at least display the latest and most successful pieces to visitors.

The showroom opened in March 2002. Architects, interior designers and specifiers can at last view and interact with the lights in the flesh and are able to deal with a dedicated sales team who are knowledgeable and passionate about Artemide products and brand status. The showroom is mainly targeted at the trade, but the public are also encouraged to find their lighting requirements within this slick, white-walled, air-conditioned environment spread across two spacious floors. Visiting lighting shops can be monotonous, but by viewing exclusively

Artemide creations, customers can step away from the sheer functional elements and begin to truly understand the intelligent thought process and technological expertise that go into the ranges. At the core of product development is a deep understanding that light is a source of physical pleasure and mental comfort.

The flexible and adaptable nature of Artemide's systems is well demonstrated by the staff who fully comprehend the difficulty of choosing the right lighting to enhance or complement a particular atmosphere or daily activity. Always on the cutting-edge of new technology and material capabilities, Artemide has more recently introduced lighting solutions that incorporate energy-efficient LEDs and digitally programmable mood settings.

The sheer enormity of choice can be experienced only by visiting the showroom in person. Don't be intimidated by using the buzzer to gain entry – any nervousness quickly dissipates as you adjust your eyes to the dazzling display within.

ATOMIC
INTERIORS

Atomic Interiors
Furniture Showroom
Plumptre Square
Nottingham
NG1 1JF
0115 941 5577
Open: Mon – Sat 9:30 – 5:30

Accessories & Gifts
14 Exchange Arcade
Nottingham
NG1 2DD
0115 979 9940
Open: Mon – Sat 9.30 – 5:30

www.atomicinteriors.co.uk

The entrepreneurial owner of Atomic, Simon Siegel, started his career selling twentieth-century originals before expanding into the world of contemporary furniture and lighting design. Initially opening in 1990 in Nottingham, Simon's business has grown steadily over the years to become arguably the town's best retailer of modern interior products. Knowing how difficult it is to successfully combine expensive furniture with small affordable accessory items, Simon has two shops to separate these markets. Atomic's furniture and lighting division finally moved to a larger showroom space at the beginning of 2000, offering more room for customers to properly admire the collections. This is home to head office where Simon and his team also operate a strong contract division.

Located in prominent corner premises on a busy stretch of road at the edge of Nottingham's Lace Market, the items on display at Atomic benefit from plenty of natural light pouring into the split-level showroom space. Despite a long list of high-end European suppliers, such as Kartell, Punt Mobles, B&B Italia, Flos, Foscarini, Vitra, Living Divani, Emmebi, Zanotta, Hitch Mylius, Fritz Hansen, and Tonelli, thankfully not too many choices are crammed into their displays. With a stronghold on classic modern designs, displays manage to carefully marry styles in various tantalizing room sets to help spark your imagination.

Showcasing only a fraction of what Atomic can supply, the friendly and knowledgeable staff will carefully assist in finding a number of options to suit your criteria. The Atomic team insists on consistent quality, professionalism and efficiency from their suppliers, and also applies these standards to its own service, ensuring that every customer leaves fully satisfied with the experience, whether buying or browsing.

B&B Italia
250 Brompton Road
London SW3 2AS
020 7591 8111
www.bebitalia.co.uk
Tube: South Kensington
Open: Mon–Sat 10–6
Sun 12–5

B&B ITALIA

DESIGNERS INCLUDE:
B&B Italia
Flos
Maxalto

SERVICES:
Bespoke Orders
Contract Division
Interior Design

CLOSE TO:
The Conran Shop
(Fulham Road)
De La Espada
The London Lighting Co
Oggetti
Rabih Hage

The major Italian furniture producer B&B Italia opened their first London showroom to much acclaim in September 2001 amid the swanky fashion boutiques and restaurants of Brompton Cross. The impressively slick glass-fronted entrance with its beautifully styled window is a bold contrast to the traditional British pub opposite and makes an eye-catching view for the alfresco drinkers. Even so, the size of this former luxury car showroom is deceiving from the outside and most definitely demands further inspection.

On entry you might qualify for a smile from the receptionist as you make your way into the space that is invisible from the street. Led through a narrow area dominated by a long gently sloping ramp and lined with a selection of B&B creations, you get a taster of the styles of furniture that are about to unfold in the main space. The immense double-height cathedral-like interior with its huge curved ceiling and mezzanine level is an awe-inspiring environment in which to display the latest furniture and kitchen

collections from B&B Italia and sister company Maxalto. The understated sharp-lined pieces designed by the cream of international talents are organized into carefully styled room-sets and illuminated by select Flos lighting, and benefit from plenty of open space for optimum communication to visitors. If only the staff sustained these communication levels, rather than modelling themselves on the stereotype of their snooty Italian counterparts. Despite being ignored, it is quite soothing to browse the furniture alone, the cool music completing this company's overall image.

If B&B Italia is what you want, then you must visit this high temple to design. Many would label this company as being the epitome of Italian manufacturing prowess. Couple that with the splendour of the space, and you have a retail environment unique to London.

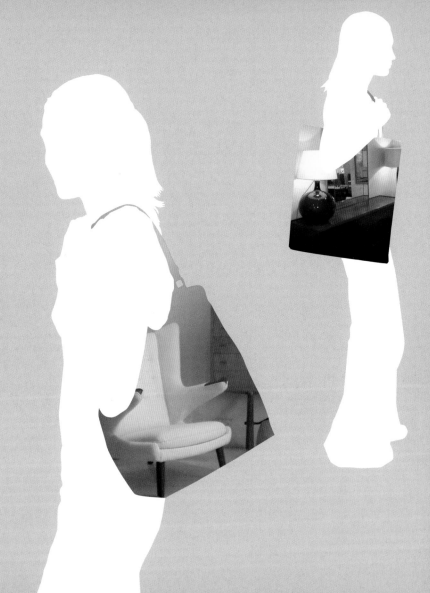

BABYLON

DESIGNERS INCLUDE:
Arne Jacobsen
Claudio Silvestrin
Hans Wegner
Matthew Hilton
Michael Anastassiades
Orrefors
Poul Kjaerholm
Raymond Loewy
Simon Maidment
Torsten Neeland
Vogt + Weizenegger

SERVICES:
Bespoke Orders
Contract Division
Gift Vouchers
Interior Advice
Sourcing
Wedding List

CLOSE TO:
Conran 2
Designers Guild
Poliform

Babylon
301 Fulham Road
London SW10 9QH
020 7376 7255
www.babylonlondon.com
Tube: South Kensington
Open: Mon – Sat 10 – 6
Sun 12 – 5

Birgit Israel and Peter Wylly are the dynamic couple behind the constantly evolving Babylon on London's fashionable Fulham Road. Originally working as a design consultancy producing lighting and accessory items on the other side of town, in autumn 1999 they decided to open a shop in this affluent area of the capital as a way of showcasing their own range to a retail audience. Their intention was always to combine their pieces with other complimentary designs, resulting in a unique fusion of styles within this white-walled and painted-wood-floor environment.

Babylon's own range comprising designs from Vogt + Weizenegger, Michael Anastassiades, Matthew Hilton, Simon Maidment, Claudio Silvestrin and Torsten Neeland, is mixed effortlessly with original Danish teak sideboards and desks, immense 1930s French gilded mirrors, and original chairs from the likes of Wegner, Kjaerholm, and Jacobsen.

Within the light and airy premises hang stunning original antique chandeliers that help illuminate some of the smaller items of glass, ceramic and tableware such as old Orrefors glass vases, a Danish rosewood cutlery set, or a Raymond Loewy-designed tea set. Should you be in search of a particularly hard-to-come-by item, the knowledgeable staff can help source it for you.

Any respectable interior designer will tell you how difficult it is to successfully combine antique with new, but a visit to Babylon illustrates just how well it can be achieved. Never the type to stand still, Birgit and Peter's latest venture is the conversion of a sixteenth-century chateau into a small luxury hotel called Chateau de Massillan (www.chateau-de-massillan.com) in the heart of Provence. It is the perfect base to relax and admire the stunning interiors and temporarily enjoy living amid impeccable taste.

BACK 2
MY PLACE

DESIGNERS INCLUDE:
Alessi
Caterina Fadda
Catherine Tough
David Design
Fiam
Flos
Fritz Hansen
Fusion
Hub
Meshman
Nelson
Scabetti
SCP
Suck UK
Sukie
Totem Design
Vitra
Zanotta

SERVICES:
Bespoke Orders
Contract Division
Gift Vouchers
Gift Wrapping
Interior Advice
Wedding List

CLOSE TO:
Momentum
Seduti

Back2myplace
5 Ivor House
Bridge Street
Cardiff CF10 2EE
029 2040 0800
www.b2mp.com
Open: Tues – Sat 10 – 6
Thurs til 7
Sun 11 – 5

Back2myplace is Cardiff's latest design shop boldly opened by Simon Robinson in spring 2002. Selling a well-selected array of contemporary furniture, lighting and accessories from a diversity of new and established designers, B2MP is certainly a shop worth visiting should you be feeling starved of cutting-edge interior products. Ignore the rather drab exterior on entering this former bank: you will feel instantly uplifted manoeuvring through the well-displayed items that surround you.

Greeted by friendly, knowledgeable staff and the cool sounds of background music, even the most design-savvy customer is likely to develop a child-like feeling of excitement as the choice of products unfolds across the two floors of the shop. There are, of course, items from well-known international suppliers such as Vitra, Fritz Hansen, SCP, Zanotta, Alessi, Flos, Fiam, and David Design, but Simon has also introduced products

from home-grown talents like Caterina Fadda, Nelson, Fusion (p 266), Suck UK (p 288), Catherine Tough, Meshman, Hub, Sukie, Scabetti and Totem Design, to name a few.

Simon makes purchasing decisions based on the initial emotional reaction he has to a product. You can sense that he is not just driven by consumer opinions, as he has managed to create a personal design message throughout the shop.

The vast shop windows on this corner location open up the space to the passing trade, with the slick window displays sure to lure you in. Driving past at night, slow down to admire the offerings strategically illuminated to celebrate the shop's finest elements. It won't be long before you're tempted to adopt some at home.

BATIK

Batik
Metthr-Hoose Raa
The GasWorks
Belfast BT7 2JA
028 9024 9311
www.batikonline.co.uk
Open: Mon–Fri 10–6
Sat 10–1:30

Batik was founded by Doug and June Elliott in 1980, and since then has retained its position as Northern Ireland's leading contemporary design store. After more than 20 years spent in a number of Belfast's wonderful converted Victorian and Edwardian warehouses, Batik moved into a fantastic new three-storey building extending over 12,000 sq ft on the former gasworks close to Belfast city centre in early 2003.

The new building was designed by twenty two over seven architects and developed by Ormeau Gasworks, both companies founded and managed by Doug and June Elliott. They led the design and project management process for this building and six others at the gasworks site, and have worked on various award-winning Victorian restoration and conversion projects in Belfast.

Batik's showroom provides a very special experience – one of structure, space and light. Venture through the ground and first-floor rooms with their visible concrete frame and ceiling plates and you will reach the magnificent top-floor white-painted attic space, with its large roof volume and clerestory lighting. Pay attention to the details – porcelain stone floors, concrete, steel, painted render, dark stained timber and natural oak comprise the material vocabulary, and that's before you admire what's on sale.

Not surprisingly, it is possible to buy a table light or a single chair, or have your home, office or restaurant fully furnished and designed by Batik. The store's product collection for home, office and leisure is extensive and reflects its longstanding partnerships with many of Italy's leading design manufacturers. I am told that the showroom presents the largest collection of Zanotta furniture to be seen in the UK. There are kitchens and bathrooms by Boffi and Schiffini and storage systems and bedrooms by Porro and Interlübke, as well as living and dining furniture from both long-established and newly emerging brands. Technical and decorative lighting, carefully chosen textiles, wall and floor tiles, outdoor furniture and various contemporary objects reinforce the quality and depth of service provided by the friendly, experienced and highly trained sales staff. Without a doubt, Batik is well worth a journey from anywhere in Europe.

BOOM!
INTERIORS

DESIGNERS INCLUDE:
David Anderson
Christiansen
Georg Jensen
Gio Ponti
Hitch Mylius
Merrow Associates
Sinnjuhl

SERVICES:
Bespoke Orders
Gift Wrapping
Interior Design
Sourcing

BOOM! Interiors
115 – 117 Regents Park Road
London NW1 8UR
020 7722 6622
www.boominteriors.com
Tube: Chalk Farm
Open: Daily 12 – 6

Boom! Interiors, owned by Phil Cowan, was originally based on the main road between Camden Town and Chalk Farm before making the decision to move to considerably larger premises in Primrose Hill in January 2003. The friendly and informative owner sells a gorgeous array of unusual twentieth-century furniture, lighting, glass, ceramics, jewellery and artwork to an ever-growing customer base looking for either generic or iconic pieces to complement their homes. I suspect the shop's name originates from the explosion of light from well-displayed floor, table, pendant, wall and task lights that hits you as you enter. These illuminate the furniture within and also help to heat the interior.

The offerings at Boom! are spread spaciously across the various levels and rooms of the shop and have been configured like room sets to help customers imagine them placed in situ at home. Indeed, browsing the shop is rather similar to exploring an immaculate house, though the beautiful clean and uncluttered display approach acts as a reminder that you are in a commercial environment. When not busy running the interior design service, Phil makes a point of being present in the shop as much as

he can. His passion for twentieth-century design is infectious and is backed up by his extensive knowledge of the subject.

The nature of his business is such that the collection on display constantly changes, giving Phil and his staff the opportunity to reconfigure the store on a regular basis. For this reason, the shopping experience always feels different – on my visit, for example, Phil had just acquired a number of slick chrome lighting designs from Gio Ponti. These were offset by some beautiful Murano glass vases positioned on a textured rosewood cabinet from Danish company Christiansen. Successful recent introductions are sofas and beds from the British company Hitch Mylius. A variety of styles and material finishes is employed in Boom! ranging from sharp-lined black leather sofas to quirky and colourful decorative objects. Driving past by day or night, the vast, vibrant window displays always catch your eye. Pay them a visit and you will undoubtedly agree that Boom! Interiors is one of the UK's finest retailers of twentieth-century design.

BOWLES
AND LINARES

Bowles and Linares
32 Hereford Road
London W2 5AJ
020 7229 9886
www.bowlesandlinares.co.uk
Tube: Notting Hill Gate or Bayswater
Open: Tues–Fri 11–5

DESIGNERS INCLUDE:
all own brand

SERVICES:
Bespoke Orders
Interior Design

CLOSE TO:
Flow
Mission
Themes & Variations

Sharon Bowles and Edgard Linares, designers of interiors as well as furniture, lighting and glassware, are the creative force behind this small Notting Hill showroom. Opened in 1997, the space is the perfect forum to display the full gamut of their work while attracting new commissions. The duo saw the sense of opening their own commercial premises after launching their debut collection of furniture in 1996 at 100% Design to great acclaim. Every year, they introduce new additions to a range that never fails to impress. One of their best-known pieces is the Espiga floor lamp of fine reeds of metal held in a cluster by an adjustable ring, which has now been developed into a smaller table version.

The roots of modernism largely influence their designs as Sharon and Edgard place emphasis on the manufacture and diligence of detailing that is unachievable unless done by hand. Much of this production takes place in their West London workshop where there is a strong belief that the hand production of the piece is as important as the design itself. The stunning glassware range comprises champagne flutes, tumblers, wine glasses, shot glasses, coffee and teacups, all hand-blown from clear or amber borosilicate glass.

Bowles and Linares use other notable materials, such as concrete, wood, and metals in a gorgeous collection that clearly communicates their commitment to quality and craft. Why not go and see their work for yourself? You will soon realize that everything is superbly manufactured to stand the test of time.

BOW WOW

BOWWOW
0 Princedale Road
London W11 4NL
020 7792 8532
www.bowwow.co.uk
Tube: Holland Park
Open: Tues – Fri 10 – 6
Sat by appointment only

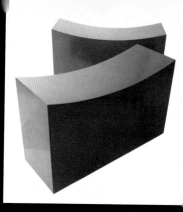

BOWWOW is a tucked-away shop feel privileged to know. It is the sort of place where there won't be masses of customers at one time; where you can expect one-on-one attention from the immensely hospitable owners Ahmed Sidki and Catherine Butler. Undertaking interior design projects or individual product commissions from the cosy offices at the back, Ahmed and Catherine use the tiny shop space at the front to showcase a stunning collection of their own unique designs alongside only a handful of other like-minded creatives.

BOWWOW commands such high standards of quality in products that these can be achieved only by employing skilled professionals to carefully hand-craft beautifully proportioned must-have designs. Ahmed's knowledge of materials and techniques would put a lot of designers to shame – his passionate attention to detail is indeed a far cry from the sometimes-lacklustre quality of mass-production.

The sharp-lined sculptural forms of Ahmed's bronze curved seats on concealed rollers (pictured) are offset by the serene yet fluid ceramic vases from Vivienne Foley and softened further with sumptuous one-off Mongolian lambswool throws and cushions by Samson Soboye. Gordon Mitchell's immaculately crafted turned wooden bowls are gently illuminated by Jean-Christophe le Greves' elegant lamps that cast light onto glass-beaded hand-stitched fabric designs from Alev Salğam. Unusually, all of the available objects are made in the UK, clear testimony of the skills that are available within our own shores.

On my visit, the new face behind the shop greeted me, that of Minnie the resident Newfoundland puppy (pictured). She now graces the pages of the website where the full extent of BOWWOW's offerings can be seen. But only by visiting the shop will you fully appreciate their level of service, hospitality and quality

BUDGE + COWARD

DESIGNERS INCLUDE:
Caroline Vidal
Dagmar Radmacher
Daniel Smith
Gill Usher
Kathleen Hills
Klementina Galcik
Paul Kennerley
Samantha Sweet

SERVICES:
Bespoke Orders

Budge + Coward
67 Roman Road
London E2 0QN
020 8980 8837
www.budgeandcoward.com
Tube: Bethnal Green
Open: Sat 10 – 6
Sun 10 – 4
Weekdays by appointment

Two RCA graduates Amelia Coward and Mark 'Budge' Hay set up a design gallery in London's East End in summer 2002 to exhibit and sell one-off or batch-produced contemporary ceramics, glass, textiles, artwork, lighting, jewellery and some furniture from a range of talented new designers. Taking over from the previous gallery owners within a building that used to be an old Victorian pub, Amelia and Mark have filled the shop with an eclectic ever-changing selection of interior products that veer away from the usual well-known brands. At Budge + Coward the focus is on the individual creator, with items from mainly new graduates and UK designer-makers whose work, in some instances, is available only through the gallery. Even to the trained eye, browsing always reveals new discoveries and acts as a reminder of new talent emerging in the industry.

A few minutes' walk from Bethnal Green tube station in an area where you wouldn't usually expect to find a shop of this sort, Budge + Coward provides a warm welcome in a rather dreary neighbourhood. Greeted by one of the friendly owners on entry, you are left to explore the desirables on display, with help always at hand should you need it. No two visits are ever the same as the display constantly evolves when pieces are sold. On my visit I was presented with vibrant digital prints by Paul Kennerley, quirky embroidered canvases by Dagmar Radmacher, bulbous hand-blown glass vases by Samantha Sweet, tactile felted pebbles by Gill Usher and ceramic tableware and lighting from Kathleen Hills, Daniel Smith, Caroline Vidal and Klementina Galcik. This is only a handful of the designers on show; there are textile designs and ceramic creations from the owners themselves. Offering varied price points and design styles, Budge + Coward has become one of London's hidden gems and makes a great place to find a unique and special gift or home addition.

CAPSULE

Capsule
126 Charles Street
Leicester LE1 1LB
0116 262 6932
www.capsulefurniture.co.uk
Open: Mon – Sat 10 – 5:30

Simon Siegel, the owner of Atomic Interiors in Nottingham (p 26) and Stuart Delahoy, the owner of Set, a design-led Leicester gift shop, joined forces to open a furniture and lighting showroom in a newly developed commercial and residential scheme in central Leicester in November 2002. Occupying a 3,000 square foot open-plan space in a former knitwear factory, the duo have merged their refined knowledge of the retail and contract design markets and filled a showroom with a variety of well-known mid- to high-end European brands.

Just outside the main throng of city centre shops, Capsule attracts design-conscious destination shoppers. The huge selling space could seem intimidating to some passers-by as its super-slick spacious interior oozes exclusivity. Shed your inhibitions and enter, for you will promptly be met by the friendly and knowledgeable staff, who will happily guide you around the showroom and assist you with product selection. Illuminated by plenty of natural light through the immense old industrial windows at the front and back of the store, Capsule stocks a good variety of modern sofas, loungers, chairs, dining tables, coffee tables and stools from the likes of B&B Italia, Molteni & C, Kartell, Vitra, Punt Mobles, Porada, Fritz Hansen, Magis and Arper. Various glass and ceramic tableware items are strategically placed around the store to add context to the furniture and soften the displays. Colourful rugs and different lighting solutions from Flos, Foscarini and Luceplan add warmth to this tranquil and airy showroom while cool music sets a calming mood.

To the trained eye, Capsule is selling pieces from many of the major usual suspect European brands. That said, one could not find any of these items in Leicester before the showroom opened so the owners must be congratulated for boldly introducing contemporary design to this Midlands city.

DESIGNERS INCLUDE:
Arper
B&B Italia
Flos
Foscarini
Fritz Hansen
Kartell
Luceplan
Magis
Molteni & C
Porada
Punt Mobles
Vitra

SERVICES:
Contract Division
Gift Vouchers
Interior Advice

CLOSE TO:
Abode Interiors

CAZ SYSTEMS

DESIGNERS INCLUDE:
Alessi
Artemide
Flos
Foscarini
Herman Miller
Kartell
Luceplan
Magis
Mobles 114
Rexite
Seven Salotti
Zack
Zanotta

SERVICES:
Contract Division
Gift Vouchers
Gift Wrapping
Interior Advice
Wedding List

CLOSE TO:
Mojoe
Roost

Caz Systems
17–19 Church Street
Brighton BN1 1RB
01273 326 471
www.cazsystems.com
Open: Mon–Sat 10–6

Owner Neil Davies has been steadily supplying big-name designs to an ever-expanding south-coast customer base since he opened Caz Systems in 1985. His presence on Church Street is significant, as he has now spread across three shop units, each with vast windows allowing passers-by to gape at the huge array of items on display.

The sheer quantity of products on offer in the store is mind-blowing. As you enter, you are greeted by a selection of small, affordable accessories, tableware, kitchen utensils and clocks from the likes of Alessi, Zack, Rexite and many others. As you move through the store into the next two rooms, you are met by the numerous lights that have been crammed into the space: spotlights, pendant lights, uplighters, downlighters, table lights, wall lights, task lights, ambient lights and chandeliers from the usual big-boy, Italian suppliers such as Foscarini (pictured), Artemide, Luceplan and Flos. Occupying the floor space is furniture – chairs, tables, consoles and

storage from more big names, like Kartell, Zanotta, Magis, Herman Miller, Seven Salotti and Mobles 114. These names may not mean anything to you but if you are after items from designers of the calibre of Starck, Morrison or Arad, then you would do well to visit this store.

With so much to choose from you can be forgiven for indecision. As you would expect, knowledgeable staff are nearby to advise. If it is big design brands that you are looking for, Caz Systems is a good place to find everything from small iconic gifts to a complete interior overhaul.

CENTRAL

Central
33–35 Little Clarendon Street
Oxford OX1 2HU
01865 311 141
www.central-furniture.co.uk
Open: Mon–Sat 9:30–6
Sun 11:30–5:30

DESIGNERS INCLUDE:
Alessi
Driade
Flos
Hitch Mylius
Kartell
LSA International
Magis
Montis
Vitra

SERVICES:
Contract Division
Gift Vouchers
Gift Wrapping
Wedding List

CLOSE TO:
Ligne Roset Oxford

Inhabitants of the historic city of Oxford are fortunate to have access to a big central contemporary design store, something of a rarity in other UK cities of a similar size. Trading since 1997, owner Geoff Taylor has clearly found his market selling a huge selection of what some might dub designs from the main players on the international scene. Here you'll find many of the newest pieces to reach the market from European brands such as Kartell, Driade, Montis, Magis, Vitra, Alessi, iittala, LSA International and Flos. Many iconic creations from new and established designers grace this open-plan furniture, lighting and accessory outlet, with something for every budget.

Making use of all available space, Central thankfully refrains from putting items on a pedestal, encouraging consumer interaction with the products instead. Giving equal status to the display of stock creates an unpretentious environment and in turn attracts passing trade. Customers are generally left alone to browse, but the seemingly busy staff are always on hand to help. Should you be looking for a bespoke interior design service without the hassle of travelling to London, Central can also offer this.

Running a successful business selling to the everyday consumer, Geoff is not one to stand still. He has recently moved into the contract market supplying bars, restaurants, offices and schools. He also owns a Ligne Roset store (p 130) on the same street. It's a relief that a city steeped in tradition has embraced the world of contemporary design.

CENTURY

Century
68 Marylebone High Street
London W1U 5JH
020 7487 5100
www.centuryd.com
Tube: Baker Street
Open: Mon – Sat 10 – 6

Century was opened in 1996 in tiny premises at the top end of increasingly fashionable Marylebone High Street. Occupying two floors, with a hairdresser sharing the basement, Andrew Weaving's store is so small it seems almost reserved for those in the know. Andrew is an expert in the field of mid-century Modernism. His shop combines many original iconic and generic designs from a handful of British and US designers, such as Eames, Nelson and Noguchi, with new items from across the Atlantic. Very few UK retailers sell new US designs, which makes for some diversity of styles within Andrew's premises.

That said, don't expect to find shelves full of products. Due to lack of space, there is a controlled number of items that change from visit to visit. Century is the UK agent for Canadian company Pure Design, which manufactures unobtrusive furniture, lighting and accessories from Karim Rashid, Stephen Burks, Butter, Mark Naden, Procter:Rihl, Richard Hutten, Boym Partners, Douglas Coupland, Andrew Tye and Paul Baber. Other products in stock include David Weeks lighting, Biproduct screens, Judy Ross graphic textiles, Jonathan Adler ceramic vases and Brian Willsher sculptural wooden reliefs.

The tiny premises ensure one-on-one attention from either Andrew or his staff to assist you in sourcing particular items. Unfortunately, the shop always feels like it is in a permanent state of transition, with the basement space often used as a storage dumping ground. Don't let this put you off – there are some goodies to be found here.

DESIGNERS INCLUDE:
Andrew Tye
Biproduct
Boym Partners
Brian Willsher
Butter
Charles & Ray Eames
David Weeks
Douglas Coupland
George Nelson
Jonathan Adler
Judy Ross
Karim Rashid
Mark Naden
Procter:Rihl
Paul Baber
Richard Hutten
Stephen Burks

SERVICES:
Sourcing

CLOSE TO:
The Conran Shop
(Marylebone)

CHAPLINS

Chaplins
477–507 Uxbridge Road
Hatch End, Pinner
Middlesex HA5 4JS
020 8421 1779
Train: Hatch End
Open: Tues – Sat 10 – 6

17–18 Berners Street
London W1T 3LN
020 7323 6552
Tube: Goodge Street or Oxford Circus
Open: Mon – Sat 10 – 6
Thurs til 8

118–120 Brompton Road
London SW3 1JJ
020 7589 7897
Tube: Knightsbridge
Open: Mon – Sat 10 – 6
Wed til 8

www.chaplins.co.uk

Chaplins opened the doors to their first showroom in London's suburban Hatch End, at the north-west fringe of the city. Supplying a huge diversity of contemporary designs from major high-end European furniture and lighting brands, it is one of the UK's largest stores of its kind. The company extended its presence to two new central premises in the capital at the end of 2000.

Opening a bright and spacious showroom spread across two floors on the expensive Brompton Road, Chaplins has cleverly tapped into the wealth that is evident in the area and introduced new contemporary styles to a typically traditional local market. Nevertheless, the Knightsbridge store still remains on the more reserved side of contemporary living, with high-quality brands such as Giorgetti, Rolf Benz, Ronald Schmitt, Tonelli, De Sede, Porada and Cor easing

DESIGNERS INCLUDE:
Cappellini
Cassina
Cor
De Sede
Edra
Giorgetti
Kartell
Moroso
Porada
Rolf Benz
Ronald Schmitt
Tonelli
Zanotta

SERVICES:
Contract Division
Interior Design

CLOSE TO:
Berners Street:
Artemide
CVO Firevault
Habitat
Heal's
Ligne Roset West End
Purves & Purves

customers into a more modern yet unobtrusive aesthetic. If you want to buy modern classics, then most of the main brands are available. Alternatively, you could check out designs from the likes of Cassina, Edra, Kartell, Moroso and Zanotta. The more exciting up-to-the-minute creations from the ultimate Italian cutting-edge furniture brand Cappellini (pictured) can be seen at the Berners Street store.

Located opposite Schrager's super-cool Sanderson hotel, this W1 store attracts a wide variety of customers who are increasingly buying into the allure of adventurous and experimental pieces to liven up their interiors. It is encouraging to see a major retailer like Chaplins wholeheartedly embracing edgier design and a sure indication that the attitudes of British consumers are progressing.

The Chaplins interiors are predominantly white, providing a carte blanche on which the furniture, lighting and select accessories can shine. Professional teams of smartly dressed sales executives always seem to be working busily within the slick showroom environments and can be guilty of forgetting to welcome you on arrival at the store. Don't let this deter you: they are keen to ensure that all of your questions and concerns are dealt with before you make any decisions.

CHARLES PAGE

Charles Page
61 Fairfax Road
London NW6 4EE
020 7328 9851
www.charlespage.co.uk
Tube: Swiss Cottage
Open: Mon – Sat 9:30 – 5:30

Furniture retailer Charles Page founded his company in 1921, selling traditional well-made pieces to a discerning clientele. More than 80 years later, and now owned by the larger company Clement Joscelyne, the store still adheres to the same standards as a purveyor of quality, understated design.

Under the direction of store manager Robert Iaccino, Charles Page continues to successfully trade high-end European furniture brands such as Minotti, Molteni, Dema, Casa Milano, Flexform, Bellato, Rimedesio, Maxalto and Tonelli. Ignoring the occasionally garish appearance of some avant-garde design, the onus is on the creation of a clean,

DESIGNERS INCLUDE:
Bellato
Casa Milano
Dema
Flexform
Maxalto
Minotti
Molteni
Rimedesio
Tonelli

SERVICES:
Bespoke Orders
Interior Design

unchallenging, modern interior aesthetic in this store. The location, away from the traffic of nearby Finchley Road, does not attract a lot of passing trade, so the majority of business is generated from clients who already know about the store and who are in the market for new additions to their homes. So don't be surprised to find that you have the full 10,000 sq ft showroom spread across two floors all to yourself.

Browse around the showroom of subtle, clean-lined sofas, beds, sideboards, dining tables and chairs and you will pass the desks at the rear of the space that are the hub of business activity – the team of interior designers.

If you haven't already been offered assistance, don't hesitate to ask for it. Making decisions about your own interior among the large selection of items on display in this serene, open-plan showroom can be daunting, which is why an interior design advisory service is offered to clarify your ideas. Serving a large contingent of London's 'cash-rich, time-poor' inhabitants, Charles Page will undertake as little or as much of the 'hassle' of interior overhaul as you require. If you're after a high specification interior that sidelines any fickle 'of-the-moment' trends in preference for clean-lined, longer-lasting modernity, then Charles Page is a suitable option for you.

CHRISTOPHER FARR

DESIGNERS INCLUDE:
Allegra Hicks
Christopher Farr
Gary Hume
Georgina von Etzdorf
Kate Blee
Michael Sodeau
Rifat Ozbek
Romeo Gigli
Sarah Morris
Tony Bevan

SERVICES:
Bespoke Orders
Contract Division

CLOSE TO:
Designers Guild
Habitat (Chelsea)
Heal's (Chelsea)
Poliform
Rabih Hage

Christopher Farr
6 Burnsall Street
London SW3 3ZJ
Tel: 020 7349 0888
www.cfarr.co.uk
Tube: Sloane Square
Open: Mon – Fri 11 – 6

In 1988, Christopher Farr founded his company, designing and producing high-quality contemporary rugs suitable for modern interiors, and quickly earned an international reputation. Operating with co-director Matthew Bourne from their Notting Hill showroom since 1996, the business relocated to a new gallery-like space in Chelsea in early 2003. Art-trained Farr can now boast a sizeable collection of his own rug designs and those specially commissioned from artists and designers. Introducing new and established creatives to the art of rug design has resulted in a truly diverse range from the likes of Romeo Gigli, Rifat Ozbek, Allegra Hicks, Georgina von Etzdorf, Gary Hume, Tony Bevan, Sarah Morris (pictured), Kate Blee and Michael Sodeau. Soft and understated or bold and highly patterned, the collection comprises designs that appeal to a variety of modern aesthetic tastes at the high-end prices you would expect for such quality. Every rug is made from highest quality wool, hand-dyed then hand-spun by skilled weavers in central Turkey. As a result, every rug or flatweave has subtle variations of tone and texture.

Christopher Farr rugs are so beautiful that you almost feel disrespectful for walking on them. Many of the latest creations are hung like paintings. Rug dimensions vary massively; some

designs up to 4 x 3m would suit an open-plan loft environment or could be hung across an expansive wall in a double-height room. Employing rugs as artwork celebrates their sheer beauty of colour and texture, and signifies their collectible status. The quiet showroom attracts mainly interior designers and architects, who are regularly drawn back by the unique qualities a Christopher Farr rug adds to their projects, sometimes commissioning custom-made designs for a particular space and setting. In addition to the rugs, the company introduced a collection of carefully selected fabrics and printed cloth in 2000.

Staging regular exhibitions in London and in his showrooms in Los Angeles, New York, San Francisco and Chicago, Christopher Farr has generated an international following through his consistently excellent designs that never fail to sustain high levels of quality and beauty.

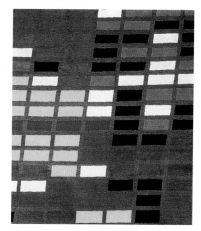

COLSTON + CO

colston+co

DESIGNERS INCLUDE:
B&B Italia
Cattelan
Driade
Fasem
Flexform
Flos
Frighetto
Gallotti & Radice
Lumincentre
Maxalto
MDF Italia
Montis
Naos
Pallucco Italia
Penta
Tonelli

SERVICES:
Bespoke Orders
Contract Division
Interior Advice

Colston + Co
4 West Centre
St Helier
Jersey JE2 4ST
Channel Islands
01534 510 300
www.colstonandco.co.uk
Open: Mon – Sat 9 – 5:30

It came as a surprise to me to discover that the small UK island of Jersey in the Channel Islands is home to a contemporary design store selling high-end furniture, lighting and kitchens. The island, with its own offshore tax laws, attracts affluent residents, not to mention tourists in the summer months. Spanning only twelve miles from east to west and four miles north to south, you might imagine that the market for modern interior products in Jersey is relatively limited. Directors Adrian Colston-Weeks, Leeana Taft and Mike Moyse would argue otherwise, claiming that the inhabitants of Jersey and neighbouring islands are falling over themselves to buy these contemporary items.

Located in a pedestrianized square in the heart of the capital St Helier, Colston + Co occupies premises that span two spaciously configured floors. Showcasing an impressive list of furniture designs from big-boy European suppliers, like B&B Italia, Maxalto, Fasem, Frighetto, Cattelan, Tonelli, Naos, Gallotti & Radice, Flexform, Montis, Driade, and MDF Italia, as well as lighting from Flos, Pallucco Italia, Penta and Lumincentre, this Jersey store is capable of offering its customers a range of choices. Clean displays, lifted by the occasional accessory, allow each product enough space to be properly examined. So as to not scare off new customers timidly approaching the contemporary design market, the owners manage to balance understated modern aesthetics with more daring examples of avant-garde design. Opened in October 2001, the store has had a positive response so far and the customer base continues to grow. The trio seem to have established a stronghold on the interior design market on this picturesque island.

CONCRETE
BUTTERFLY

DESIGNERS INCLUDE:
Block
Cor Unum
Emily Quinn
56 North
Fissler
Giancarlo Piretti
Hans Wegner
Iform
iittala
Illy Collection
Jenny Duff
Marcel Breuer
Pandul
Pick One
Scabetti
Snowcrash
Swedese
Tessuti

SERVICES:
Bespoke Orders
Contract Division
Gift Vouchers
Gift Wrapping
Interior Design
Wedding List

CLOSE TO:
Tangram

Concrete Butterfly
317–319 Cowgate
Old Town
Edinburgh EH1 1NA
0131 558 7130
www.concretebutterfly.com
Open: Tues – Sat 12 – 6

In Edinburgh's Old Town, close to the castle, Alasdair Gall opened Concrete Butterfly in 2000 as a retail forum for an interesting mix of products from international brands and individual designers alike. A designer of interiors and furniture himself, Alasdair is responsible for creating the understated, clean-lined shop space that provides a suitably unobtrusive backdrop for the interior offerings. Lured in by the appealing floor-to-ceiling window displays, you are likely to be attracted by any number of design goodies on entry. I was drawn to the slick angled wood wall with illuminated glass shelving that showcases glass, ceramic and kitchenware from iittala, Illy collection, Scabetti, Block, Cor Unum and Jenny Duff, and Fissler cooking instruments. Occupying the floor space are some classic furniture pieces such as Giancarlo Piretti's Plia chair, Hans Wegner's Three-legged Plywood chair, and Marcel Breuer's Chaise Longue for Isokon Plus, illuminated by occasional lighting from Pandul and Snowcrash. Sitting next to them with equal pride of place are contemporary designs, such as Yuriko Takahashi's modular Twister stools for Swedese and Iform's refined plywood-stacking chairs.

As you may have already gathered, there is a definite preference towards elegant fine-tuned Scandinavian design. But Alasdair is also keen to support talented local companies, displaying tableware and handprinted scarves and cushions from Tessuti, handmade lambswool throws by Pick One, functional storage units from 56 North, and graphic Irish linen and wool cushions from Emily Quinn. Designing furniture for commercial interiors, Alasdair has the added opportunity to incorporate some of his own pieces into the shop, as well as trial a few prototypes.

Recently the adjoining space has become Concrete Wardrobe, selling an eclectic array of clothing items to accompany the homewares. Staff throughout are approachable, helpful and enthusiastic – many of them are designers or artists working part time. For something a bit different, a visit to this friendly shop is warmly recommended.

THE CONRAN SHOP

The Conran Shop
Michelin House
81 Fulham Road
London SW3 6RD
020 7589 7401
Tube: South Kensington
Open: Mon – Sat 10 – 6
Weds, Thurs til 7
Sun 12 – 6

55 Marylebone High Street
London W1U 5HS
020 7723 2223
Tube: Baker Street
Open: Mon – Fri 10 – 6
Thurs til 7
Sat 10 – 6.30
Sun 12 – 6

12 Conduit Street
London W1S 2XQ
020 7399 0710
Tube: Oxford Circus
Open: Mon – Fri 10 – 6
Thurs til 7
Sat 10 – 6.30
Sun 12 – 6

Conran 2
350 King's Road
London SW3 5UU
020 7559 1140
Tube: Sloane Square
Open: Mon – Sat 10 – 6
Sun 11 – 5

www.conran.com

DESIGNERS INCLUDE:
Anne Kyyrö Quinn
Clarissa Hulse
Dieter Rams
Jasper Morrison
Jorge Pensi
Mario Bellini
Ou Baholyodhin
Philippe Starck
Ron Arad
Shin & Tomoko Azumi

SERVICES:
Bespoke Orders
Contract Division
Gift Vouchers
Gift Wrapping
Wedding List

CLOSE TO:
(FULHAM ROAD):
B&B Italia
De La Espada
The London Lighting Co
Oggetti
Rabih Hage
(MARYLEBONE):
Century
(CONDUIT STREET):
Alma
(CONRAN 2):
Babylon
Designers Guild
Poliform

Terence Conran, founder of Habitat, opened the first Conran Shop on London's Fulham Road in 1973, when he was discovering many interesting interior items too expensive or too esoteric for the Habitat range. He has always been concerned with opening individual stores that bring together a timeless selection of homewares within architecturally significant buildings, such as Michelin House, which was designed in 1911. The company's initial philosophy has not altered since its beginnings. The Conran style is instantly recognizable and the stores incorporate a variety of aesthetics, from the latest offerings from contemporary designers to classic designs, as well as the comfortable unobtrusive modern look synonymous with the Conran Shop brand.

The Conran shop's aim is to make good design accessible to all, and in order to achieve this the buying team scour the world for new and exciting objects that fulfil this brief.

Products are the core of the business, but the calm atmosphere of the stores, the clean presentation and innovative display of the items, and the friendly attitude and knowledge of the staff are all crucial components in the overall shopping package. People are not intimidated by entering a Conran Shop – quite the opposite, encountering a visual feast without feeling overwhelmed. A vast selection of different types of products caters for all inevitable modern needs for home or office. Traditional modern styling is combined with hip contemporary pieces, offering an opening for many into the world of 'good design'. This variety of ideas and suggestions helps customers create individual interiors with confidence.

The success of The Conran Shop in the UK has witnessed the opening of several stores around the world in Paris, Tokyo, Fukuoka and New York. Add to this Terence Conran's extensive portfolio of restaurants, numerous other projects and businesses, and it is no surprise that the Conran name is so widely received and globally recognized.

CRAFTS COUNCIL
GALLERY SHOP

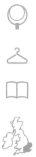

DESIGNERS INCLUDE:
Amy Cushing
Andrew Wicks
Ben Dunington
Catherine Hough
Jessie Higginson
Hub
Kate Malone
Kathryn Roberts
Keiko Mukaide
Louise Raven
Marianne Buus
Rupert Spira
Samantha Sweet
Sophie Cook

CLOSE TO:
Area Squared Design
Aria
Fandango
Living Space
Twentytwentyone
(warehouse)

Crafts Council Gallery Shop
44a Pentonville Road
London N1 9BY
020 7806 2559
Tube: Angel
Open: Tues–Sat 11–5:45
Sun 2–5:45
Closed Mon except in December

Crafts Council Shop at the V&A
Victoria & Albert Museum
South Kensington
London SW7 2RL
020 7589 5070
Tube: South Kensington
Open: Mon 12–5:30
Tues–Sun 10–5:30
Wed 10–9:30

www.craftscouncil.org.uk

The Crafts Council was founded in 1971 as a national organization for the promotion of contemporary British crafts. Funded by the Arts Council of England, it has showcased a vast array of outstanding exhibitions over the years in the gallery within its Islington headquarters. Aiming to promote crafts and applied arts 'of the highest quality in all media including new and challenging work by established and emerging artists', the Crafts Council can claim credit for increasing public awareness of contemporary crafts. It has also squashed any notion that applied arts are part of a bygone industry superseded by mass production. The Council has witnessed and encouraged the emergence of UK 'designer-makers' over the past twenty years and has used the gallery shop to sell this work to a captive audience.

On approaching the impressive building, you will immediately notice the colourful display of objects in the left-hand ground-floor shop window. Enter the front door and you will be met by tantalizing glassware, ceramics, jewellery and textiles, in well-lit display cases that succeed in luring you into the shop. Occupying only a small space, the shop has still found room for plenty of creations – colourful glassware from Samantha Sweet (pictured), Kathryn Roberts, Marianne Buus, Keiko Mukaide, Amy Cushing, Catherine Hough, Ben Dunington and Louise Raven, and tactile ceramics from Andrew Wicks, Jessie Higginson, Rupert Spira, Hub, Sophie Cook and Kate Malone. There is also an excellent range of design-related books and periodicals.

You can spend a long time browsing in this quiet shop. If indecision gets the better of you, think about your potential purchase while taking in the latest exhibition in the gallery next door. Next time you visit the Victoria & Albert Museum, look out for the Crafts Council shop there, too.

DESIGNERS INCLUDE:
Bodo Sperlein
CVO Fire
Hive
Ochre
Salviati

SERVICES:
Bespoke Orders
Contract Division
Gift Vouchers
Gift Wrapping

CLOSE TO:
Artemide
Chaplins
(Berners Street)
Ligne Roset West End
Noel Hennessy
Furniture

CVO Firevault
36 Great Titchfield Street
London W1W 8BQ
020 7580 5333
www.cvofirevault.co.uk
Tube: Oxford Circus
Open: Mon – Fri 9:30 – 6
restaurant and bar til 10:30
Sat 12 – 6

Set up by husband and wife duo Carolyn and Christian van Outersterp in autumn 2000, CVO Firevault is a unique home and lifestyle concept showroom a few minutes walk from Oxford Circus. The company's main focus is the design and development of its own range of contemporary fireplaces. Bored with the dominance of traditional designs in the fireplace market, the couple spotted the need for fires that are relevant to modern lifestyles and domestic environments. Identifying the 'symbolism, spirituality, and dynamism of fire', the owners wanted to radically reinterpret the essence of fire, its uses, and our responses to it within an unusual showroom space. Here they have created a welcome oasis of comfort, calm and style away from the hustle and bustle of everyday life.

Everyone is drawn to fire – it not only brings warmth to a room, but also provides a focus for interaction and intimacy. At CVO, the pieces surrounding the beautiful fires play an important part in the overall experience: in the showroom you can sink into a sumptuous leather sofa or a luscious cord armchair while enjoying anything from a frothy cappuccino to a three-course meal from the restaurant in the basement.

The cosy dark space has become an extremely tactile experience through the use of materials such as velvet, suede and leather, combined with steel, bronze, ceramic, concrete and stone fireplaces. Browse the showrooms quirky nooks and crannies to encounter delicate porcelain tableware from Bodo Sperlein, Italian crystal from Salviati, handmade furniture and lighting from Ochre, fire accessories from Hive, as well as clothing from fresh UK designers, throws and cushions from the CVO own-label collection and a good range of design-led books.

What you see from the street is not the complete picture – you need to fully explore this calming environment to entirely appreciate the way of life advocated by CVO.

DALLAS + DALLAS

Dallas + Dallas
18 Montrose Street
Glasgow G1 1RE
0141 552 2939
www.dallasanddallas.com
Tube: Buchanan Street
Open: Mon – Fri 9:30 – 5:30
Sat 10 – 6

Husband and wife owners Ian and Elaine Dallas have always worked in the furniture and lighting contract market. In December 2000, they decided to expand into retail as well, when they moved into premises in Montrose Street in central Glasgow. The stunning spacious showroom with smaller basement space benefits from simple white walls and wood floors throughout, providing a serene backdrop for the products. Huge glass windows at the front flood the interior with plenty of natural light, creating a calming atmosphere.

The owners and their friendly staff greet you on entry and offer help or leave you to browse if you prefer. Furniture choices are well edited, with high-quality sofas, chairs and storage from brands like Minotti, Frighetto, Baleri Italia, Fasem, Vitra, Alivar, Offecct, Artifort, Kartell, Mobles 114, Matteograssi, and Tisettanta.

Illumination comes from Flos, Luceplan and Foscarini, with some wackier alternatives from Ingo Maurer that add a splash of humour to the sometimes sterile room sets. Ian and Elaine Dallas have thankfully refrained from cramming the showroom, and have instead opted for plenty of manoeuvrable space for customers to properly admire the items. Too much choice can be overwhelming so if you are looking for a particular type of interior solution, be sure to ask the staff for advice – they are more than likely to be able to source the right piece for you.

Furniture and lighting involve careful decision making, but for spontaneous purchases, smaller accessories are also available. Displayed in a dedicated area by the reception desk, you'll find tableware from Boda Nova, Goods, Stelton, Hub and Alessi, as well as other desirable pieces from Oliver Hemming, Mathmos, Magis, Lily Latifi, Suck UK (p 288), Hive, and Anne Kyyrö Quinn (p 254).

Customers are always more likely to purchase high-end goods when satisfied with the level of in-store assistance. Ian and Elaine Dallas fully recognize this fact and take great care to ensure that Dallas + Dallas maintains a consistently professional service.

DESIGNERS INCLUDE:
David Mellor
Julie Goodwin
Jerpoint Glass
Ray Key
Richard Batterham
Svend Bayer

SERVICES:
Gift Vouchers
Gift Wrapping
Wedding List

CLOSE TO:
The Conran Shop

David Mellor
The Round Building
Hathersage
Sheffield S32 1BA
01433 650 220
Open: Mon – Sat 10 – 5
Sun 11 – 5

4 Sloane Square
London SW1 8EE
020 7730 4259
Tube: Sloane Square
Open: Mon – Sat 9:30 – 6

www.davidmellordesign.com

Twelve miles from Sheffield, amid the stunning landscape of Derbyshire's Peak National Park, the small village of Hathersage is the creative centre of David Mellor's cutlery production. Born and bred in the steel city, the award-winning designer continues to oversee the manufacture of his famous cutlery collection in the celebrated Round Building factory, designed in 1989 by architect and friend Sir Michael Hopkins.

David Mellor is best known for his metalwork skills. This Royal Designer for Industry has applied his talent to a diversity of pieces, from modern craft silver to the familiar traffic lights we drive past everyday. David Mellor is recognized by many as one of the top success stories of the UK manufacturing industry, namely for his range of designs on those humble tools the knife, fork and spoon. If you wonder why anyone would get excited about everyday utensils, you

need to witness the meticulous attention to detail in the design stages and the processes involved in production. After a tour of the factory, the balance, weight and hand-polished precision of every piece can be appreciated at the neighbouring shop, and also bought.

Selling the full collection alongside numerous other kitchenwares, the Hathersage store possesses much more of a country-craft atmosphere than the London retail premises. Opened in 1969 in fashionable Sloane Square, this larger glass-fronted shop on two floors portrays a more contemporary image, displaying an impressive selection of kitchen and tableware. Helpful staff explain how the Mellor masterpieces are produced. This sophisticated shopping environment in affluent Chelsea houses the entire collection from the family business, including bent plywood furniture by David's son Corin.

A talented craftsman and designer with an assertive passion for perfection and a forward-thinking entrepreneur and businessman, David Mellor is a creator of extraordinary vision.

De La Espada
60 Sloane Avenue
London SW3 3DD
020 7581 4474
www.delaespada.com
Tube: South Kensington
Open: Mon – Sat 10 – 6
Wed til 7
Sun 12 – 5

De La Espada opened its first showroom in 1996 on fashionable and expensive Sloane Avenue, selling a beautifully refined collection of understated sofas, chairs, dining and coffee tables, desks, beds, cabinets and wardrobes. Using solid American oak and walnut, the company is intent on showing these superb materials at their best by manufacturing orders to the highest specification at its factory near Madrid. Controlling the complete chain, from processing and selection of timber to final point of sale, De La Espada is able to keep a tight rein on time and cost efficiency. Every aspect of design and production is undertaken in house, culminating in a top level of service for the customer.

The design team is not concerned with groundbreaking material manipulation or invention of new functions and forms. Instead, they focus their attentions on combining three distinct elements: a sleek and minimal design, durability and fair prices. The company philosophy has clearly caught on with a loyal band of customers, and there are now stores now in Amsterdam, New York and San Francisco. Side-stepping short-term fashion, the company places huge importance on consistency and function by choosing to work with only two solid woods and a careful selection of fabrics and colour ranges. Employing an aesthetic positioned somewhere between modern and traditional, De La Espada succeeds in attracting customers who are seeking durable timeless furniture of a style that won't fight for attention in the home.

The familiarity of natural materials in the serene, spacious and airy showroom and the use of earthy tones like chocolate, beige, cream, white and grey create a serene environment for customers. Displays are enhanced with occasional accessories, while graphic posters and soothing contemporary music lift the atmosphere. Customers are content spending time carefully contemplating the furniture choices, comfortable in the knowledge that the friendly and informative staff will deliver a standard of service only to be expected from such a professional and finely tuned business.

DESIGNERS INCLUDE:
all own brand

SERVICES:
Bespoke Orders
Interior Design

CLOSE TO:
B&B Italia
The Conran Shop
(Fulham Road)
The London Lighting Co
Oggetti
Rabih Hage

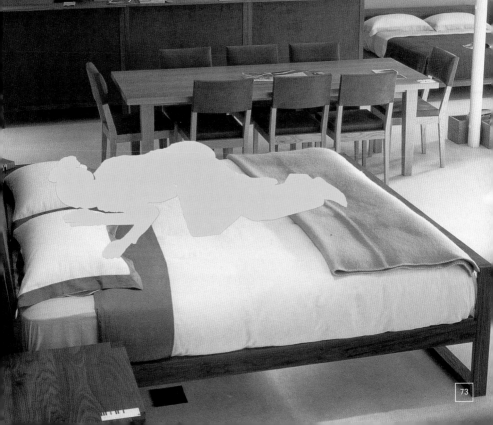

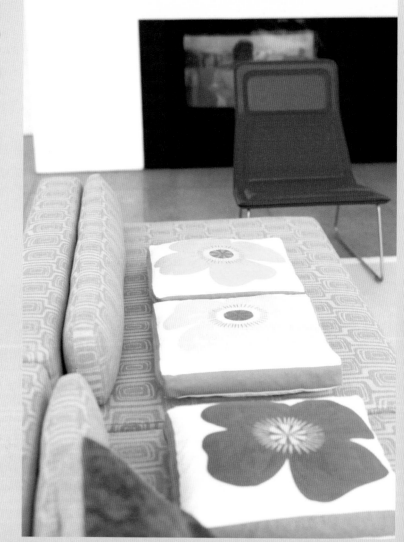

DESIGNERS INCLUDE:
Designers Guild
Emily Todhunter
Ralph Lauren
William Yeoward

SERVICES:
Contract Division
Gift Vouchers
Gift Wrapping
Interior Design
Wedding List

CLOSE TO:
Babylon
Christopher Farr
Conran 2
Poliform

Designers Guild
267 – 271 & 275 – 277 King's Road
London SW3 5EN
020 7351 5775
www.designersguild.com
Tube: South Kensington
Showroom open: Mon – Sat 10 – 6
Shop open: Mon – Sat 10 – 6
Sun 12 – 5

Since establishing Designers Guild in 1970, Tricia Guild has built up an award-winning, international company specializing in the design and wholesale of furnishing fabrics, wallcoverings, upholstery, and bed and bath collections. Processing around 600 orders a day and selling more than two million metres of fabric and wallpaper a year, Tricia Guild and group chief executive Simon Jeffreys have clearly implemented an impressive corporate strategy and management system. In the past ten years, annual turnover has climbed to more than £30 million, with the company selling to interior designers, department stores, retailers and the hotel and contract market. Impressive facts aside, you know that you are in capable hands when you step into the London showroom.

Occupying sizeable premises on busy King's Road in Chelsea, the Designers Guild emporium is split into two entities. The corner showroom is home to the company's high-quality range of 3,000 plus fabrics and more than 2,000 wallpaper choices – printed florals and geometric patterns, plains, checks, stripes, jacquards, tapestries, silks, velvets, trimmings and children's collections. Keen to place her unique style into a lifestyle

context, Tricia Guild has a shop next door that fuses her latest seasonal designs with other carefully selected interior products, such as furniture, glassware, ceramics, tableware and smaller accessories. Tricia Guild sets personal style precedents by defining her own trends, without getting wound up in the sheepish restrictions of fashion. This is confirmed in the regular publication of her style books, which aim to promote and share her recent individual interior inspirations.

In the beautifully composed room-sets and window displays across two floors, you can find inspirational home additions to suit all budgets – from an elegant vase to a colourfully upholstered three-seater sofa. At Designers Guild, customers are given a finely honed package of quality in design, product, and service, combined with a friendly, committed and motivated team. Inevitably the store won't appeal to everyone's tastes, but Designers Guild must be congratulated for maintaining a clear-cut vision while constantly reinventing trends to stay ahead of the game.

DESIGN
MUSEUM SHOP

Design Museum Shop
28 Shad Thames
London SE1 2YD
020 7940 8773
www.designmuseum.org
Tube: London Bridge / Tower Hill
Open: Daily 10 – 5:45

Entrepreneur Sir Terence Conran is known globally for his support and contribution to modern industrial design over the past 50 years. He was responsible for founding The Conran Foundation, which organized exciting exhibitions in the Victoria & Albert Museum's Boilerhouse yard from 1982–86, showcasing innovative functional design creations as interesting and stylish artefacts. These shows became extremely popular and confirmed the need for a permanent museum space, which took the form of the Design Museum in 1989. Located next to Conran's empire at Butlers Wharf near Tower Bridge, the stunning Bauhaus-inspired building hosts a changing programme of internationally touring exhibitions and features a restaurant, café and shop.

As the first museum in the world to be dedicated to twentieth- and twenty-first-century design, you can expect high standards from the gallery shop. Located on the ground floor next to the Konditor & Cook café and admissions desk, it offers a variety of smaller classic and contemporary design items, from curvaceous glassware from iittala, dinky miniature classic chairs from Vitra and slick stainless-steel tableware from Stelton to colourful watering cans by Jerszy Seymour, glowing Pigeon lights by Ed Carpenter, futuristic dish drainers by Marc Newson and irresistible ceramics by Hella Jongerius. Many of these items are behind glass but customers are free to pick up some of the more affordable items as well as browse through the comprehensive selection of books on design-related topics.

The calm, light and airy shop space benefits from plenty of natural illumination and great views across the Thames, and customers can spend time browsing and flicking through the books. The staff, typically all dressed in black, are friendly and informative and more than happy to help.

The Design Museum is an institution that contributes to our education and to our appreciation of the world's best contemporary designs. It's shop is an entirely worthy accessory.

DESIGNSHOP

Designshop
116 Causewayside
Edinburgh EH9 1PU
0131 667 7078
www.designshop.eu.com
Open: Mon – Sat 9:30 – 6

Opened in February 2002, Designshop is a retail extension to Patrick Haddad's architectural practice Designlab. Realizing that many people find it intimidating to walk into an architectural practice, Patrick Haddad formed a retail design division as a way of attracting everyday customers to his practice within a normal shop environment. Apparently this approach has succeeded in establishing new commissions for the firm – but it's not everyday someone comes in to buy a chair and leaves having arranged a roof extension.

Designshop sells an ever-changing selection of contemporary furniture,

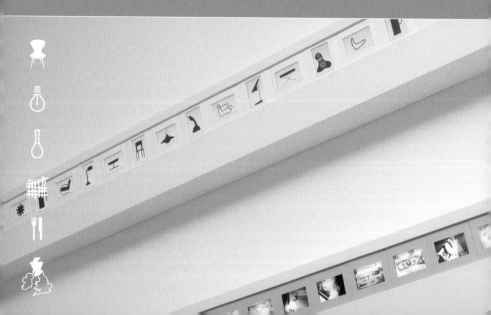

DESIGNERS INCLUDE:
Artemide
Bozart
David Design
Eurolounge
Flos
Foscarini
Guzzini
Inflate
j-me
Kartell
Magis
Marimekko
Mayday
Stelton
Suck UK
TYE3D

SERVICES:
Bespoke Orders
Contract Division
Gift Vouchers
Gift Wrapping
Interior Design
Wedding List

lighting, ceramics, glass, tableware, textiles and artwork. Without significant street presence in an area away from the city centre, it is a pleasant surprise to find this treasure trove of modern design in an unexpected location. Opting for slick presentation of fun and colourful objects, the shop is a welcome place where people can buy small inexpensive items from the likes of Suck UK (p 288), Inflate, Bozart, Mathmos, Stelton, Propaganda, Guzzini, Marimekko, or j-me. Larger furniture and lighting by designers such as Kartell, Magis, David Design, Snowcrash, Eurolounge, TYE3D, Foscarini, Flos, Mayday and Artemide

can also be bought. The white-walled interior is enlivened by strategic splashes of colour and the tidy displays hold just the right amount of products – neither cluttered nor sparse. Every six to eight weeks, the theme of the stock changes thereby remaining constantly fresh. On my visit during the Edinburgh festival, the theme was orange – everything from sweets, chess sets to transparent furniture. This well-branded venture is staffed on rotation by the friendly architectural team in the office, allowing them a refreshing break from the drawing boards. This is an upbeat, vibrant shop that certainly warrants a visit.

DOMANE INTERIORS

DESIGNERS INCLUDE:
Artifort
B&B Italia
Driade
Flos
Foscarini
Kartell
La Palma
Magis
Montis
Pallucco Italia
Porro
Vitra
Ycami
xO

SERVICES:
Bespoke Orders
Contract Division
Interior Design

CLOSE TO:
Mason

Domane Interiors
Union House
5 Bridge Street
Leeds LS2 7RF
0113 245 0701
www.domaneinteriors.com
Open: Mon – Fri 9 – 5:30
Sat 10 – 5

Observing the revolution in inner-city living in Leeds, Ben Ritson and Ashley Thornton quickly identified a gap in the market to supply property owners with contemporary furniture and lighting. This came to fruition in 1998 in the form of Domane Interiors, and in early 2000 the duo found they needed to expand, moving to their current corner-location, Bridge Street premises.

Both qualified designers, Ben Ritson and Ashley Thornton can identify quality in design products. They stock a variety of modern chairs, sofas, tables, storage, lighting, and various accessories, and on the open-plan ground floor there is a collection of pieces that will appeal to different budgets and tastes. They will happily talk you through the options available from their suppliers to ensure that you are happy with your final purchase. Supplied by strong European furniture brands like Porro, Ycami, Kartell, Driade, Vitra, Montis, B&B Italia, La Palma, Magis, Artifort and xO, as well as lighting from Flos, Foscarini and Pallucco Italia, you won't have any problems finding suitable additions for your home or office. But if you need the expertise of an interior designer to advise on your interior overhaul, look no further than the professional and efficient in-house services at Domane.

Committed to effective design solutions, Ben Ritson and Ashley Thornton have recently opened an industrial-style basement showroom that acts as a flexible space to create changing room-set displays. Away from the busy high-street stores, Domane is a calm retreat where you can make a considered purchase, aided by expert specialist attention.

DESIGNERS INCLUDE:
Alessi
Alivar
E15
Diseño
Eva Solo
Julie Nelson
Kartell
Kristalia
Leonardo
LSA International
Magis
Oliver Hemming
Rosendahl
Rosenthal
Tagliabue
Unique Interieur
WMF cutlery
Zack

SERVICES:
Contract Division
Gift Vouchers
Gift Wrapping
Wedding List

Domus
Constance House
117 High Street
Norton
Stockton-on-Tees TS20 1AA
01642 649 411
Open: Mon – Sat 10 – 5

Domus opened in 1998 and for several years was the only good contemporary design retailer between Leeds and Edinburgh. On the leafy High Street in Norton at the edge of Stockton-on-Tees, Domus sells a large selection of tableware and accessories married with select items of furniture and lighting.

Owner Emma Kench is all too aware that her collections must combine modern design aesthetics with suitable price points, knowing that garish, avant-garde and expensive alternatives are unlikely to sell significantly to local customers. The welcoming sky blue shop front attracts the eye and succeeds in luring customers in. On entry, you are greeted by clean displays showcasing a selection of unobtrusive tableware from familiar brands such as Rosenthal, LSA, Leonardo, Rosendahl, Zack, WMF cutlery, and Eva Solo, and a well-edited choice of Alessi offerings. Welcomed by the friendly staff, you can then turn the corner into the lighting and furniture section, an area cheerfully illuminated with plenty of natural light, as well as by designs from the likes of Unique Interieur (pictured). Showcasing various dining tables, shelving and storage units, with chairs and loungers, the selection has been

organized into room-sets and livened up by the addition of strategically positioned tableware to help customers visualize how pieces might unite in their own homes. With quantity on display restricted by space, Domus staff are happy to guide you through the furniture catalogues from suppliers like Magis, Kartell, Alivar, Kristalia, Diseño and Tagliabue and to explain the numerous ordering options. Be sure to ask about the stunning solid-wood furniture creations from German company E15, which are made with high-quality natural materials, such as European oak and cherrywood, American walnut and maplewood, combining them elegantly with stainless steel, leather and felt to produce timeless, refined furniture for the modern interior.

Emma Kench's understanding of her customers has resulted in a collection of contemporary products that appeals to a diverse range of tastes, including the design-wary. The unintimidating environment at Domus makes for a pleasantly relaxed shopping experience.

EAT MY
HANDBAG BITCH

DESIGNERS INCLUDE:
Arnolfo di Cambio
Bozart
Carlo De Carli
Ernest Race
Frank Guille
Gio Ponti
Karim Rashid
Robin Day
Yoshitomo Nara

SERVICES:
Sourcing

CLOSE TO:
Overdose On Design
Unto This Last

Eat My Handbag Bitch
6 Dray Walk
The Old Truman Brewery
91–95 Brick Lane
London E1 6QL
020 7375 3100
www.eatmyhandbagbitch.co.uk
Tube: Aldgate East or Liverpool Street
Open: Daily 11–5

Concession at Selfridges, London (p 208)

George and Georgina are the friendly couple behind the provocatively named Eat My Handbag Bitch in London's East End. Opened in May 1999, the store occupies a split-level unit in The Old Truman Brewery on Brick Lane and is home to a continually changing selection of vintage furniture, lighting, ceramics and glass from a range of designers from the 1950s to 1980s. Sourcing pieces from across Europe is an ongoing task for the energetic duo – however, they tend to place emphasis on English and Italian designers of the 1950s and 1960s, such as Gio Ponti, Ernest Race, Carlo De Carli, Frank Guille and Robin Day. In 2001, the business grew to incorporate a concession in the basement of Selfridges in London's Oxford Street.

More recently new objects have been introduced to the shop floor. These include the stunning crystal glass collection designed by pioneers Joe Columbo, Enzo Mari and Ettore Sottsass for Arnolfo di Cambio, as well as certain pieces from US company Bozart, such as a colourful chess set by Karim Rashid or humorous ashtray and bookends by Yoshitomo Nara. With a changing display of pieces in their East London store, it is no surprise that the space looks different from visit to visit. Sometimes cluttered, sometimes sparse, the display often depends on the couple's ability to source a cross section of products that they are happy with, as they insist that high quality is sustained across their collection.

Compare the East London store with the concession in Selfridges and it is evident that the different locations largely dictate what is sold. The Selfridges customer calls for a polished space with a variety of styles and price ranges to suit the varying tastes and budgets. The Brick Lane premises cater more for the design-savvy buyers who are often able to identify the designer, era or origin of a piece on their own. If you want something in particular, check the website or phone in advance to avoid disappointment. Make your purchasing decisions quickly – hesitation could result in someone else buying it before you.

EQUINOX

DESIGNERS INCLUDE:
Alessi
Design House
Stockholm
Georg Jensen
Global
iittala
Kosta Boda
Ritzenhoff
Rosenthal
Stelton
Thomas Goode
WMF

SERVICES:
Contract Division
Gift Vouchers
Gift Wrapping
Wedding List

CLOSE TO:
Lounge

Equinox
32 Howard Street
Belfast BT1 6PF
028 9023 0089
www.e-equinox.co.uk
Open: Mon – Sat 9:30 – 5:30
Thurs til 9

Owners Kay and Jan Gilbert have established a firm foothold in retail tableware since opening a shop in central Belfast in 1985. Tapping into the higher end of the market, Equinox supplies customers with an interesting and diverse choice of well-made beautiful crockery, cutlery and kitchenware, complemented by some bathroom accessories, clocks, watches and jewellery.

Housed on a busy street, Equinox attracts a significant number of visitors looking for a quality alternative to the usual department store pickings. The large selection of clean-lined crockery from German company Rosenthal is sure to catch your attention, alongside colourful glass vases from Kosta Boda. With every item given equal pride of place within the black-and-white interior of this well-presented store, it's hard to resist the carefully chosen stock from recognized brands such as Stelton, iittala, Hackman, Global, WMF, Thomas Goode, Ritzenhoff, Design House Stockholm and Alessi.

Equinox is a superior store. The displays are clean, slick, uncluttered and well lit, and the ambience within the space is calm and professional. Good-looking staff, all clad in black, are available to help with any enquiries and offer crucial assistance with difficult decision making. The shopping experience is further soothed by the euphoric music piped around the shop, and by the food and drink from the café at the rear. Kay and Jan Gilbert's business has been cleverly refined over the years and is well worth a visit.

FANDANGO

DESIGNERS INCLUDE:
Arne Jacobsen
Charles and Ray Eames
Hans Wegner
Holmegaard
Poul Henningson
Tapio Wirkkala
Vennini
Verner Panton
Vistosi

SERVICES:
Sourcing

CLOSE TO:
Area Squared Design
Aria
Crafts Council
Gallery Shop
Living Space
Twentytwentyone

Fandango
50 Cross Street
London N1 2BA
020 7226 1777
www.fandango.uk.com
Tube: Angel or Highbury & Islington
Open: Tues – Sat 11 – 6

Fandango was originally based at the Angel-end of Essex Road but in March 2001 moved to their cosier and more polished location on Cross Street. Owners Henrietta Palmer and Jonathan Ellis deal in original twentieth-century design and decorative furniture. A limited changing display of pieces continually comes into the tiny shop before eager purchasers snap up these hard-to-find items.

Henrietta Palmer and Jonathan Ellis have the exhausting task of sourcing pieces of furniture, lighting, glassware and prints from across Europe, buying items that are then restored to their former glory by the experts in the workshop at the back of the shop. The day I visited, the back door was open for ventilation and I was able to witness the restoration of a Danish rosewood sideboard. The workshop is usually fairly active during the week in preparation for the Saturday rush of customers. If you are lucky, you can lay claim to an object from the workshops before it is ready for purchase, safely ensuring no one else gets in there first. All new additions are regularly uploaded onto the website, with many collectors from abroad using this virtual tool to buy pieces.

I would always recommend visiting the shop so that you can experience the items first-hand: the combination of iconic designs with many generic offerings means that you never quite know what to expect. I always enjoy this level of anticipation – perhaps it will be a 1950s Danish sideboard, a stunning Italian glass chandelier, or a Holmegaard or Vennini glass vase. Don't be too hesitant – pieces don't hang around for long.

FERRIOUS @ HOME

DESIGNERS INCLUDE:
Claire Norcross
Ferrious
Jeremy West
Jonathan Woolley
Jorrit Kortenhorst
Jurgen Bey
Marcel Wanders
moooi
Piet Boon and the
Monkey Boys
Tom Kirk

SERVICES:
Bespoke Orders
Contract Division
Interior Design

CLOSE TO:
Innerform

Ferrious @ Home
Arch 61 Whitworth Street West
Manchester M1 5WQ
0161 228 6880
www.ferrious.co.uk
Open: Tues – Sat 11 – 6

You would be hard pressed to find a UK design company producing better high-quality contemporary furniture for the contract and domestic markets than Manchester-based Ferrious. It was founded by Jeremy West and Paul Tempest in 1993, who have managed to consistently design and manufacture their own range of cool sofas and chairs in this country. Most people assume Italy is the only place to source original modern furniture, but Ferrious is one reason to start your search closer to home.

The company began by supplying mainly commissioned furniture and some lighting to the trade. Establishing its own range from these projects, it can now boast a sizeable collection, which is always well received by the international design community. The company's base is in a spacious double-height arched showroom under the railway line into Oxford Road station in central Manchester, the slick entrance and interior providing a refreshing contrast to the exposed brick exterior. Unfortunately, entry is by an intimidating buzzer, but once inside you will be greeted by one of the friendly and hospitable owners. Browse the selection of furniture and you'll immediately notice the level of quality. Pieces are hand-assembled in the workshop behind the showroom. Paul Tempest controls a lot of the business logistics, while most design and production work is undertaken by Jeremy West, who has implemented a slick commercial aesthetic with subtle touches of his quirky British humour. Occasionally impressed by the work of newer UK designers, Ferrious has taken on gorgeous designs from local talents, namely the 850 light by Claire Norcross and the Pipe sofa by Jonathan Woolley (p 272).

At the time of going to press, Ferrious was embarking on renovation work to the showroom space to incorporate a mezzanine level displaying other contemporary pieces that complement its range. You can not only order good-looking additions for your home or office but also expect professional service and efficiency from the team, delivered with a smile.

FLIN FLON

DESIGNERS INCLUDE:
Alvar Aalto
Arabia
Hans Wegner
iittala
Josef Frank
Kinnasand
Kobolt
Marimekko
Oiva Toikka
Robin Day
Svenskt Tenn
Torsten Neeland
Tapio Wirkkala

SERVICES:
Interior Design
Sourcing

CLOSE TO:
Her House
Vitra

Flin Flon
138 St John Street
London EC1V 4UA
020 7253 8849
www.flinflon.co.uk
Open: Thurs – Fri 12 – 6
Sat 12 – 4

You will be forgiven for passing by this discreet gallery-like shop on Clerkenwell's St John Street as it has extremely subtle street presence. Bonnie Kennedy and Marianna Wahlsten opened this 'hidden gem' in October 2000 and chose to name it after a Canadian town situated at the edge of human civilization. The shop originally occupied a relatively small space, so the owners decided to take out the ground floor to reveal and utilize the basement, at the same time creating the impression of more space with increased room height. On entry to the shop, admire the selection from street level before descending the stairs to be greeted by the friendly staff. The entire space is kept very raw with textural plywood boarding used to clad the walls and bare bulbs to illuminate the mainly original Scandinavian mid-century furniture and fabric designs.

Bonnie Kennedy and Marianna Wahlsten source a constantly changing collection of personally chosen interior items that catch their eye on trips to Finland and Denmark. Their network of dealers and suppliers is extensive and varied, making for a constantly changing choice of items that have been selected for their 'soft-modernist' design qualities. Original Alvar Aalto No 60 three-legged stools and his Y-leg stool are positioned next to an iconic upholstered chair by Robin Day, or an armchair design by Hans Wegner. A mahogany chair by Josef Frank for Svenskt Tenn is lifted by hand-embroidered linen cushions by Jaana Wahlsten and illuminated by the new Eclipse light by Torsten Neeland. Vibrant graphic fabric designs, both reissued and vintage, mainly from Marimekko and Kinnasand, play a large part in the shop by adding colour to large expanses of blond wood panelling. Dotted around the shelving displays are pieces of vintage glass from Kaj Franck for iittala, Tapio Wirkkala, and Oiva Toikka as well as ceramic tableware from Arabia and Kobolt and a few specialist old and new design books. The owners are attracted to nature and wilderness, and source items that possess soft organic elements while retaining obvious functional benefits.

The atmosphere in the shop is calm and exclusive without feeling pretentious. Prices suit various budgets, but even if you leave empty-handed, you are sure to remember this shop and mention it to your close friends. Unless you prefer to keep it a secret…

DESIGNERS INCLUDE:
Alison Crowther
Amy Cushing
Andrew Wicks
Anthony Bryant
Barry Griffiths
Hans Stofer
John Lewis
Liam Flynn
Lulu Sylvest
Zoe Hope

SERVICES:
Bespoke Orders

CLOSE TO:
Bowles and Linares
Mission
Themes & Variations
Vessel

Flow
1–5 Needham Road
London W11 2RP
020 7243 0782
www.flowgallery.co.uk
Tube: Notting Hill Gate
Open: Mon–Sat 11–6

Founding director of Flow, Yvonna Demczynska, opened her contemporary applied arts gallery in October 1999 on a side street off London's fashionable Westbourne Grove in Notting Hill. Fed up with the stark minimalism and mass-produced nature of so many design products of today, Yvonna Demczynska was keen to introduce an eclectic mix of both functional and non-functional objects of a softer aesthetic. Selecting objects that are inspired by nature's organic curvilinear forms and a palette ranging from neutral tones to rich and earthy colours, Flow has succeeded in attracting customers seeking more unusual additions to their homes.

Flow works with a number of British artists to bring ceramics, jewellery, metalwork, wood, textiles, paper and glass to a tranquil gallery setting. There is always a new choice of beautifully crafted pieces to capture your attention, from talents, such as John Lewis, who makes colourful and curvaceous glass vases. You'll also find Anthony Bryant's unique, fragile wooden vessels, Andrew Wicks' muted textural ceramics, Zoe Hope's

ethereal textiles, and Barry Griffiths' moiré-effect functional sculptures (pictured). At Flow, the selection manages to blur the distinctions of what is functional and decorative, reinforcing the ambiguity that surrounds the relationship between craft and design.

In addition to the permanent uncluttered displays that occupy the wall space, Flow holds six exhibitions a year, such as the 'Field of Silver' show that was staged across the main floor space. In an expensive location and premises, you expect everything to cost a fortune. While this can be the case, Yvonna Demczynska tries to strike a balance with products at prices to appeal to a range of budgets.

The retail environment at Flow feels entirely accessible and welcoming. It inspires casual browsing and the appreciation and, often, purchase of work by some of Britain's leading contemporary applied artists.

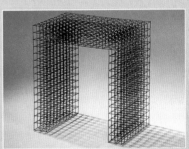

FORM

Form (Glasgow)
First Floor
The Lighthouse
11 Mitchell Lane
Glasgow G1 3LX
0141 225 8422
www.thelighthouse.co.uk
Tube: Buchanan Street
Open: Mon – Sat 10:30 – 5
except Tues 11 – 5
Sun 12 – 5

In 1999, during Glasgow's year as UK City of Architecture and Design, The Lighthouse opened in a Charles Rennie Mackintosh-designed building in the city centre, revitalized by architects Page & Park to become one of Europe's largest architecture and design centres. Situated down a narrow lane off busy Buchanan Street, this impressive building houses four floors of exhibition space, conference facilities, an education centre, a café, restaurant and a panoramic viewing platform at the top. Staging fabulous changing exhibitions of the work of talented designers and architecture practices, what was missing from The Lighthouse was a retail division for visitors to actually buy some of the items on display in the galleries. December 2001 finally saw the opening of Form, the centre's very own design shop.

Attracting a large number of people every year creates an ideal opportunity to introduce design to a wider audience by offering contemporary products that don't break the bank. The majority of items are designed by UK talents such as Nelson, Benis, Black & Blum, Suck UK (p 288), Isabel Stanley, Kate Allsop, One

Foot Taller, Happell, Peppermint, Oliver Hemming, Geraldine McGloin, Innermost, Sukie, Fossil and Charlie MacPherson.

Form occupies a sizeable double-height room on the first floor, and you enter the raw textural old-industrial space along 'the catwalk' lined with various lighting and accessory items. There is furniture from Vitra (p 242), which utilizes half of the room as its Scottish office and showroom. Some floorspace features saleable products that coincide with the exhibitions upstairs, such as the Alessi range on my visit. Glaswegians agree that The Lighthouse is a unique venue for the celebration of contemporary design, and Form is a far cry from the stereotypical gallery shop and another good reason to visit this inspiring cultural destination.

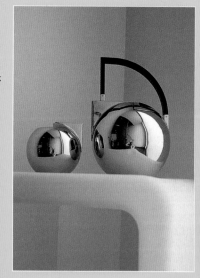

DESIGNERS INCLUDE
Alessi
Benis
Black & Blum
Charlie MacPherson
Fossil
Geraldine McGloin
Happell
Innermost
Isabel Stanley
Kate Allsop
Nelson
Oliver Hemming
One Foot Taller
Peppermint
Suck UK
Sukie
Vitra

SERVICES:
Bespoke Orders
Contract Division
Gift Wrapping

CLOSE TO:
Vitra (Scotland)

FORM

Form (Sheffield)
6 The Plaza
West One
8 Fitzwilliam Street
Sheffield S1 4JB
Tel: 0114 275 8700
www.formliving.com
Open: Mon – Weds 9:30 – 6
Thurs 9:30 – 7
Fri-Sat 9:30 – 6
Sun 10:30 – 4:30

DESIGNERS INCLUDE:
Alvar Alto
Artek
Asplund
Boda Nova
Bodum
Cath Kidston
David Design
iittala
LSA International
Marimekko
Melin Tregwynt

SERVICES:
Contract Division
Gift Vouchers
Gift Wrapping
Interior Advice
Wedding List

CLOSE TO:
The Humble Abode
Prego

The massive West One residential and commercial development in the heart of Sheffield opened in March 2003 and with it launched Form, a lifestyle design store owned by John Booth and Matt Carr. Occupying a 1,400 sq ft split-level retail unit fronting onto Cavendish Street, the store features a contemporary mix of mainly smaller homewares and some carefully chosen furniture and lighting. Form benefits from high ceilings and plenty of natural light flooding through floor-to-ceiling glazed windows. The owners have succeeded in creating a welcoming, warm and stylish backdrop on which to display a selection of modern interior products for increasingly design-conscious Sheffield residents.

Room-set displays combine furniture with soft furnishings, ceramics and glassware, inspiring customers to imagine how the gorgeous creations could be incorporated into their own homes. Who can resist sinking into a slick low-level Alfa sofa from Zanotta graced with fabrics from Marimekko? Classic Alvar Aalto chairs and stools from Artek are brightened up by colourful glassware from iittala and LSA under the warm illumination of David Design and Max Watt lighting.

While local attitudes towards contemporary design are progressing, the owners of Form are all too aware that the introduction of high-end designs needs to be complemented with a large selection of affordable accessories and gift ideas. Form stocks a huge variety of functional items for every room in the home, each piece adhering to the owners' design sensibilities. As part of a large commercial development, Form attracts a variety of customers, from the curious browser to the design-savvy. Resisting any garish avant-garde designs, John Booth and Matt Carr have selected a simple, clean, classic and carefully priced collection of designs with broad appeal in a friendly and hospitable shopping environment.

14 HOLLAND STREET

14 Holland Street
14 Holland Street
London W8 4LT
020 7938 2244
Tube: High Street Kensington
Open: Mon – Fri 9 – 6

DESIGNERS INCLUDE:
Mark Humphrey

SERVICES:
Bespoke Orders
Contract Division
Gift Vouchers
Gift Wrapping
Interior Design
Wedding List

Located at the end of a stretch of shops and boutiques on elegant Holland Street is Brent Jackson and James Davies' latest joint venture. Occupying a stunning quirky old Georgian house, 14 Holland Street is their unique three-storey showroom designed by interior and product designer Mark Humphrey. He has blended his individual interior concept of space into the seductive environs of this new showroom, launched in December 2002. Mark Humphrey has redefined our preconceptions of space by tailoring every interior detail and product specifically for the showroom's overall scheme, designing all of the elements to work together in an ingenious multifunctional space. After all, why not transform your hallway into a formal dining room? Or combine your sleeping area with a Kevlar fibre and Masur birch bath and bathing cabinet? Couldn't your office and drawing room become the guest bedroom with careful space management? At 14 Holland Street, they are eager to demonstrate how to take advantage of such possibilities.

Humphrey has created his own designs exclusive to the showroom, designing most of the fittings as well as a refined and luxurious furniture, lighting and accessories collection that draws on the skills of specialist craftsmen around England.

He works closely with the underused resources that are available in this country, and his collection unusually combines a plethora of classic and modern materials, such as stainless steel, nickel, carbon fibre, marble, limestone, granite, leather, fibre optics and eglomise mirror, in the creation of richly textured and patterned additions for the home. Insisting that customers should be more expressive and bold in their interior decisions, Humphrey has created an eclectic environment that oozes sexy couture glamour.

Met by the welcoming owners, you are instantly impressed by the sheer quality and attention to detail that has gone into the scheme. You can peruse the fabulous bespoke interior offerings while benefiting from the dedicated attention of the knowledgeable proprietors, whose passion and enthusiasm for their industry is immediately evident. They offer a service that caters for a single purchase or a complete interior overhaul, delivering to you new and imaginative solutions with the utmost professionalism and care.

DESIGNERS INCLUDE:
Alvar Aalto
Brionvega
Charles and Ray Eames
Danese Milano
David Design
Eero Aarnio
Flos
iittala
Marimekko
Mario Bellini
Oluce
Pure Design
Stelton
Vico Magistretti

SERVICES:
Contract Division
Gift Vouchers
Gift Wrapping
Wedding List

CLOSE TO:
XU

**Fusion
30 Church Street
Birmingham B3 2NP
0121 236 1020
www.fusionlifestyle.co.uk
Open: Mon – Sat 9:30 – 6**

Over the past few years, a huge amount of investment has gone into the Midland's capital city of Birmingham, bringing it in line with other similar size European cities. As the cityscape becomes increasingly modernized, so, too, do the inhabitants who are eager to incorporate modern living into their homes. Catering to this demand is Fusion, in a new development called Innovation Square opposite the sumptuous Hotel du Vin. Occupying a high-ceiling corner unit and benefiting from decent passing trade in the business quarter, Paul Maycock's new venture is a welcome addition to the Midland's retail design market, bringing with it mainly Scandinavian and Italian furniture, lighting and accessory products.

Although he hails from a background in automotive design, Paul Maycock's exposure to other design influences over the years has introduced him to the sort of design products that haven't previously been available in the area… until now.

With 1,400 sq ft of retail space spread across two levels, Fusion offers a range of furniture, from re-editions of twentieth-century design classics from Alvar Aalto,

Eero Aarnio, Charles and Ray Eames, Mario Bellini and Vico Magistretti to works from more contemporary design companies like Sweden's David Design and Canada's Pure Design. To accompany the larger items there is a good selection of accessories such as iittala glassware, Stelton stainless steel tableware, vibrant Marimekko fabrics, Danese Milano desk objects, Brionvega TV and radios, as well as lighting from Oluce and Flos.

The diversity of designs at Fusion suits varying budgets, from more expensive furniture to accessible gifts or impulse buys. Introducing an attractive lifestyle to a variety of customers, from the design-conscious to the everyday consumer, Fusion has put vivacity and colour back into the sometimes sterile and self-aware design industry, turning shopping here into an enjoyable experience.

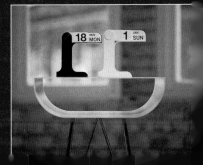

GEOFFREY DRAYTON

Geoffrey Drayton
85 Hampstead Road
London NW1 2PL
020 7387 5840
Tube: Warren Street or Euston Square
Open: Mon – Sat 10 – 6

104 High Street
Epping
Essex CM16 4AF
01992 573 929
Open: Mon – Sat 9 – 5:30

www.geoffrey-drayton.co.uk

In 2002, the modern furniture and lighting retailer Geoffrey Drayton celebrated forty years in the business. He first opened in 1962 in Walthamstow, with the aim of providing well-designed contemporary furniture and lighting that was not otherwise available outside central London. Selling mainly Scandinavian pieces, the shop rapidly developed a loyal following in the area, prompting the opening of a second shop on Epping High Street in 1964. Then, in 1989, he opened another showroom near St Katherine's Dock, which was relocated to Hampstead Road when the complex closed. Standing out among lesser furniture stores, the eye-catching 5,000 sq ft retail space is home to an extensive range of leading European furniture from major brands like Cassina, B&B Italia, Interlübke, Vitra, Zanotta, Emmebi, Kartell, Magis, Ycami and Montis. A huge selection of products crammed into the sizeable showroom

can prove to be a visual maelstrom as you manoeuvre around gorgeous offerings illuminated by lighting options from Artemide, Flos, Ingo Maurer, Lumina, Luceplan, Oluce and Tobias Grau.

Geoffrey Drayton supplies both trade and public with a considerable choice of high-quality designs temptingly displayed. Understandably, the store has developed a good reputation over the years, boasting an impressive base of customers who appreciate the professional and courteous service. Always setting his sights on quality lasting designs, Geoffrey Drayton still sells some of the pieces of furniture he first stocked in 1962, proving that good design will always stand the test of time. Having experienced the fluctuations in the design industry over the years, Geoffrey Drayton is delighted that modern design is at last attracting larger audiences as more people embrace a contemporary lifestyle.

DESIGNERS INCLUDE:
Artemide
B&B Italia
Cassina
Emmebi
Flos
Ingo Maurer
Interlübke
Kartell
Luceplan
Lumina
Magis
Montis
Oluce
Tobias Grau
Vitra
Ycami
Zanotta

SERVICES:
Interior Design
Contract Division

(EPPING):
Gift Vouchers
Gift Wrapping
Wedding List

CLOSE TO:
Planet Bazaar

Cassina

Cass

HABITAT

DESIGNERS INCLUDE:
Andrew Davies
Bethan Gray
Claire Norcross
Fred Rieffel
Georg Baldele
Lance McGregor
Lisa Norinder
Matthew Hilton
Matt Hobbs
Naomi Waldman
Nick Green
Niki Jones
Norman Richards
Peter McCann
Robin Day
Ross Menuez
Shin and Tomoko Azumi
Simon Pengelly
Susanne Philippson

SERVICES:
Contract Division
Gift Vouchers
Interior Design

CLOSE TO:
Chaplins
(Berner Street)
Heal's
Ligne Roset West End
Purves & Purves

Habitat
196 Tottenham Court Road
London W1P 9LD
020 7631 3880
www.habitat.net
Tube: Goodge Street
Open: Mon – Wed 10 – 6
Thurs 10 – 8
Fri 10 – 6:30
Sat 9:30 – 6:30
Sun 12 – 6

Other stores nationwide
Call 0845 60 10 740
See website for details

Founded in May 1964 in London's Fulham Road by Terence Conran, Habitat marked the start of bold new beginnings in the British homestyle market. During the swinging Sixties, Conran opened the eyes of the British public to modern 'simple, functional, beautiful and affordable' designs sourced from across the world. Over nearly forty years, Habitat has experienced some turbulent changes within its business structure and ownership but has always maintained its commitment to its original holistic brand values, creating a collection of accessible interior products. With stores worldwide, the company's creative vision is now led by design director Tom Dixon, who has appointed a seven-strong team to steer the chain comfortably into the twenty-first century. Working with a global network of suppliers and craftspeople, Dixon has the huge task of commissioning products that stay abreast of contemporary tastes

while still appealing to a broad spectrum of customers. In addition to Habitat's range of stable unobtrusive sellers are pieces from prolific designers like Robin Day, Simon Pengelly, Shin and Tomoko Azumi, Ross Menuez, Georg Baldele and Lisa Norinder, which are marketed strongly to retain a 'cool' image.

Operating nearly 40 stores around the UK in city centre locations, Habitat can boast good nationwide reach to everyday consumers. While the collections remain consistent throughout the network, general upkeep and standards seem to fluctuate considerably from city to city. During the past five years Habitat has redefined its collections; perhaps the next move will see it reconfigure its in-store identity.

Selling everything from tableware to lighting and textiles to furniture, Habitat has successfully maintained its reputation for affordable modern design, and has contributed significantly to the shift in attitude of design-conscious everyday consumers.

HEAL'S

DESIGNERS INCLUDE:
Alessi
Guzzini
Hackman
Heal's
Ligne Roset
LSA International

SERVICES:
Bespoke Orders
Contract Division
Gift Vouchers
Interior Design
Wedding List

CLOSE TO:
Chaplins
(Berners Street)
Habitat
Ligne Roset West End
Purves & Purves

Heal's
196 Tottenham Court Road
London W1T 7LQ
020 7636 1666
www.heals.co.uk
Tube: Goodge Street
Open: Mon – Weds 10 – 6
Thurs til 8
Fri til 6.30
Sat 9.30 – 6.30
Sun 12 – 6

Stores in Chelsea, Guildford
and Kingston Upon Thames
See website for details

For most people in the south-east of England, Heal's is a recognizable retail brand that has served the interior needs of many generations of consumers since it was founded on London's Tottenham Court Road in 1810. Initially a family-run bedmaking firm, the store grew considerably under the sixty-year reign of Sir Ambrose Heal, who worked as craftsman, designer and finally chairman from 1893 to 1953. Combining beauty and function with high-quality yet commercial production techniques, he expanded the company's trading activities to incorporate retailing, contracting, fabric conversion and wholesaling, cabinet furniture manufacture, and beds and bedding manufacture. After various acquisitions and management buy-outs over the past twenty years, Heal's is once again a private company that has recently embarked on a revitalization of its brand.

The impressive 45,000 sq ft flagship store on Tottenham Court Road (pictured), is home to organized and tidy displays of interior products that span a variety of budgets and functions.

Appealing to a core customer base of young professionals in their late twenties and early thirties, Heal's has achieved a merchandise style that succeeds in drawing in other demographics, too. This savvy retailer has tapped into a design style that refrains from being overtly avant-garde in favour of a more subtle and elegant contemporary aesthetic. Favouring natural materials, uncomplicated forms and functionalism – all at the right price – Heal's manufactures pieces and sources companies that fit these popular criteria.

With four stores in the south east, all in prime retail locations, it is no real surprise that Heal's retains a core of loyal customers. If you are unfortunate enough not to be based near a store, bridge the gap by shopping online.

HER HOUSE

Her House
30d Great Sutton Street
London EC1V 0DU
020 7689 0606
www.herhouse.uk.com
Tube: Farringdon
Open: Tues–Fri 12–7
Sat 11–4

DESIGNERS INCLUDE:
Her House
Luke Morgan
LuLu Guinness
Scott Batty
Uptight

SERVICES:
Bespoke Orders
Gift Wrapping

CLOSE TO:
Flin Flon
Vitra

I don't know about you but the idea of having a bunch of strangers traipsing through my house every day fills me with horror. After all, it's my private space. But Her House owner Morag Myerscough would disagree. She has turned her kitchen into an intimate living-space gallery where you can buy new artworks, designs, textiles and products from a changing selection of emerging artists and designers, as well as own-brand items. As it has a normal shop front, you could be forgiven for not even realizing you are actually wandering round someone's home. Not until you spot the oven (meticulously polished every day) and fridge, along with a few dog-eared cookbooks, do you understand where you are. Any momentary pangs of guilt for invading Morag Myerscough's kitchen soon disappear once you become absorbed by the quirky selection of objects on sale.

What better than to nose around someone else's space and have the opportunity to buy everything in it? After opening hours, the blinds come down and life in the Myerscough household returns to normal, which magnifies the feeling of privilege of intruding on this routine. Spotting the kettle on the sideboard, you wonder whether it would be cheeky to ask for a cup of tea. After all, you can easily spend a long time looking at the eclectic offerings that make up the regularly changing themed exhibitions.

Spread across the simple shelving displays are all sorts of unusual small kitsch or humorous accessory items that you are unlikely to find elsewhere, as well as various clothing items and specially commissioned artwork adorning the walls. Morag Myerscough is a graphic designer by training and has collaborated with the likes of Luke Morgan and Scott Batty on a Her House product range, such as a lamp made from colourful surgical tubing and curving steel, a coffee table with 'Bollocks' graffiti-slashed across the top, a tongue-in-cheek bird box and a flat-pack table made from 100% recyclable materials.

Without a doubt, a visit to Her House will put a smile on your face and a dent in your wallet. No two visits are ever the same, which makes a change from the repetition and complacency sometimes experienced in other shops.

THE HOME

DESIGNERS INCLUDE:
Alessandro Mendini
Alvar Aalto
Charles Eames
Enzo Mari
George Sowden
Harry Bertoia
Le Corbusier
Marcel Breuer
Memphis
Natalie du Pasquier
Philippe Starck

SERVICES:
Contract Division
Gift Vouchers
Gift Wrapping
Wedding List

The Home
Salts Mill
Victoria Road
Saltaire
Bradford BD18 3LB
01274 530 770
www.saltsmill.org.uk/thehome.htm
Open: Daily 10 – 6

Salts Mill is not the first place you might expect to find a huge selection of contemporary design items. This immense looming mid-nineteenth century converted textile factory situated on the edge of Bradford in Saltaire is one of the area's most visited tourist attractions, mainly due to the fact that it houses the world's largest public collection of work from locally born artist David Hockney. The collection may be big, but the building is bigger, allowing room for commercial opportunities such as a bookshop, restaurant and design shop.

Robin and Pat Silver's design emporium was opened in 1994 and occupies a vast long open-plan space lined with factory windows that cast plenty of natural light onto the objects within. Selling a mix of classic and contemporary furniture alongside ceramics, glass and tableware, you might easily leave with more than just the Hockney print you had anticipated. Attracting a mix of customers, the husband and wife duo have made sure that they carry a stock of items that will appeal to both design aficionados and public alike. However, with annual visitor numbers exceeding 500,000, their obvious problem is protection of the goods from damage and general wear-and-tear. Against their wishes, the solution has been to display products on plinths, behind rope, or in glass cases with DO NOT TOUCH signs, rather like a museum. This approach, while necessary, doesn't especially encourage people to buy and unfortunately contributes to the ongoing myth that good contemporary design pieces should be reserved for the privileged. The Home showcases exciting innovative creations to a wider audience and displays the prices clearly for those who understandably succumb. Friendly staff are on hand to retrieve your chosen items from the stock room.

You have to visit The Home to appreciate the impressive quantity of goods from mainly European designers. Claiming they would like even more space to show other design pieces, the charismatic owners must know that their store offers the most comprehensive on-the-spot design choice in the country.

THE HUMBLE ABODE

The Humble Abode
7 Garden Street
Sheffield S1 4BJ
0114 272 8999
www.thehumbleabode.co.uk
Open: Tues – Fri 11 – 7
Sat 10 – 7
Sun 11 – 5

The Humble Abode is a fabulous new interiors store located slightly off the beaten track in the centre of Sheffield within a 1,000 sq ft former car repair garage. Gone are the oily rags and smell of petrol in favour of an extensively refurbished retail outlet that has been instigated by The Big Fish Corporation. Having worked in the music industry for ten years, owners Iain Kelly and Dickon Fletcher, set up The Humble Abode in spring 2003. Their aim was to sell quality design items that side-step those normally found in the mainstream.

The street presence is deliberately understated. All that remains of the building's former occupation is two huge wooden doors. The old inspection pit in the small ground-floor space now plays host to platinum koi carp swimming

DESIGNERS INCLUDE:
Charles and Ray Eames
Erno Goldfinger
Flameboy
Isokon Plus
Marcel Breuer
Michael Sodeau
Pure Design
Scabetti
Vitra

SERVICES:
Bespoke Orders
Contract Division
Gift Vouchers
Gift Wrapping
Wedding List

CLOSE TO:
Form
Prego

elegantly beneath toughened glass. The silver-grey space around them is occupied by funky plastic chairs and sultry artwork. Climb the narrow metal staircase to the first-floor showroom and you will be met by a huge white loft-style space benefiting from high eaves and exposed metal work, plus a cosier mezzanine area showcasing comfy low-level seating arrangements.

Greeted by friendly staff, you are free to browse the array of modern and understated furniture, tableware and soft furnishings on display. The cool strains of minimalist electronica put customers at ease in an engaging atmosphere that feels somewhat separate from the outside world. On my visit, the space held pieces from up-and-coming designers, such as Flameboy and Scabetti alongside immaculately produced plywood furniture by Marcel Breuer, Michael Sodeau, and Barber Osgerby from Isokon Plus (p 124). Understated elegance from Canadian company Pure Design sits effectively next to various classic chair designs from Charles and Ray Eames and Arad for Vitra, not to mention iconic furniture creations from Erno Goldfinger. Accessories and books accompany the larger, more expensive and exclusive items, and a changing display of contemporary artworks occupy the vast back wall. The owners describe themselves as 'environment enhancers' as they have created a space that appeals to all of the human senses. Take a seat, engage in conversation and you will inevitably be reluctant to leave this hidden gem.

INDISH

DESIGNERS INCLUDE:
Bim Burton
Caterina Fadda
Corin Mellor
Finn Stone
Fiona Davidson
Flos
Foscarini
Gitta Gschwendtner
Helen Rawlinson
Indish
Innermost
Isabel Stanley
Kartell
Magis
Max Watt
Meshman
OCP
Oliver Peake
Orian
Ruth Franklin
Suck UK

SERVICES:
Gift Vouchers
Wedding List

Indish
13 & 16 Broadway Parade
London N8 9DE
020 8342 9496
www.indish.co.uk
Open: Mon – Sat 10:30 – 5:30

Located in Crouch End in north London, Indish has managed to successfully tap into the area's growing first-time buyers' market. Owners Melanie Silgardo and Kasha Dalal opened the doors to their first contemporary homewares store in 1996, selling a mix of affordable contemporary textiles, accessories, and lighting, with the occasional small piece of modern furniture, from their cosy retail premises on busy Broadway Parade. The shop didn't have quite the right backdrop, let alone the space, to show really contemporary furniture alternatives, so in 1999, they snapped up an available retail space a few doors down. Simply decorated with white walls and wood floors, these new lighter and airier premises were to be home to a selection of funkier interior alternatives.

Buying decisions combine usual-suspect brands and products with lesser-known, more individually chosen pieces. To the untrained eye this won't be apparent. To the design-savvy, it is encouraging to see big-boy European furniture and lighting brands like Kartell, Magis, Flos, and Foscarini mixed with equal emphasis alongside designs from UK talents. Encountering lighting from Suck UK (p 288), Fiona Davidson and Gitta Gschwendtner, Isabel Stanley, Helen Rawlinson, Orian and Max Watt, as well as ceramics from Innermost, Caterina Fadda and Ruth Franklin, or furniture from Corin Mellor, Oliver Peake, Finn Stone, OCP, Bim Burton and Meshman, you can't help feeling a sense of pride at the achievement of the designers in this country who haven't disappeared to easier manufacturing climates. More retailers need to embrace the creative talent within the UK before automatically targeting the safe Italian brands.

Indish buys in products with affordable price tags and welcomes a steady flow of customers. Unfortunately, the newer store always has a permanent clutter of boxes at the rear of the shop that give it a messy and unfinished appearance, and the staff seemed mildly bored and somewhat clueless when I visited. Don't be put off: this is probably not always the case, and you will surely enjoy simply browsing the displays for gifts or contemporary home additions.

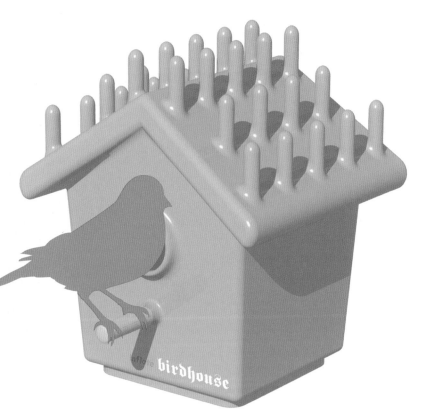

INFLATE

DESIGNERS INCLUDE:
Artomatic
Eurolounge
Inflate
Magis

SERVICES:
Bespoke Orders
Contract Division

CLOSE TO:
Applied Arts Agency
Lowe Interiors
Mac London
Viaduct

Inflate
28 Exmouth Market
London EC1R 4QE
020 7713 9096
www.inflate.co.uk
Tube: Farringdon
Open: Mon – Fri 10 – 6
Sat – phone first

Most of us are familiar with the clever, inflatable products from the Inflate studio, founded by Nick Crosbie and Mark Sodeau in London in 1995. Tapping into a niche market, the company has gone from strength to strength, starting with its own-brand selection of inflatable egg cups, pendant light shades, postcards and cushions. It then went on to produce PVC designs, such as salt and pepper shakers, toothpick dispensers, candlesticks, soap dishes, condom holders and mouldable beanbags, before cleverly incorporating polyethylene into designs for bed bases and lighting.

Since opening its shop in August 2001, Inflate has moved offices from its old Clerkenwell premises into the back of the retail space. This move has conveniently allowed the staff to work in closer proximity to their end user – the everyday customer. They now have the benefit of being able to trial new prototypes to both public and trade customers in the small showroom. Accompanying Inflate's own inimitable range are other products that complement the company ethos and aesthetic, including designs from Eurolounge, Magis and Artomatic.

Since the beginning, Inflate has earned itself a strong reputation and considerable international sales. So, it feels like a privilege to enter the creative hub of this company and speak directly to the team. After all, most design firms are normally tucked away behind closed studio doors. Uniquely, the introduction of a shop has created the unusual scenario of designer as retailer. Although the show space is only small, it has had a big impact on the company, enabling it to define what appeals to the consumer via first-hand experience. When you disappear down bustling Exmouth Market with an Inflate product in your hand, you will have made a small contribution to the company's ongoing market analysis.

INHOUSE

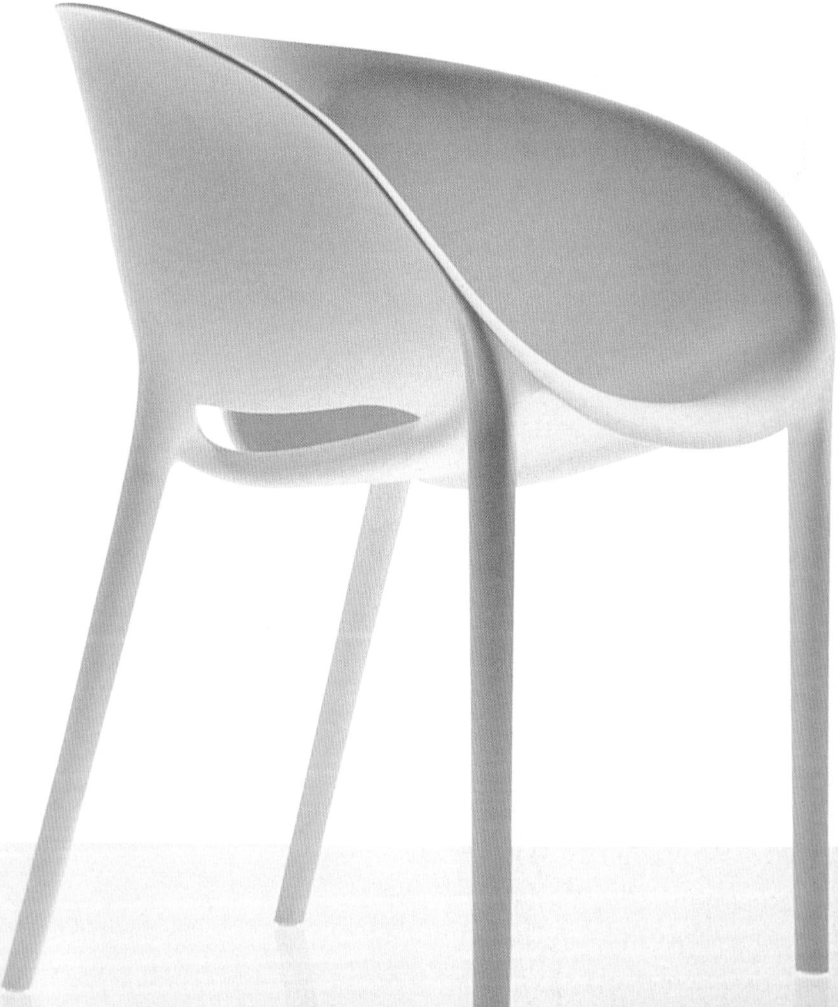

DESIGNERS INCLUDE:
Artek
Artemide
Bellato
Cassina
Driade
Fiam
Flos
Living Divani
Luceplan
Lumina
Mobles 114
Molteni & C
Oluce
Porro
Seven Salotti
Tobias Grau
Zanotta

SERVICES:
Contract Division
Gift Vouchers
Gift Wrapping
Interior Design
Wedding List

CLOSE TO
(GLASGOW):
Dallas + Dallas
Tony Walker Interiors

Inhouse
Inhouse Edinburgh
28 Howe Street
Edinburgh EH3 6TG
0131 225 2888
Open: Mon – Fri 9:30 – 6
Thurs 10 – 7
Sat 9:30 – 5:30

Inhouse Glasgow
24 – 26 Wilson Street
Glasgow G1 1SS
0141 552 5902
Tube: Buchanan Street
Open: Mon – Fri 10 – 6
Thurs til 7
Sat 9:30 – 5:30

www.inhousenet.co.uk

Bill and Sylvia Potter opened the first Inhouse store in Edinburgh in 1982 as one of the few companies to be importing European contemporary furniture for the retail market. Six years later, the company expanded to Glasgow to secure its position on Scotland's design map. Continuing to trade through the ups and downs of the economic climate of the past two decades, Inhouse has established a successful retail formula, sustained by a strong contract division.

Inhouse has good relationships with many large European suppliers, allowing customers a wide choice of contemporary products. Due to limited space in both stores, only a fraction of the company's portfolio is on display, from brands like Seven Salotti, Living Divani, Cassina, Bellato, Molteni & C, Porro, Zanotta, Mobles 114, Driade (pictured), Fiam and Artek. By making use of all the available space, the store has crammed in an extraordinary number of products. For many customers the resulting displays could perhaps be overwhelming. Accompanying the furniture is a cluster of lighting from Flos, Artemide, Oluce, Luceplan, Lumina and Tobias Grau, and shelves full of ceramic, glass and tableware.

In cities with relatively small populations like Edinburgh and Glasgow, the market for high-end furniture is understandably limited. Inhouse is keen to attract customers by offering items to suit all budgets in a welcoming shopping environment that destroys the myth that modern design is elitist and reserved only for the rich. In reputedly conservative Edinburgh, this approach has served Inhouse well; Bill and Sylvia Potter's business has flourished while others have come and gone.

INNERFORM

Innerform
24 Hulme Street
Manchester M1 5BW
0161 238 8558
www.innerform.com
Open: Mon – Sat 10 – 6

Paul Payne and Kevin Large founded Innerform in 1994 in Stockport just outside Manchester, selling high-end European furniture and lighting. Witnessing the growth of inner-city living taking place in Manchester over the past five years, the owners decided to expand their business into the city centre. The duo boldly moved into a 7,000 sq ft commercial property at the base of an apartment development near Oxford Road station in July 2002. They now display modern, clean-lined furniture and lighting options for both the public and contract market.

Having worked with many suppliers over the years, the owners have honed their list to ensure that each and every

DESIGNERS INCLUDE:
Artemide
Dada Flos
Foscarini
Ingo Maurer
Living Divani
Luceplan
MDF Italia
Molteni & C
Porro
Rimadesio
Rimo
Ycami
Zanotta

SERVICES:
Bespoke Orders
Contract Division
Interior Advice

CLOSE TO:
Ferrious @ Home

piece they stock is of the highest quality. With the textural exposed brick walls as a contrasting backdrop, slick yet unobtrusive sofas, chairs, tables, storage, and wardrobe units from the likes of Zanotta, Living Divani, Molteni & C, Porro, MDF Italia, Ycami and Rimadesio truly shine within these spacious surroundings.

A deliberate decision not to stock any accessory items has resulted in a refreshingly uncluttered showroom (spread across three floors), with larger items illuminated by strategic lighting options from Pallucco, Artemide, Flos, Luceplan, Foscarini and Ingo Maurer. The basement space is shared with Rimo, a handmade and custom-designed rug

concession. Paul Payne and Kevin Large also deal in optimum-quality kitchens from Dada, and flooring options. When working with expensive products customers need the process to be carefully explained in detail. This job is expertly undertaken by the knowledgeable and articulate proprietors. Innerform's rather tucked-away location means it attracts people who are in the market for contemporary design rather than aimless browsers. The result is a calm atmosphere where you usually benefits from friendly one-on-one service to decipher exactly what sort of interior solution you are looking for. If you want major additions to your modern interior, start exploring at Innerform.

ISOKON PLUS

Isokon Plus
Turnham Green Terrace Mews
Chiswick
London W4 1QU
020 8994 0636
www.isokonplus.com
Tube: Turnham Green
Open: Tues–Fri 10:30–5:30
Sat 10–6

DESIGNERS INCLUDE:
Barber Osgerby
Associates
Isokon
Marcel Breuer
Michael Sodeau
Simon Pengelly

SERVICES:
Bespoke Orders
Contract Division

The history of Isokon dates back to 1935 when British entrepreneur Jack Pritchard elevated his experience of working with plywood by founding a forward-thinking furniture business with Bauhaus extraordinaire Walter Gropius. Appointing Marcel Breuer, former Bauhaus Master of the Carpentry Workshop, the company quickly established an enviable reputation at the cutting-edge of international modernism. Breuer's designs from the 1930s and 1940s have been the stronghold of the company and are still at the core of the business today, having truly stood the test of time.

In 1982 Jack Pritchard confidently embraced the skills of the specialist makers Windmill Furniture to continue the manufacture and sales of the Isokon range from its Chiswick workshops. Husband and wife duo Lone and Chris McCourt have been manufacturing high-quality bespoke wood pieces for the contract market for more than twenty-five years, accounting for a high percentage of turnover. The iconic bent plywood creations from Breuer still sell well, but the enterprising owners have not stood still with the Isokon collection. New creations from talented UK designers of today include the beautifully proportioned 'Loop' series by Barber Osgerby Associates (BOA), which has already gained significant worldwide recognition as a future classic. More recent additions from Michael Sodeau and Simon Pengelly are destined to follow.

The Isokon Plus complex near Turnham Green tube station is located in a mews with limited available parking. The workshops are a hive of activity where a sizeable team produces a regular stream of work for both Isokon Plus and Windmill Furniture bespoke contracts. Ask nicely and you might be granted a tour of the workshops – otherwise witness the timeless designs in the tranquillity of the retail space. Occupying three floors at the corner of the factory building, the former storage space was sympathetically revamped by BOA in December 2001. Juxtaposing brick walls and old marked wooden floors with areas of slick white wall and a serene connecting staircase, allows customers to experience the full range combined with other complementary furniture, lighting, ceramic and glass, tableware and textiles. Friendly staff or the owners themselves will happily guide you around the spacious displays. But you will only experience true satisfaction when loading up your car with a timeless design for your own home.

KEY LONDON

DESIGNERS INCLUDE:
Alastair McNeill
Amy Cushing
Block Design
Edra
Extremoris
Jay Watson
Joanna Bone
Karin Schösser
Kay Thos
Kelvin Birk
Lulu Sylvest
Norbert Wangen
ogossart
Philipp Plein
Pierantonio Bonacina
Sharon Elphick
Wellis
WW Modcons

SERVICES:
Bespoke Orders
Contract Division
Interior Advice

CLOSE TO:
Mint
Noel Hennessy
Furniture
RJM Furniture
(Wigmore Street)
Selfridges
Skandium

Key London
92 Wimpole Street
London W1G 0EG
020 7499 9461
www.key-london.com
Tube: Bond Street
Open: Mon – Fri 10 – 6
Sat 11 – 6

Lethwin Kuwana opened Key London in early 2000 on a street behind busy, overcrowded, brand-orientated Oxford Street. Occupying a relatively large white-walled L-shaped retail space, charismatic Lethwin Kuwana has been able to showcase her personal choice of furniture, lighting, ceramics, glass and artwork to her clients. Her intention is to offer individualism within the realm of high-end design items, introducing many pieces that are new even to the trained eye. After all, what is the point of selling pieces that every other retailer stocks?

Designs are invariably stunning and high quality is an equally important factor in Lethwin Kuwana's buying decisions. Select pieces of furniture from the likes of Edra, Bonacina, Extremoris, Wellis and Norbert Wangen kitchens don't come cheap – but as soon as you interact with these items, you quickly realize why. This is not a store for consumers in a disposable society; rather it's a place where purchases are carefully considered with the premise that they will last a long time.

Key London also sells objects from a changing array of designers, including elegant handmade colourful glass vases

from Joanna Bone, sharp-lined tables from Kay Thos and Philipp Plein, ceramic lighting objects from Karin Schösser as well as numerous other creations from talents such as Kazuhiro Yamanaka, Block Design, WW Modcons, Amy Cushing, Sharon Elphick, Lulu Sylvest, Kelvin Birk, Jay Watson, Alastair McNeill and ogossart.

On entering the shop you are never sure what to expect, which takes the predictability out of shopping or browsing. The well-lit space has a New York gallery feel to it, especially towards the back where a glass roof structure allows plenty of natural light to flow in. Key London has approached the design market from a different angle – and it works.

LEIGH BUCKLAND

Leigh Buckland
40–42 Old Town
London SW4 0LB
020 7720 5353
www.leighbuckland.com
Tube: Clapham Common
Open: Mon–Sat 10–6
Sun 12–4

Buying furniture involves thought, time and exploration, but the results can be disappointing when you encounter mediocre craftsmanship that doesn't seem to warrant the high price tag. The prospect of commissioning a bespoke interior might seem extravagant but a trip to the Leigh Buckland store in Clapham could change your mind. Compromise is not part of the vocabulary of owners Leigh Buckland and Matthew Roberts.

Opened in September 2002, the fresh 1,600 sq ft open-plan white and grey showroom is home to their own contemporary furniture designs, crafted from solid wood, using traditional joinery and stunning solid timbers from around the world. Every piece on display has been handmade by skilled joiners in the company's state-of-the-art Dulwich workshop and provides an example of the sort of furniture produced. It is then up to you to consult Nick Hannam, head of design, to decide on the exact specifications to suit your individual space and style. Delivery is approximately six weeks after ordering.

At Leigh Buckland, staff and craftsmen understand that there is no such thing as a standard size or space. They will work with a customer's specific

DESIGNERS INCLUDE:
Allermuir
Artemide
Cherner
iittala
Kasthall
Kvist
Leigh Buckland
Louis Poulsen
LSA International
Prandina
Succession
Top Floor

SERVICES:
Bespoke Orders
Contract Division
Gift Wrapping
Interior Design
Wedding List

CLOSE TO:
Places and Spaces

needs on anything from dining and coffee tables, beds and shelving systems to bespoke kitchens and commercial installations, liaising with close partners on specialist glass manufacturing, metal working and upholstery. To complement its own furniture ranges, Leigh Buckland has sourced artwork, lighting, textiles, tableware and seating from reputable producers, such as Zanotta, Allermuir, Succession, Kvist, Cherner, Louis Poulsen, Artemide, Prandina, Top Floor, Kasthall, LSA and iittala. The combination of polished concrete floor and fresh white walls with silky wood finishes, shiny metals, sumptuous leathers and soft fluffy rugs amounts to overall textural bliss.

Sharing the same passion and belief, the friendly and welcoming owners have put a huge amount of effort into fine-tuning the unique package that they offer. Clean-lined understated modernity is favoured here over fly-by-night cutting-edge aesthetics, and all the designs are capable of standing the test of time. Leigh Buckland has identified customers' desire for individualism and is implementing the future of furniture manufacture. Expect to see more stores opening soon.

DESIGNERS INCLUDE:
Arik Levy
Christian Ghion
Christian Werner
Didier Gomez
Francois Bauchet
Jeffrey Bernett
Michel Ducaroy
Ronan and Erwan Bouroullec
Pascal Mourgue
Peter Maly
Sophie Larger

SERVICES:
Contract Division

CLOSE TO:
(West End)
Artemide
Chaplins
(Berner Street)
CVO Firevault
Habitat
Heal's
Purves & Purves

Antoine Roset first started out producing walking sticks and umbrella handles from his small craft workshop in Montagnieu, France, in 1860 before evolving into a manufacturer of furniture. Still in the hands of the Roset family more than 140 years later (under the sharp direction of Antoine's great-grandchildren Pierre and Michel Roset), the business has expanded into the big league of international contemporary furniture brands. Represented on five continents with exclusive outlets in twenty-five countries, Ligne Roset has significant market presence.

Retail presence for the Ligne Roset brand has really grown in the UK during the past five years. While selling through selected retail outlets, the expansion of exclusive franchises has done wonders to establish the Ligne Roset brand in the mind of the consumer. As well as producing many safe and rather bourgeois furniture and storage pieces, the creative headquarters in France has increasingly embraced the talents of both established and new contemporary designers, who have added more flair to the collection in recent years. New furniture, bed, lighting, rug, accessory and textile creations from French names like Pascal Mourgue, Peter Maly, Didier Gomez, Ronan and Erwan Bouroullec, Arik Levy, François Bauchet and Jeffrey

Bernett have added immense value to the brand, positioning it more powerfully in the international design limelight. Many Ligne Roset customers choose to combine different modern, unobtrusive, and functional designs with existing traditional pieces and find that the company provides a 'style de vie' that caters to this perfectly.

The full collection can be viewed at the ever-expanding network of outlets around the country. For example, the Ligne Roset store on Mortimer Street W1 houses the latest additions to the range across the two floors of a spacious well-located showroom. Browse the space, interact with the items and feel free to ask for help from the staff who live, breathe and sleep Ligne Roset. At the time of going to press, the company was on the cusp of announcing the opening of a new concept store in the East End of London. This will be one of the largest Ligne Roset stores in the world, with more than 7,000 sq ft of showroom space especially designed by renowned French designer and artist Pascal Mourgue, who also designed the outstanding New York, Miami, Chicago and Munich stores. The new East End franchise will showcase all the latest Ligne Roset furniture, tableware collection and accessories, including several pieces never previously shown in the UK.

LIVING SPACE

Living Space
36 Cross Street
London N1 2BG
020 7359 3950
www.intospace.co.uk
Tube: Angel or Highbury & Islington
Open: Mon – Sat 10:30 – 6
Sun 12 – 5
Closed Tues

Spencer White opened Living Space in spring 2000 in discreet retail premises just off Islington's Upper Street on Cross Street. Fed up with seeing retailers buying products purely based on brand names, he wanted to introduce new design items that adhere to the criteria of beauty, function and quality. Refreshingly, Spencer White buys in products that few, if no other, UK retailers supply, making for an enlightening shopping experience that sidesteps the predictable. Steering towards a sharp, clean-lined, polished, masculine aesthetic, Living Space has attracted a growing number of customers who are uninterested in frivolous fashion-dictated creations. Instead, they are

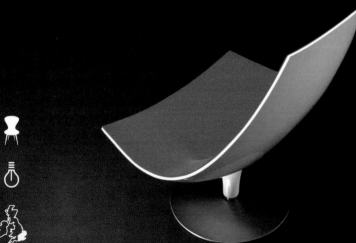

DESIGNERS INCLUDE:
Dema
Il Loft
Italcomma
Lago
Nespoli
Urbinatti

SERVICES:
Bespoke Orders
Contract Division
Interior Design

CLOSE TO:
Area Squared Design
Aria
Crafts Council
Gallery Shop
Fandango
Twentytwentyone

searching for high-end furniture that will perform its daily function for years to come while also providing an unobtrusive modern style.

Within the brilliant white environment of Living Space, the collection tends towards the multifunctional, especially the storage units and dining tables. It uses companies that have tapped into mass-customisation, so that customers are able to order many of the products in varying sizes, configurations, colours, materials and finishes – and all still within the normal eight-week delivery times.

Spencer White stresses the importance of flawless service, proper communication and careful attention to customers' needs. He and his staff will talk you through the products so that you feel confident in your final choice. These items aren't cheap, so Living Space also offers a free interior design advisory service, with a home visit to make measurements and suggestions.

Living Space offers original choices that are well presented and crucially backed up by good service.

LLOYD DAVIES

DESIGNERS INCLUDE:

Aaronson Noon
B&B Italia
Cappellini
Cassina
Driade
Eva Solo
Flexform
Fritz Hansen
Ghislène Jolivet
Kartell
Knoll
LSA International
Montis
Salviati
SCP
Stelton

SERVICES

Bespoke Orders
Contract Division
Gift Vouchers
Gift Wrapping
Interior Design

Lloyd Davies
14 John Dalton Street
Manchester M2 6JR
0161 832 3700
www.lloyddavies.co.uk
Open: Mon – Sat 10 – 6
Sun 12 – 5

Bob Lloyd Davies opened the doors to his central Manchester design store in 1997, originally occupying two floors in prominent corner premises on John Dalton Street. In 2001, the basement was extended and the area consolidated into one large room, with the upper level now a smart bar and restaurant. The store is not immediately obvious from the street. You enter down some stairs into an open-plan room to be confronted by a large choice of contemporary interior items – furniture, lighting, ceramics, glass, tableware, bedlinens and books. Driven towards the domestic interior, the different products on display should appeal to many varying budgets and tastes, whether you are looking for a gift or a completely new look for your home.

On your left is a wall of glowing shelving that houses vases, glasses, crockery, cutlery and other accessories from companies like Stelton, Eva Solo, Salviati, LSA and Aaronson Noon. Particularly striking on my visit was the elegantly formed, colourful handblown glass collection from French designer Ghislène Jolivet, positioned on a suitably sharp-lined new B&B Italia dining table. Continue through the wood-floored shop space and to various mini room-sets for living, dining or bedrooms, featuring international brands like Flexform, Cassina, Knoll, Fritz Hansen, Montis, Kartell, Driade, SCP or Cappellini. Dotted throughout the space are various complementary choices of lighting, while the far corner displays a more comprehensive clustering of illumination options from major lighting suppliers. Across another wall is a simple shelving system containing all sorts of chairs, contributing to the overall accessible feeling within the shop. The ambience in the store is welcoming and customers always feel comfortable asking for advice from the approachable staff.

LOFT

Loft
24–28 Dock Street
Leeds LS10 1JF
0113 305 1515
www.loftonline.net
Open: Mon–Sat 10–5:30
Sun 12–5

Entrepreneur Mac Maclean opened Loft during the summer of 2000 in a converted nineteenth-century warehouse in Leeds' Riverside district. Occupying two commercial spaces totalling 3,000 sq ft, the store is home to a range of furniture from the likes of Sancal, Zanotta, Minotti, Vitra, Fritz Hansen, Knoll, Punt Mobles and SCP, with lighting from Artemide, Oluce, Ingo Maurer, Flos, Luceplan and Fontana Arte, plus numerous accessory items. Combining the exposed brick walls and original beams with an unusual pea-gravel floor set in epoxy resin, the textural open-plan space is an inspiring environment in which to shop.

Many celebrated iconic design pieces are sold in Loft from the likes of Le Corbusier, Arne Jacobsen, Verner Panton and Charles & Ray Eames. But more recently a designer of equal esteem has been introduced to this selling forum. Loft has acquired the licence to manufacture various designs from Robin Day, the pioneering UK designer and global leader of well-designed affordable furniture. Entering the new realm of furniture production, the friendly and enthusiastic Loft team can hardly contain their excitement at working with this design master to reintroduce such designs as the Polo chair (pictured) in new colours and material finishes, bringing back this classic design for today's consumer. With all products manufactured in the UK to a high quality and at an affordable price, Mac Maclean is justly proud to stock Robin Day's work.

Very few contemporary design retailers would ever consider embracing the world of manufacturing, so it is inspiring to witness a company wholeheartedly tackling new territory.

DESIGNERS INCLUDE:
Arne Jacobsen
Artemide
Charles and Ray Eames
Flos
Fritz Hansen
Ingo Maurer
Knoll
Le Corbusier
Luceplan
Minotti
Oluce
Punt Mobles
Robin Day
Sancal
SCP
Verner Panton
Vitra
Zanotta

SERVICES:
Bespoke Orders
Contract Division
Gift Vouchers
Gift Wrapping
Interior Advice
Wedding List

THE LONDON
LIGHTING CO.

The London Lighting Co.
135 Fulham Road
London SW3 6RT
020 7589 3612
Tube: South Kensington
Open: Mon – Sat 9:30 – 6
Sun 12 – 5

Many domestic interiors, and especially hotel rooms, suffer from a lack of well-thought-out lighting solutions. A room can be full of stunning furniture and accessories but can look staid, dull, cold and even depressing without the mood-enhancing possibilities light can offer. Like most markets, the lighting industry has been saturated with millions of variations of ways to use the humble light bulb. As technology has progressed, the range has dramatically increased, making choosing a daunting task. So where can you go to find a well-edited selection? Most dedicated lighting shops try to cram in as many alternatives as possible and end up dazzling customers in a retail space that can get as hot as a sauna. One store that has found a successful formula is The London Lighting Company, opened in 1973 on upmarket Fulham Road.

On my visit on a warm day in the summer, I was dreading the inevitable heat wave emitted from hot bulbs. So I was pleased to be blasted with a jet of cold air from the air-conditioning unit at the entrance. Unlike most other interior environments, lighting shops do not benefit from natural light, which you are reminded of when venturing deeper into this darkened space. In The London Lighting Co, there is enough space to look at the well-edited selection of lights in comfort – floor lamps, table lamps, up-lighters, down-lighters, pendants, spot lights, wall lights, occasional lights, ambient lights, task lights and outdoor lights. The interior may consist of rather dated shades of brown, but the displays remain uncluttered with each light given equal pride of place. Should you need advice, ask one of the somewhat deadpan members of staff to assist.

The atmosphere in the store leaves a little to be desired, but there is no denying that the lighting ranges from top suppliers and designers, such as Ingo Maurer, Philippe Starck, Michele de Lucchi, Vico Magistretti, Ettore Sottsass, Isamu Noguchi, Richard Sapper, Achille Castiglioni, Paolo Rizzatto, and Torsten Neeland will not disappoint.

LOUNGE

DESIGNERS INCLUDE:
Alessi
Alva
Block Design
Bodum
Driade
Dualit
Inflate
Kartell
Krosno
Magis
Menu
Mibo
Room
Rosendahl
Wireworks

SERVICES:
Contract Division
Gift Vouchers
Gift Wrapping
Interior Advice
Wedding List

CLOSE TO:
Equinox

Lounge
13 Wellington Place
Belfast BT1 6GB
028 9024 4474
Open: Mon – Sat 9:30 – 5:30
Thurs til 9
Sun 1 – 5

Angela Murray and Steve Brown opened their store on a busy street in Belfast city centre in June 1999. They were certain that the Northern Ireland capital was ready for contemporary design objects and quickly realized that they were right. Instead of pitching themselves at the high end of the market, the owners sell a selection of the better-known brands that inspire customer confidence and don't break the bank.

Treading carefully at first, Angela Murray and Steve Brown have recently introduced some slightly more garish design items from Italian colour giants Magis (pictured) and Kartell in the new small furniture space at the back of the shop. Lining the shelving units are

a whole array of affordable accessory and tableware items from international companies such as Alessi, Driade, Rosendahl, Menu, Bodum, Dualit and Krosno glass, as well as offerings from UK companies such as Inflate, Mibo, Alva, Room, Wireworks and Block Design, to name but a few.

Lounge is not pitching itself just to the design-savvy consumers of Belfast – the market wouldn't be large enough for them to survive with high-street overheads. The slightly predictable selection is geared towards the everyday shopper seeking contemporary additions to their living environment. The store layout and displays succeed at remaining approachable and, with friendly staff to reinforce this, it is no surprise that there is a steady flow of customers.

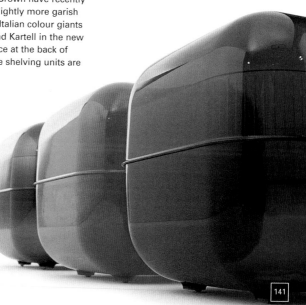

LOWE INTERIORS

DESIGNERS INCLUDE:
Black + Blum
Ferrious
Geraldine McGloin
Hive
Jona Hoad
Julie Nelson
Junilda Ross
Kaya Hoang
Mark Finzel
OCP Design
Phörm
Sasha Gabbe
The Unnatural
Lighting Company

SERVICES:
Bespoke Orders
Contract Division
Gift Wrapping
Interior Design
Wedding List

CLOSE TO:
Applied Arts Agency
Inflate
Mac London
Viaduct

Lowe Interiors
18 Exmouth Market
London EC1R 4QE
020 7278 1140
www.loweinteriors.co.uk
Tube: Farringdon
Open: Mon – Sat 10 – 6

Anyone who has set foot in Clerkenwell over the years could be excused for thinking that Lowe Interiors is an antique store. Owner Andrew Lowe originally dealt in older original pieces and did some restoration. In autumn 2001, however, he turned his attention to the world of contemporary design, and now sells new furniture alongside an eclectic selection of lighting, glass, ceramics, textiles and a range of accessories.

As you enter the store, you can see immediately that mainstream design products do not ring any bells for this retailer. Andrew Lowe's background dealing in originals has influenced his buying decisions for this new venture, with an unusual array of items on display that all maintain his core purchasing criteria of quality, durability and function.

On wandering through the space, you can't help but be struck by the textural contrasts – exposed brick walls juxtaposed with beautifully finished glowing acrylic lighting from Jona Hoad. Lighting from The Unnatural Lighting Co.

highlights the beauty of the raw unfinished plastered wall, which in turn forms the backdrop for serene, organically shaped ceramic lighting from Julie Nelson. Other pieces to grace the space are from talented designers, such as Phörm (p 281), OCP Design, Geraldine McGloin, Kaya Hoang (p 274), Hive, Sasha Gabbe, Mark Finzel, Ferrious, Junilda Ross and Black + Blum.

Lowe Interiors offers domestic and commercial clients a bespoke design service. Andrew Lowe is keen to stock work from UK designers who are able to make pieces to specification, acting as the crucial link between customer and designer. The totally white basement space is used as a carte blanche environment to help clients visualise a particular room-set and, with the careful attention of the staff to aid your decision, you might well walk away with a unique new addition for your interior.

MAC LONDON

DESIGNERS INCLUDE:
Cappellini
Christophe Delacourt
C+B Italia
De Sede
Giovanna Josephine
Jac Calum
Lothair Hamann
Lucas Twins
Mac
Mdina
Minotti
Mozzee
Murano
Studio 212
Susannah Shaw
Vittoria Aquilina

SERVICES:
Bespoke Orders
Contract Division
Interior Advice
Sourcing

CLOSE TO:
Applied Arts Agency
Inflate
Lowe Interiors
Viaduct

Mac London
142 Clerkenwell Road
London EC1R 5DL
020 7713 1234
www.mac-london.com
Tube: Farringdon
Open: Mon – Fri 10 – 5
Sat 10 – 3
Or by appointment on 07771 765 123
or 07775 560 055

Mac was opened in 1998 by Louis McCullough in response to a growing demand for quality leather furniture from many loft apartment dwellers, following the redevelopment of numerous old industrial buildings in Clerkenwell. Located strategically in the centre of loft territory, Mac London's prominent corner premises are home to an ever-changing display of leather sofas and armchairs, as well as some exuberant retro chandeliers and iconic posters – not to mention a few handblown glass vases and platters. Without a huge amount of space to work in, the shop often has a rather cluttered appearance because of its fast turnover.

We are all aware of the value and desirability of leather. Often its best characteristics are brought on with age, and many consumers will only purchase used leather furniture, preferring a worn look and feel to brand new offerings. Mac London sources original pieces, which are then reconditioned where

necessary. The company also produces its own collection of new leather furniture in a range of sizes particularly popular with the restaurant and bar industry. With its own manufacturing and restoration process in London, quality is assured and delivery times are fast – resulting in satisfied customers.

Mac London's sales policy means that should you want to change a piece of furniture, the company will exchange it or buy it back from you for the price you paid, dependent on condition and resale value, of course. Pieces are also available for interior designers and stylists to hire.

Louis McCullough is usually on hand to greet customers, and his welcoming and laid-back approach immediately puts everyone at ease. Touches of humour such as the Playboy bunny on the back wall lighten the atmosphere, and it is no surprise that the company has a loyal following.

MAISONETTE

DESIGNERS INCLUDE:
Hub
LSA International
Maisonette
Scabetti

SERVICES:
Bespoke Orders
Gift Vouchers
Gift Wrapping
Interior Advice

Maisonette
79 Chamberlayne Road
London NW10 3ND
020 8964 8444
www.maisonette.uk.com
Train: Kensal Rise
Open: Tues – Sat 11 – 6:30

Amanda Sellers and Martin Barrell opened the award-winning interior boutique Maisonette in September 2000 after many years of working in the fashion industry. Moving into the realm of products for the home, the duo have developed a collection of fashion-related, decorative interior pieces that are displayed alongside vintage and contemporary glass, ceramic, lighting and furniture designs. The clean white-walled retail space provides a calm and unobtrusive backdrop for the seductive combination of homewares and accessories. Focusing on colour and pattern, it is an uplifting experience to enter this retreat off a nondescript north-west London street. Browse the small shop space and you will quickly pick up on the unique way of life that the friendly owners and staff are trumpeting by stocking items that appeal to all of the human senses.

Located in an unexpected area of the capital, Maisonette stands out like a sore thumb amid the other shops in Kensal Rise. The individual nature of the selection has made the shop into a destination that people will travel to visit. Normally you share the space with just a few other customers, allowing for a more personal service from the staff. While old and new pieces are showcased together, the distinctions between them aren't always that obvious, making visitors re-examine their preconceptions of the past. On my visit, I was met by a Louis XIV chair upholstered with fluffy sheepskin and a 1970s smoked glass coffee table graced with ceramics from Scabetti and Hub, all illuminated with a striking hanging Murano light. Next to that, on the white pebble-textured wall, was one of the many large format paint-it-yourself graphic paintings (viewable on website) developed by Maisonette that have proved extremely popular with its predominantly female customers. It also produces unique cushions made from decorative vintage scarves that add vibrancy to the white displays.

The lifestyle package is completed by up-market home fragrances, sexy lounge music and own-collection loungewear. All in all, Maisonette is a sexy, sensuous and individual retreat, where you can browse for gorgeous objects feeling comfortably separated from the chaos of city life. Shoppers in Sheffield can now find a Maisonette concession at Prego (p 182).

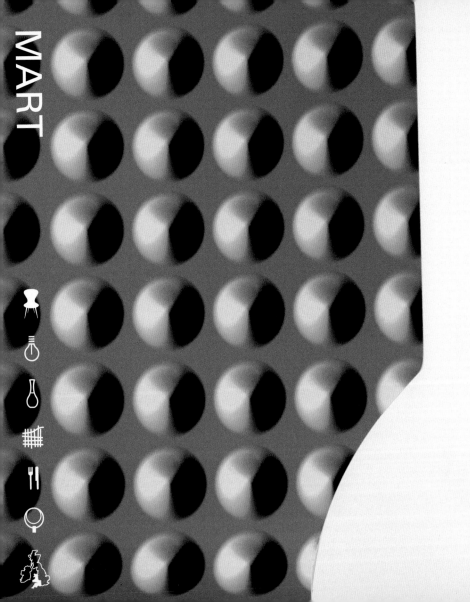

DESIGNERS INCLUDE:
Bakebean
Claire O'Hea
Geraldine McGloin
James Bullen
Karen Smith
Linus Pell
Mart
Mibo
Paul Johnson
Simple Simon
Stella Corrall

SERVICES:
Bespoke Orders
Gift Vouchers
Gift Wrapping
Interior Advice
Wedding List

Mart
8 Jacobs Wells Road
Hotwells
Bristol BS8 1EA
0117 904 3245
Open: Tues – Sat 11 – 6
Sun 1 – 5

Situated slightly out of Bristol's immediate town centre at the base of a very steep hill below Clifton Village, Mart occupies a very small retail space that you are likely to miss if you're driving. Make an effort to park around the corner and visit owners Samantha Purnell and Jaine Bevan in their treasure-trove of design goodies. Mart's selection of ceramics, tableware, period glass, lighting, jewellery, soft furnishings and prints has had to be well edited to prevent the appearance of clutter. The owners have chosen pieces based on their own styles and preferences, instead of opting for brands with a proven sales record. Even to the trained eye, the result is refreshing, as they are not afraid to showcase new designs from a diversity of UK designers, some unknown.

The shop displays a striking number of pieces. Ceramics from Geraldine McGloin, Karen Smith, Bakebean and Linus Pell are deftly complemented by Stella Corrall's multi-coloured rubber placemats and some vibrant retro glass vases. Furniture includes Simple Simon's plastic stools and Paul Johnson's clean-lined modular shelving units, softened by Claire O'Hea's bright cushions. Overhead illumination comes courtesy of Mibo's well-known pendant light shades.

There is a definite graphic element running through the range of pieces. Most notable are the digitally designed textiles from James Bullen. These have been applied to Amtico laminate panels, and Mart was fortunate to have an exclusive range of one-off chairs (pictured) and panels on my visit.

I can't help feeling that the discreet location of Mart doesn't fully benefit the business, but this may soon change as there are plans for growth and expansion. With this in mind, it may be wise to phone ahead before visiting Mart for the first time.

MASON

DESIGNERS INCLUDE:
Arflex
Baleri Italia
Bellato
Desalto
Fiam
4orm Design
Cristalia
Melia
Meshman
Mobileffe
Molteni & C
Richard Williams
Furniture
Rimadesio
Robots
Seven Salotti
Tagliabue
Tonelli

SERVICES:
Bespoke Orders
Contract Division
Interior Advice

CLOSE TO:
Domane Interiors

Mason
70 North Street
Leeds LS2 7PN
0113 242 2434
www.masonfurniture.com
Open: Mon – Fri 9:30 – 5:30
Sat 10 – 5

Mason is a large contemporary furniture showroom on a busy stretch of road in Leeds' northern quarter and was opened by Robert Mason in autumn 1998. The premises look deceptively small from the street but once past the modest entrance display area, you enter a vast open-plan warehouse-like space that is home to a range of modern furniture items. Since opening, Robert Mason has increased his collection of unobtrusive European sofa, storage and chair designs from reputable suppliers like Seven Salotti, Kristalia, Tagliabue (pictured), Molteni & C, Fiam, Tonelli, Mobileffe, Bellato, Arflex, Baleri Italia, Rimadesio,

Desalto and Robots. He isn't afraid to mix international brands with pieces from UK design companies such as Meshman, Melia, 4orm Design and Richard Williams Furniture. The selection refrains from the predictable with the combination of sharp-lined Italian pieces and quirkier lesser-known items.

Experiencing this mix of styles and materials could be a little confusing if you are looking for a particular interior aesthetic. But you can always discuss your requirements with the friendly owner who is happy to advise.

The natural light flooding through the bank of windows on the back wall is backed up by the rather harsh artificial illumination from fluorescent strip lights. Don't let this bother you, however, as Robert has created an environment that simply displays products as they are without any of the unnecessary pretence that can sometimes shroud the design industry.

MINT

DESIGNERS INCLUDE:
BD
Darkroom Architecture
De Padova
Peter Ghyczy
Sabine Bürk
Tom Dixon

SERVICES:
Gift Vouchers
Gift Wrapping
Interior Advice
Wedding List

CLOSE TO:
Key London
Noel Hennessy
Furniture
RJM Furniture
(Wigmore Street)
Selfridges
Skandium

Mint
70 Wigmore Street
London W1U 2SF
020 7224 4406
Tube: Bond Street
Open: Mon – Sat 10:15 – 6:15
Thurs til 7:15

Visiting every design retailer in the country, it's no surprise that I encounter a lot of the same brands and designers on sale. But on stepping into the treasure-trove that is Lina Kanafani's Mint, my spirits lifted at the sight of a totally individual and unique product selection. Bored by our obsession with classics and labels, Lina showcases an ever-changing array of one-off or production pieces of furniture, lighting, ceramics, glass, tableware and textiles to her growing band of loyal customers.

The shop occupies a former wine store, and many of the original details such as the old brickwork and tiles remain, providing a beautifully textured backdrop for the items on display. Lina Kanafani, who sources products from around the world, simply wants to sell what she loves best, boosting her own and her staff's enthusiasm and making the shopping experience that little bit more personal for customers. Discovering designs I've not seen before gives me the feeling that I have discovered something special.

Spread across two floors, the rather quirky, irregular-shaped shop housed on my visit stunning creations, such as Peter Ghyczy's 1968-designed Novo chair, Sabine Bürk's Chair of Roses, Vico Magistretti's Vidun table for De Padova, concrete modular furniture from Darkroom Architecture, Pepe Cortez's Olvidada lamp for BD, and Tom Dixon's Fresh Fat plastic-extruded bowls (all pictured). The knowledgeable and welcoming staff take pride in the service they offer, making sure you leave the store with a smile on your face.

MISSION

DESIGNERS INCLUDE:
Clare Twomey
Julie Cockburn
Julie Nelson
Melanie Trievnor
Michael Wolfson
Patrick Fredrikson

SERVICES:
Bespoke Orders
Interior Design

CLOSE TO:
Bowles and Linares
Flow
Themes & Variations

Mission
45 Hereford Road
London W2 5AH
020 7792 4633
www.intomission.com
Tube: Notting Hill Gate or Bayswater
Open: Please phone for opening times

Mission was opened by design PR Yvonne Courtney and architect Misha Stefan in 1998, with the intention of fusing commerce and culture in a unique environment that blurs the boundaries of showspace, shop, PR agency, architecture and design studio. Located on a side street off busy Westbourne Grove, Mission is one of London's hidden gems, visited only by those in the know.

Misha Stefan designed Mission's stunning 2,000 square foot soft modern interior, applying his 'function follows form' ideology to create a fluid space that is a destination in itself. The interior has been used as a location for television programmes, ads, photo shoots and exhibitions. So is it really a design shop within the scheme of this book?

I would suggest it's more of an experience destination that showcases an eclectic selection of objects. Retail is not the major part of the business,

so Mission doesn't have to succumb to the usual commercial sales pressures. Instead it can display unusual examples of iconic and contemporary furniture and artworks from designers such as Patrick Fredrikson, Julie Nelson, Melanie Trievnor, Julie Cockburn, Clare Twomey and Michael Wolfson. Yvonne Courtney's real passion is for books so Mission stocks a fantastic array of publications on design and popular culture.

Mission celebrates life as it should be lived – as a visit is sure to confirm.

Mojoe
24 Church Street
Brighton BN1 1RB
01273 208 708
www.mojoe.co.uk
Open: Tues–Sat 10–6
Sun 12–5

Mojoe is Brighton's newest addition to the design scene. Friendly, down-to-earth owners Moses Kisubika and Jessica Joe opened in spring 2001 selling an interesting selection of affordable tableware, accessories, furniture and lighting from small premises on the hill leading up Church Street. Since their debut, I have visited the store several times and have always been struck by the changes to the stock. New pieces from local and European designers are regularly introduced and product presentations are often restyled, making for new expectations each time you walk through the door.

That said, the store never alters drastically as this would frighten off the existing client base. Instead,

DESIGNERS INCLUDE:
Caterina Fadda
Covo
Droog
Fusion
Inflate
Innermost
Keith Brymer Jones
Kerry Marriott
One Foot Taller
Ozgen
Paul Johnson
SRF Hantverk
Tim Parson

SERVICES:
Bespoke Orders
Gift Vouchers
Gift Wrapping
Interior Advice
Wedding List

CLOSE TO:
Caz Systems
Roost

any changes occur within the boundaries of the owners' distinct vision. The Mojoe ethos is to make good contemporary, yet affordable design more accessible to the public, via a welcoming retail environment manned by friendly and knowledgeable staff. By creating an informal setting in the store, Mojoe cleverly avoids the common preconception that the design world is snobbish, elitist, and expensive.

You can find some fantastic quirky designs from the experimental talents of Dutch company Droog, as well as beanbags from Inflate, great-looking brushes from SRF Hantverk, armchairs from One Foot Taller, tableware from Fusion (p 266) and Caterina Fadda, lighting from Innermost, ceramics from

Tim Parson, coffee cups from Covo, ironic pieces from Ozgen, as well as creations from local talents like Paul Johnson, Keith Brymer Jones, and Kerry Marriott to name but a few.

The basement is open occasionally for exhibitions of local artists and designers, when drinks are served and new contacts made. Pop in, join the mailing list, and don't leave empty handed.

DESIGNERS INCLUDE:
Arper
Artemide
B&B Italia
Driade
Flexform
Gallotti & Radice
Ingo Maurer
Kartell
Lammhults
Magis
MDF Italia
Montis
Pallucco Italia
Porada
Punt Mobles
Robots
Sare
SCP
Vitra

SERVICES:
Interior Design
Bespoke Orders
Contract Division

CLOSE TO:
Back2myplace
Seduti

Momentum
31 Charles Street
Cardiff CF10 2GA
029 2023 6266
www.momentumcardiff.com
Open: Tues – Sat 10 – 6

Husband and wife team PJ and Lyn Statham have worked in interior design and contract furnishings for many years, but in September 2001, decided to open a retail outlet dedicated to well-designed European contemporary furniture and lighting. Noting changes in the market over several years, they thought that Cardiff residents were ready to adapt their living environments to a more modern aesthetic.

Four floors of the showroom on Charles Street are dedicated to well-known European furniture brands, such as Magis, Punt Mobles, Porada, Sare, Vitra, Robots, MDF Italia, SCP, Arper, Flexform, Driade, Montis, Kartell, Lammhults, B&B Italia, Artemide, Gallotti & Radice, Ingo Maurer, and Pallucco Italia, to mention only a handful. From working in the contract market, PJ and Lyn Statham have built up a considerable suppliers' list and are able to offer customers a huge choice of items from their product database. And advice is always on offer from Momentum's knowledgeable staff.

From street level, Momentum seems to occupy a relatively small space visible through floor-to-ceiling showroom windows – a spiral staircase is the only clue that there are more floors. Only on entering do you realize that the showroom occupies the whole premises. The building is configured like a house but the furniture is left to speak for itself, displayed with a sterility that reminds you that you are in a commercial space. The range and diversity of items are superb, but you can't help feeling that the setting would benefit from being warmed up a little with furniture and lighting styled into identifiable room-sets, to give customers a better feeling for their application in a domestic setting. But if you can picture what you are after, Momentum should succeed in serving your interior needs.

MOOCH

DESIGNERS INCLUDE:
Artemide
Bookan
Dada
Felicerossi
Flexform
Flos
Fontana Arte
Foscarini
Living Divani
LSA International
Luceplan
Moooi
Penta
Porro
Rimadesio
Stelton
Vibieffe

SERVICES:
Bespoke Orders
Contract Division
Interior Design

Mooch
321 Bradford Street
Birmingham B5 6ET
0121 622 0390
Open: Mon – Fri 10 – 6
Sat 10 – 5

Timber Wharf
28 – 29 Worsley Street
Castlefield
Manchester M15 4LD
Open: Mon – Fri 10 – 6
Sat 10 – 5

www.mooch.eu.com

Owners David Currin and Colin Graham's contemporary furniture and lighting showroom, formerly called Living, moved to larger premises in autumn 2001, filling just over 5,000 sq ft of an impressive open-plan show space with clean-lined European designs. Mooch's new larger venture is situated slightly beyond Birmingham's city centre – a store that people make the effort to visit. Whether you want a slick Italian sofa or an elegant set of dining chairs, you will enjoy browsing through the big-brand Italian suppliers. Rather than combining pieces from different furniture companies, areas of the store are allocated for room-set displays of particular brands, such as Living Divani, Felicerossi, Porro, Flexform or Vibieffe.

Benefiting from the light that pours through the immense floor-to-ceiling glass windows on two sides of the showroom, Mooch is fully exposed to passing traffic on this busy road. While attracting an ever-growing number of public orders,

commercial orders for the contract market form a significant part of the business. Operating from offices at the back of the showroom, the team also undertake an interior design service, offering advice and guidance on how to integrate the latest ideas into your home.

Furniture dominates the space but various lighting configurations are also on display, from Luceplan, Artemide, Flos, Foscarini, Penta and Fontana Arte. Storage facilities and room dividers are supplied by Rimadesio, as well as slick, functional kitchen set-ups from Dada, illustrating Mooch's commitment and ability to work on various elements of the home interior. A showroom of this size can feel sterile and intimidating but Mooch aims to offset this with various ceramic, glass, and stainless steel items from LSA, Stelton, Bookan and Moooi to soften the look, accompanied by funky music to define a mood.

Business for the company has increased in Manchester, so in spring 2003, the directors opened another showroom in one of the commercial units in an Urban Splash development near Deansgate Locks.

MORRIS&CO

DESIGNERS INCLUDE:
Annie Sherburne
Driade
David Trubridge
Flos
Knoll
MDF Italia
Rosenthal
Sasha Bunbury
Vitra
Zanotta

SERVICES:
Bespoke Orders
Contract Division
Gift Wrapping
Interior Design
Wedding List

CLOSE TO:
SCP
Two Columbia Road

Morris & Co
387 The Arches
Geffrye Street
London E2 8HZ
020 7739 8539
www.morrisandco.co.uk
Tube: Old Street
Open: Tues – Fri 10 – 5:30
Sun 11 – 5
Mon and Sat by appointment

The relentless presence of the same high-street brands has become a depressingly familiar sight in the main shopping centres of most UK cities. To counteract the invasion of the global giants, more and more people want to discover hidden gems that offer alternatives to mass production. Morris & Co is one such example, tucked under the railway arches behind the historic Geffrye Museum in London's Shoreditch. Forget all stereotypes that surround the area and enter the world of Morris & Co.

Nick Morris has worked in the interiors and architecture industry for more than thirty years, but, in 1999 he decided to open his own store selling an eclectic array of furniture, lighting, ceramics, glass and interior products for home and office. An arched brick-walled showroom space is the perfect setting to combine the works of contemporary designers and craftspeople with twentieth-century classics and original antiques. Nick Morris is an energetic character, just as eccentric as his showroom collection, and he personally selects every item on display. By simply buying the things he loves, Nick has successfully created his own haven in east London, combining a number of interior styles of differing character and ambience.

On my visit he showed me his latest fusion of products – a slender-legged round slate-top table sitting on Astroturf surrounded by black steel Bertoia chairs, straw-filled Perspex cubes by Sasha Bunbury and a translucent Tom Vac chair by Ron Arad for Vitra. On the table French-style milky-white glazed tableware was complemented by Italian pewterware. To the side, a curvaceous lounger by New Zealand designer David Trubridge was draped in a felt 'cobble' throw from Annie Sherburne, while a slick MDF Italia shelving system displayed porcelain from Driade and Rosenthal, illuminated by recent additions from Flos.

At Morris & Co, the belief is that outstanding designs will respond well to the careful mixing of ages and styles. All that is left is for you to decide which combination of pieces you would like to take away.

NOEL HENNESSY
FURNITURE

DESIGNERS INCLUDE:
Amat
Bernini
Ceccotti
Dux
Flos
Fontana Arte
Foscarini
Living Divani
Nueva Linea
Matteograssi
Porro
Santa + Cole
Wittmann
Zanotta

SERVICES:
Bespoke Orders
Contract Division
Gift Vouchers
Gift Wrapping
Interior Design
Wedding List

CLOSE TO:
Artemide
CVO Firevault
Key London
Mint
RJM Furniture
(Wigmore Street)
Skandium

Noel Hennessy Furniture
6 Cavendish Square
London W1G 0PD
020 7323 3360
www.noelhennessy.com
Tube: Oxford Circus
Open: Mon – Fri 10 – 6
Sat 10 – 4

Noel Hennessy, the man behind this W1 store, started trading in furniture and lighting in early 1998. He had become frustrated always working for other people and was determined to create a business generated from his own vision and personal passion. Having found the perfect location in central London, Noel Hennessy now operates a thriving retail business from his beautiful furniture showroom in Cavendish Square.

Refreshingly, he doesn't hide behind the safety of the usual big-brand suppliers; instead, he travels extensively to seek out the best of European design. His final selection is based not only on the quality of an item but also on the simple premise that he likes it. Noel Hennessy loves to be surrounded by beautiful things and believes that consumers should be buying timeless pieces that 'afford you pleasure each time you see and touch them'. All too aware of the importance of helping customers make the 'right' choice for their home or office, he and his staff are well informed about their entire stock and guide clients professionally through the available pieces. Customers

go home confident that their purchase has been well researched and that they have been carefully advised. A free interior design service is also offered.

Browse around the large two-floor showroom and you will discover a well-composed mix of contemporary furniture and lighting from companies such as Porro, Zanotta, Ceccotti, Wittmann, Nueva Linea, Living Divani, Matteograssi, Bernini, Amat, Dux, Flos, Fontana Arte, Foscarini and Santa + Cole. If these names mean nothing to you, that's all the better – you might find something you haven't seen before among the organized, uncluttered changing displays. Neatly bearded and bow-tied Noel Hennessy is adamant that customers shouldn't feel intimidated entering his modern furniture shop. The space has been softened with the addition of various unique accessories or fine art pieces and enlivened with plenty of exciting interior choices.

OGGETTI

DESIGNERS INCLUDE:
Alvar Aalto
Antonio Citterio
Arne Jacobsen
Björn Dahlström
Carina Seth-Andersson
Enzo Mari
Ettore Sottsass
Jasper Morrison
Kaj Franck
Marianne Brandt
Tapio Wirkkala
Timo Sarpaneva

SERVICES:
Gift Vouchers
Gift Wrapping
Wedding List

CLOSE TO:
B&B Italia
The Conran Shop
De La Espada
The London Lighting Co
Rabih Hage

Oggetti
143 Fulham Road
London SW3 6SD
020 7581 8088
Tube: South Kensington
Open: Mon – Sat 9:30 – 6

Oggetti is located just a few doors from its sister lighting showroom, The London Lighting Co, on London's Fulham Road. Oggetti is a modest-sized shop selling a stunning collection of tableware desirables for anyone who enjoys good food and drink and wants to enhance a sense of occasion through presentation.

Drawn in by the window displays, customers are put at ease in what could be seen as an intimidating space by classical music. The black-and-white interior provides a sharp yet unobtrusive backdrop for the pieces on display, which are all behind glass. Although this makes the shop look like a museum, it's simply a precaution against breakage, so don't let it deter you from asking for assistance if you are interested in any particular items. The well-illuminated displays hold timeless designs from the likes of Alvar Aalto, Tapio Wirkkala, Arne Jacobsen, Timo Sarpaneva, Marianne Brandt, Kaj Franck, Enzo

Mari, and Ettore Sottsass, designed decades ago but still as popular as ever. Contemporary designs from today's talents like Jasper Morrison, Antonio Citterio, Carina Seth-Andersson and Björn Dahlström have also reached the displays, selected for their ability to side-step whimsical fashion-dictated design principles. While most of the designs in the store are industrially produced, Oggetti also sells select pieces of unique Murano glass vases and platters, as well as vibrant Swedish and German glassware.

This well-presented gift emporium is a reminder of the beauty of everyday objects. Steering clear of the garishly avant-garde, Oggetti is an ideal place to purchase lasting designs.

ONE PONTCANNA STREET

One Pontcanna Street
1 Pontcanna Street
Cardiff CF11 9HQ
029 2038 8499
www.onepontcannastreet.com
Open: Tues–Fri 9–6
Sat 10–6

Finding a unique design store slightly off the beaten track is always a pleasure and one that you don't necessarily want to share with others. Alas, my job is to reveal these places to you, such as One Pontcanna Street. It was during a chance meeting with Darkroom Architecture's co-director Glen Thomas over a gin and tonic that I learned of his new venture with partner Steven Gheorghiu-Currie. The architectural duo opened a furniture showroom in a small and rather intimate environment in Cardiff's Pontcanna area, renowned for its pubs, restaurant nightlife and deli's. They have introduced a laid-back showroom atmosphere to an industry that is typically perceived as inaccessible and elitist. A quirky old bookshop was transformed into a new dynamic venue where you can view furniture designs, sit down on concrete, solid Welsh oak and brushed stainless steel seating with an espresso, and browse through an array of old and new publications illuminated by a classic slender Paolo Rizzatto 265 light. Caffeine-charged, customers can then wander down the narrow staircase to see more furniture and a monthly exhibition of talented artists in the slick white and grey basement gallery.

Opened in August 2002 the shop has managed to attract a range of customers who are intrigued by the seemingly ambiguous activities at One Pontcanna Street. Challenging the notion of what a furniture shop can be, the owners have introduced elements that might appeal even if you're not currently in the market for furniture. Perhaps you need some artwork for your bare walls? Or maybe you simply want to gather your thoughts over a coffee? Perhaps you are really after a bespoke dining table or even a total architectural overhaul of your home? If so, One Pontcanna Street sets no boundaries, rejects preconceptions and provides a welcoming forum for your imagination. Away from the brash consumerism and branding overdose of the city centre, One Pontcanna Street is one of Cardiff's hidden gems.

OVERDOSE
ON DESIGN

Overdose on Design
182 Brick Lane
London E1 6SA
020 7613 1266
www.overdoseondesign.com
Tube: Aldgate East or Liverpool Street
Open: Daily 11 – 6

DESIGNERS INCLUDE:
Arne Jacobsen
Charles and Ray Eames
Eero Saarinen
Erwin and Estelle Laverne
George Nelson
Giancarlo Piretti
Harry Bertoia
Joe Columbo
Mario Bellini
Peter Ghyczy
Pierre Paulin
Rodney Kinsman
Tobia Scarpa
Verner Panton
Ynge Eckstrom

SERVICES:
Contract Division
Sourcing

CLOSE TO:
Eat My Handbag Bitch
Unto This Last

Brick Lane in London's East End has developed a reputation over the past few years as being one of the best streets to source original twentieth-century furniture and lighting. This is partly due to the introduction of Overdose On Design in 1999, which occupies a prominent corner location on this busy street. Spread across two cluttered floors is an ever-changing array of chairs, sofas, storage and lighting from well-known, iconic designers such as Arne Jacobsen, Harry Bertoia, Verner Panton, Pierre Paulin, Eero Saarinen, George Nelson

and Joe Columbo. In addition, OOD stocks what must be the largest quantity of Aluminium Group chairs from Charles and Ray Eames that I have ever seen. Harder-to-find items include pieces from designers like Giancarlo Piretti, Ynge Eckstrom, Erwin and Estelle Laverne, Peter Ghyczy, Tobia Scarpa, Mario Bellini and Rodney Kinsman. What you see is not everything you get. Vast amounts of stock are held in storage elsewhere, so be sure to ask the staff if you are in search of a particular piece.

The interior display is constantly changing as stock levels fluctuate. More often than not the space feels overcrowded, with stacks of objects competing for your attention. This seems to fit with the shop's name – you do in fact experience a visual 'overdose' of choice. But somehow it seems to work – in contrast to the sometimes precious environments used in the twentieth-century design sales arena. OOD also operates a successful hire service to film and TV industries.

The relaxed attitude of the staff could be interpreted as blasé. They allow the products to sell themselves, but should you need some help then of course they are available to assist. The market for original designs is still going strong, proving good design will always stand the test of time.

OXO TOWER WHARF

OXO Tower Wharf
Bargehouse Street
South Bank
London SE1 9PH
020 7401 2255
www.oxotower.co.uk
Tube: Blackfriars, Waterloo or Southwark
Open: Tues–Sun 11–6

Once the storage, processing and packing centre for the Liebig Extract of Meat Company, better known for producing OXO gravy, the riverside wharf was transformed when Coin Street Community Builders bought the site in 1984. Remarkably, the OXO Tower was refurbished rather than demolished. Now a landmark on London's South Bank – you can't miss the tower's fantastic original illuminated 'OXO' lettering – it is home to a variety of operations, including 33 retail studios for contemporary UK designers on the first and second floors.

The first-floor studio units house companies producing furniture, lighting, ceramics, glass, jewellery and textiles, plus graphic works from the likes of Hive, Bodo Sperlein (pictured), Caterina Fadda, Joseph Joseph, Alexander Taylor (p 252) and salt. You can see the designers at work, and buy or commission a wide variety of original products. Venture to the second floor to discover more designers, such as Fusion (p 266), BDM Design, Black + Blum, Kate Maestri, Miranda Watkins and Little + Collins. Each company seems to operate its own sporadic opening hours, so you can't rely on a particular studio being open on a spontaneous visit.

Even so, you won't have a wasted trip – you can always enjoy a coffee and some food in EAT, the ground-floor café, or pop into the.gallery@oxo, which has a changing programme of exhibitions showcasing innovative new applied art, contemporary design, architecture and photography. Floors three to seven are occupied with apartments, but the building's real tour de force is the rooftop OXO Tower Restaurant, Brasserie and Bar. With some of the best views in London across the Thames to the City and a balcony for summer dining, the elegant restaurant marries breathtaking cityscape with gastronomic delights.

DESIGNERS INCLUDE:
Alexander Taylor
BDM Design
Black + Blum
Bodo Sperlein
Caterina Fadda
Fusion
Hive
Joseph Joseph
Kate Maestri
Little+Collins
Miranda Watkins
Salt

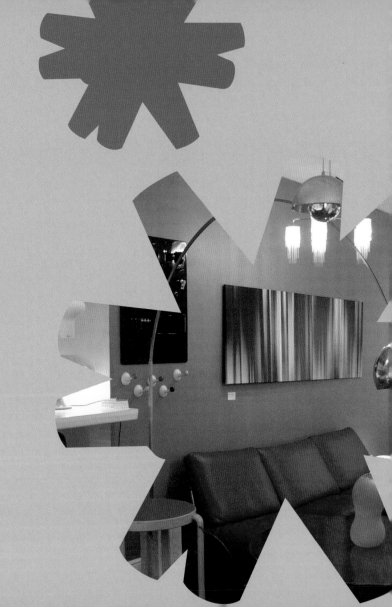

PLACES AND SPACES

DESIGNERS INCLUDE:
Artemide
Artifort
Asplund
Bim Burton
Bodo Sperlein
Catherine Tough
Eurolounge
Finn Stone
Flos
Hub
Michael Sodeau
Nelson
Nick Hannam
Tom Kirk
Vitra
Zanotta

SERVICES:
Bespoke Orders
Contract Division
Interior Design

CLOSE TO:
Leigh Buckland

Places and Spaces
30 Old Town
London SW4 0LB
020 7498 0998
www.placesandspaces.com
Tube: Clapham Common
Open: Tues – Sat 10:30 – 6
Sun 12 – 4

Places and Spaces was opened by Paul Carroll and Nick Hannam in 1997 as part of the small stretch of shops on Old Town at the north-east corner of Clapham Common and was taken over by new owners in early 2003. Occupying only small retail premises, the store manages to attract a following of loyal customers who want to buy into the individual aesthetic they offer. The shop has always offered a changing selection of original furniture, lighting and accessories mixed in with complementing new pieces. Although this remains, the balance has veered more towards new contemporary designs with a larger choice of mid-priced products from designers such as Hub, Nelson, Bodo Sperlein, Bim Burton, Finn Stone, Tom Kirk, Michael Sodeau, Catherine Tough and Eurolounge. One of the biggest sellers is the timeless, well-priced Swedish storage and drawer units from Asplund, accompanied by strategically placed lighting from Artemide and Flos. Gracing the walls above furniture from Vitra, Artifort and Zanotta is a selection of graphic-inspired artwork that completes the overall look.

Due to limited space in the shop, the stock is carefully edited to avoid cluttering and confusing the display. If you are looking for a particular design, it is worth talking to the owners who are likely to be able to find what you want. They also offer an interior design service.

Away from the activity of the high street, Places and Spaces is a destination shop that caters for anyone looking for an intimate level of service, readily available from the friendly, knowledgeable and informative owners. I look forward to charting how the store evolves under new directorship.

PLANET
BAZAAR

DESIGNERS INCLUDE:
Alvar Aalto
Annabel de Vetten
Arne Jacobsen
Charles and Ray Eames
Charlotte Perriand
Eero Aarnio
Ettore Sottsass
Gaetano Pesce
George Nelson
Harry Bertoia
Peter Ghyczy
Pierre Paulin
Tal Gur
William Plunkett

SERVICES:
Sourcing

CLOSE TO:
Geoffrey Drayton

Planet Bazaar
149 Drummond Street
London NW1 2PB
020 7387 8326
www.planetbazaar.co.uk
Tube: Warren Street or Euston Square
Open: Mon – Sat 11:30 – 7

Maureen Silverman opened Planet Bazaar in 1997 in rather small and intimate premises, selling an eclectic mix of original twentieth-century classic furniture, lighting, ceramics, glass and artwork to a loyal and ever-expanding client base. Known as London's 'top pop shop', the store sells iconic and generic items with a definite bias towards bright colours reminiscent of the 1960s and 1970s.

Stepping from London's grey pavements into this vibrant treasure-trove cannot fail to bring a smile to your face on a dreary day. A massive array of lighting options emit warmth into the shop and illuminate numerous other objects on display. Maureen Silverman personally buys in everything that she sells, ensuring that all originals first meet her quality standards before they reach her customers. Planet Bazaar has a rather cluttered feel that gives character to the store and adds to that satisfying and exciting sense of discovery when shopping.

The general feel is bright and cheerful, with designs from Verner Panton, Peter Ghyczy, Pierre Paulin, Eero Aarnio, and Gaetano Pesce. You can also find less garish pieces from Alvar Aalto, George Nelson, Arne Jacobsen, Harry Bertoia, Charles and Ray Eames, Charlotte Perriand and William Plunkett,

to name just a few. Dealing with originals, it is always difficult to predict the stock or guarantee the availability of a particular piece, so an advance phone call is always recommended. On my visit, the shop was well stocked with Memphis ceramics and lighting from Ettore Sottsass – a very collectible era of design that often provokes love or hate reactions.

Planet Bazaar also carries a number of generic creations from across Europe, such as a choice of colourful and eye-catching Murano glassware. More recently a few contemporary designs have been introduced to complement the style of other pieces, such as humorous glowing plastic figures from Israeli designer Tal Gur. As well as numerous poster prints of artwork from Warhol, Vasarély, and the Sex Pistols, there are new graphic paintings of twentieth-century icons like Elvis, James Dean and Audrey Hepburn by Annabel de Vetten (pictured). With so much on offer, be sure to visit the shop and uncover these discoveries for yourself.

POLIFORM

Poliform
278 King's Road
London SW3 5AW
020 7368 7600
www.poliform.it
Tube: South Kensington
Open: Mon – Sat 10 – 6

One of the latest major Italian furniture brands to open a dedicated showroom in the growing UK market is Poliform, which moved into an award-winning 8,000 sq ft space in March 2002. Anyone driving or walking along this stretch of London's King's Road is immediately drawn to the three-storey minimalist building designed by architect Paolo Piva. The immense floor-to-ceiling windows on the façade expose the slick sofas, chairs, wardrobes, beds, storage systems, sideboards and shelving from Poliform and Flexform, as well as the sharp-lined precision kitchen designs from subsidiary company Varenna.

This impressive Italian showspace could appear intimidating – the uncompromisingly modern exterior in this wealthy area implies that entry should be reserved for those who can afford it. But appearances can be deceptive – once through the entrance, customers are welcomed by reception staff before encountering a first taste of the Poliform world in this theatrically vast space.

First, experience the chic simplicity and functionality of a working kitchen designed by Paolo Piva, before moving on to various displays of ultra-cool storage units or comfortable understated

cubist sofas, which are all available in a choice of material finishes and fabrics. The setting is starkly minimalist, ceilings are high, and floor and wall tones are muted greys and neutral taupe, creating a rather cold showroom space. Rugs and throws in earthy colours offset the clean lines and help to recompose the senses.

With natural light playing a massive role in the building, and the luxury of plenty of floor space, you always feel relaxed when browsing, whether or not you're in the market for buying.

The style of Poliform is it is as much about minimalist elegance as about comfort and practicality. While the showroom space is a fantastic extreme addition to the often traditional Chelsea lifestyle, the understated muted nature of the collections doesn't particularly spark many feelings of excitement. All pieces are made to the highest standards while integrating clever functional features, but the highly polished displays could perhaps benefit from a few more human touches to suggest and inspire real applications within the home.

DESIGNERS INCLUDE:
Alessi
Artemide
Artifort
Bonaldo
Bontempi
Fiam
Flos
Foscarini
Frighetto
Fritz Hansen
Kartell
Magis
Montis
SCP
Vibieffe
Vitra

SERVICES:
Bespoke Orders
Contract Division
Gift Vouchers
Interior Design
Wedding List

POP UK
278 Upper Richmond Road
Putney, London SW15 6TQ
020 8788 8811
Tube: East Putney
Open: Mon – Sat 10 – 6
Sun 12 – 5

17 High Street
Wimbledon Village
London SW19 5DX
020 8946 1122
Tube: Wimbledon
Open: Mon – Sat 10 – 6

www.popuk.com

Auday and Richard Tokatly, the entrepreneurial cousins behind Pop UK, opened their latest design store on the busy Upper Richmond Road in November 2001. Their design retail career began in Croydon, then they opened a shop in Wimbledon Village in 1999 before relocating the Croydon venture to the more design-susceptible area of Putney, and this is now their flagship store. When choosing their premises, the cousins have been clever enough to set up in affluent areas but at the same time choosing locations that are far enough away from the competition and extortionate rents of more central addresses.

The Putney store benefits from more floor space than its sister counterpart, with an impressive selection of furniture, lighting and accessories displayed across two floors. The cousins manage to strike a careful blend of newer designs from Europe's hotbed of avant-garde talent with more aesthetically digestible furniture solutions from well-known brands. Select items from established suppliers along the lines of Kartell, Montis, Fritz Hansen, Artifort, Vitra, SCP, Magis, Fiam, Frighetto, Bonaldo, Bontempi, Vibieffe, Flos, Artemide, Foscarini and Alessi are all present in the space. Interspersed with objects from newer UK designers, all offerings are well presented in small room-sets that avoid the appearance of clutter.

While Pop UK is at the higher end of the market, it is careful not to frighten away customers approaching the idea of introducing modern design to their homes for the first time. The shops manage to avoid appearing intimidating to these crucial newcomers and special attention is paid to customer care and service.

DESIGNERS INCLUDE:
Artifort
B&B Italia
Bodo Sperlein
Driade
Flos
Foscarini
iittala
Kartell
Lammhults
LSA International
Maisonette
Montis
MDF Italia
Pallucco Italia
Punt Mobles
Rosendahl
SCP
Stelton
Vitra

SERVICES:
Bespoke Orders
Contract Division
Gift Vouchers
Gift Wrapping
Interior Advice
Wedding List

CLOSE TO:
Form
The Humble Abode

Prego
No 7 The Plaza
West One
8 Fitzwilliam Street
Sheffield S1 4JB
0114 275 5512
Open: Tues – Sat 10 – 5:30
Sun 11 – 4

Moving from premises in Sheffield's Victoria Quays, Prego's owners Paula and Caro Whiteside relocated to a brand new outlet as part of the West One development in the heart of the Devonshire Quarter in March 2003. Home to high-specification contemporary apartments upstairs, the development also contains commercial units at ground level, with Prego newly situated on a prominent corner location. Three sides of the shop benefit from floor-to-ceiling glass windows, which allow plenty of natural light to illuminate the contemporary offerings within, as well as enticing customers into the store.

Furniture displays showcase a large range of items from the vibrant, eye-catching brand Kartell, especially the Philippe Starck designs. As well as larger pieces, an array of elegant household accessories are displayed from LSA,

Rosendahl, iittala, Stelton, Driade and Bodo Sperlein, perfect as gifts or impulse purchases. A rising change in level on the ground floor brings you to an area overlooking Cavendish Street where you will find the first concession from London-based company Maisonette (p 146), specializing in DIY paint kits, original twentieth-century glassware and sumptuous cushions made from vintage scarves.

Climb the stairs to the mezzanine level to browse clutter-free displays of primarily furniture and lighting from the likes of Vitra, Lammhults, Montis, MDF Italia, Pallucco Italia, SCP, B&B Italia, Punt Mobles, Flos and Foscarini – these are also dotted around the rest of the store. Perch on a new Artifort (pictured) creation upstairs and people-watch through the glass balustrades onto the shop floor below while contemplating which gorgeous designs to buy. Should you require non-pushy advice from the hospitable owners, feel free to ask – they are the fount of all knowledge when it comes to their collections.

As its expansion confirms, Prego has succeeded in becoming one of Sheffield's premier suppliers of contemporary interior products.

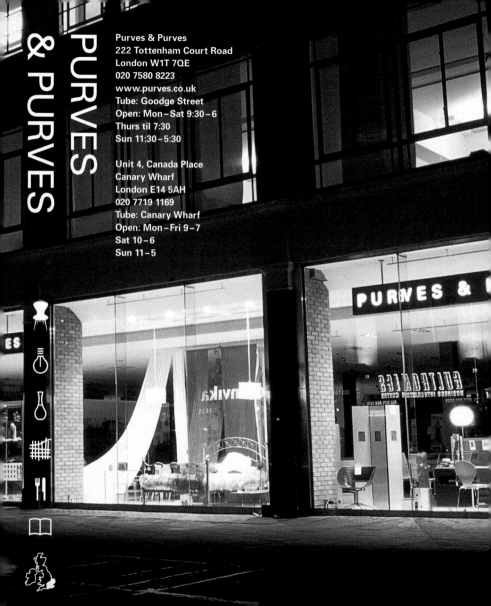

PURVES & PURVES

Purves & Purves
222 Tottenham Court Road
London W1T 7QE
020 7580 8223
www.purves.co.uk
Tube: Goodge Street
Open: Mon – Sat 9:30 – 6
Thurs til 7:30
Sun 11:30 – 5:30

Unit 4, Canada Place
Canary Wharf
London E14 5AH
020 7719 1169
Tube: Canary Wharf
Open: Mon – Fri 9 – 7
Sat 10 – 6
Sun 11 – 5

DESIGNERS INCLUDE:
Alessi
Artifort
B&B Italia
Driade
Edra
Hitch Mylius
Kartell
Magis
MDF Italia
Punt Mobles
Riva

SERVICES:
Bespoke Orders
Contract Division
Gift Vouchers
Interior Design
Wedding List

CLOSE TO:
Chaplins (Berners St)
Habitat
Heal's
Ligne Roset (West End)

Purves & Purves started life on bustling Tottenham Court Road in 1992 as a bold new venture established by Andrew and Pauline Purves. At that time, competition for the retail of quality contemporary European furniture was scarce and the store's popularity grew quickly. Starting with just furniture, lighting and rugs, the range of products expanded two years later to incorporate home accessories and kitchenware, building the store's reputation for contemporary design at affordable prices.

Tottenham Court Road is best known for electronics shops and furniture emporiums. Firmly established in the latter but eager for expansion, in autumn 2000 Andrew and Pauline Purves jumped at the chance to move into larger better-situated premises in a redevelopment further down the street. In the same year, they chose to expand beyond the West End, launching their first satellite store in the new shopping centre at the base of the Canary Wharf tower. The shop here sells mainly smaller accessory items for the gift market or impulse buyer.

For furniture and lighting you need the huge open-plan flagship store on Tottenham Court Road, with its selection of sofas, loungers, chairs, stools, dining tables, coffee tables and storage options from reputable European brands like B&B Italia, Kartell, Driade, Artifort, Riva, Punt Mobles, MDF Italia, Edra and Hitch Mylius, to name just a few. At the back of the store you'll find affordable ceramics, glassware, kitchenware and accessories, including well-designed

items from the likes of Alessi and Magis as well as rather tacky cheap plastics and gadgets. Enjoy a coffee and some food in the café or continue down the central stairs to the basement for more furniture choices and the lighting department.

With a prominent location on one of London's main shopping streets, Purves & Purves flagship store attracts a variety of customers and creates a welcoming environment free from any of the pretence that can sometimes taint the design industry. But I couldn't help feeling slightly disconcerted by the combination of high-end expensive furniture and so many smaller items that seem to somewhat lower the tone. Staff aren't always totally clued up on the stock, and clarity of presentation can be inconsistent. However, Purves & Purves have successfully tapped into the everyday consumer market and must be congratulated for successfully promoting contemporary design in what has now become an increasingly competitive industry.

RABIH HAGE

Rabih Hage
69–71 Sloane Avenue
London SW3 3DH
020 7823 8288
www.rabih-hage.com
Tube: South Kensington
Open: Mon–Sat 10–6

French-Lebanese interior designer Rabih el Hage opened his first retail space in September 2002, selling exclusive pieces of furniture, lighting and contemporary art sourced from an international selection of new and established designers. The shop on Chelsea's Sloane Avenue sells a selection of high-quality interior objects that stimulate the senses with a range of materials, unique forms and sculptural yet functional visual clarity.

Trained as an architect at the Ecole des Beaux-Arts in Paris, Rabih el Hage's early work was characterized by high-tech commercial projects for large practices in the French capital. In recent years, his focus has shifted almost entirely to interiors, working on a variety of residential refurbishment projects in London, where he has implemented his clean, modern and comfortable interior aesthetic while paying careful attention to clever yet unobtrusive functional efficiency. Such criteria are evident in works from European designers like Julie Prisca, Eric Gizard and Jean-Pierre Tortil, who create well-made furniture and lighting that maintain an understated modern appearance while employing and celebrating traditional craftsmanship and production values. In addition, you'll find one-off or limited edition art pieces that blur the boundaries between sculptural products and functional objects. These include Mark Harvey's linear Wave and Block benches and Johnny Swing's breathtaking amoeba-shaped Nickel Coach, constructed over four months entirely from welded nickel coins. The fusion of different materials used in these UK-exclusive products manages to gel into a coherent and luxurious schematic style, and Rabih el Hage and art consultant Annick Lashermes strive hard to ensure that it continually evolves.

The business also operates a successful bespoke interior design and architectural service for those wanting to integrate Rabih-Hage style into a home environment.

DESIGNERS INCLUDE:
Eric Gizard
Jean-Pierre Tortil
Johnny Swing
Julie Prisca
Mark Harvey
Rabih el Hage

SERVICES:
Bespoke Orders
Interior Design

CLOSE TO:
B&B Italia
Christopher Farr
The Conran Shop
De La Espada
The London Lighting Co
Oggetti

187

RAISBECK & REASON

Raisbeck & Reason
29 Regent Street
Leamington Spa
Warwickshire CV32 5EJ
01926 889 879
www.raisbeckandreason.co.uk
Open: Tues – Sat 10 – 5:30

You might not expect to find a modern furniture and lighting design shop in the historic town of Leamington Spa in Warwickshire. But inhabitants of this picturesque town have increasingly chosen to fit out their homes with comfortable contemporary items. Saving them the trip to Birmingham thirty miles away, Raisbeck & Reason stocks a digestible quantity of high-quality unobtrusive European brands offering sofas, coffee tables, dining tables, chairs, beds, storage and lighting options and, more recently, kitchens.

Opened on a relatively busy shopping street in the town centre in November 2000, Helen and Alan Bainbridge's store attracts passing customers by clean unintimidating displays of tempting interior items. With more people making the transition from traditional interiors to the clean lines of modernism, Raisbeck &

Reason has succeeded in satisfying those who want to make that change gently. Suppliers like Porada, Desalto, Flexform, Ronald Schmitt, Presotto, Fiam and Pianca fulfil these criteria, producing functional and often clever design solutions that don't visually clamour for attention. Adding colour to the two floors of this small store are a few recognizable items from Kartell and Vitra, as well as lighting from Flos, Foscarini, Oluce and the ever-innovative Ingo Maurer, whose new take on the chandelier is guaranteed put a smile on your face. Occasional accessories and artwork also grace the displays to help soften the look, giving the store a slightly cosier appearance and a sense of context for the larger pieces.

In addition to retail sales to local and nationwide customers, the owners also undertake interior design work for customers unsure of how to integrate new pieces into their homes. Talk to the informative staff about your needs and they will suggest solutions, offering you a professional and efficient service. If you are in the market for good-quality interior additions that won't break the bank, Raisbeck & Reason is certainly the right place to look.

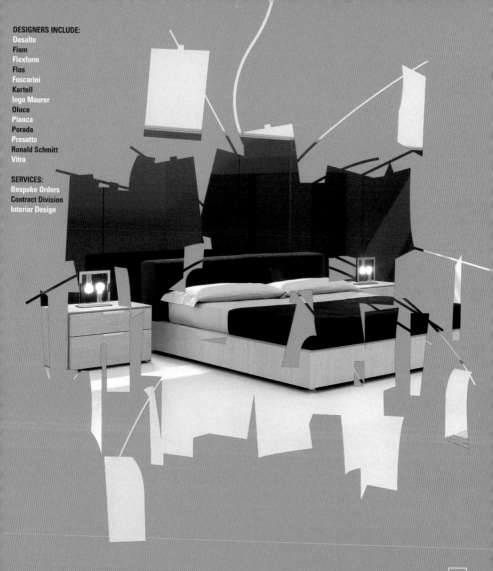

DESIGNERS INCLUDE:
Desalto
Fiam
Flexform
Flos
Foscarini
Kartell
Ingo Maurer
Oluce
Pianca
Porada
Presotto
Ronald Schmitt
Vitra

SERVICES:
Bespoke Orders
Contract Division
Interior Design

RHA FURNITURE

DESIGNERS INCLUDE:
Architects
Cattalan
Driade
Emmemobili
Fantoni
Flexform
Frighetto
Gallotti & Radice
Gervasoni
Guiliomarelli
Fritz Hansen
Kartell
La Palma
Magis
Pierantonio Bonacina
Porada
Punt Mobles

SERVICES:
Bespoke Orders
Contract Division
Interior Design

RHA Furniture
133 – 135 Kew Road
Richmond
Surrey TW9 2PN
020 8332 8715
www.rhafurniture.com
Tube/train: Richmond
Open: Mon – Sat 10 – 6:30

RHA Furniture owners Richard and Caroline Hunt have been supplying the contract market with furniture and lighting for many years, but in February 2002 they made the decision to expand into retail. Working with architects Design LSM of Brighton, the result is a sizeable new showroom spread across two floors that acts as a light and spacious backdrop for contemporary collections.

Designs from approximately thirty-five suppliers are displayed to the trade and public six days a week, showcasing a diversity of styles and material finishes to appeal to varying tastes and preferences. With such a huge choice available, the showroom is regularly updated to accommodate new pieces, always maintaining a mix of seating, upholstery, lighting, storage, rugs, beds, dining and garden furniture. Understandably, the space will never be big enough to display everything, so be sure to browse through the library of catalogues if you can't see what you want. The knowledgeable staff are all from design backgrounds and will offer you the advice you need.

While showing well-known iconic creations from the big-name designers with companies like Driade, Fritz Hansen, Kartell and Magis, refreshingly RHA provides a backdrop for manufacturers such as Pierantonio Bonacina (pictured), Cattalan, Emmemobili, Frighetto, Gallotti & Radice, Gervasoni, La Palma, Porada, and Punt Mobles. The definitive list and product portfolio can be found on RHA's surprisingly comprehensive website, allowing you to choose from the comfort of your home or office.

While the contract division is the main arm of the business, RHA is equally helpful to those who want a single item, encouraging discussion before decisions are made. Orders are processed and delivered quickly, concluding a professional and satisfying experience.

RIGHT ANGLE

DESIGNERS INCLUDE:
Alessi
Base d
Bookan
De Sede
Fabbian
Flos
Isabel Stanley
Kartell
Kim Greenaway
Lexon
Magis
Naos
Oluce
Room
Santa + Cole
Targetti

SERVICES:
Gift Vouchers
Interior Design
Wedding List

Right Angle
34 Tranquil Vale
London SE3 0AX
020 8852 8857
www.therightangle.co.uk
Train: Blackheath
Open: Mon – Sat 10 – 6
Sun 11 – 5

Right Angle occupies extremely narrow retail premises on a busy stretch of road running through the centre of London's village-like Blackheath. As it's not necessarily the sort of area where you would expect to find items of contemporary design, owner Anthony Banks has had to make sure that his shop isn't going to intimidate his many local customers. Lack of space has resulted in a rather cluttered appearance, where furniture, lighting and accessories, as well as design books and artwork, fight for your attention. To some this might be off-putting, while others might find it alluring, but at least this treasure-trove of design goodies thankfully lacks any unnecessary pretence.

Familiar and eye-catching brands like Alessi, Kartell and Flos help to pull customers through the door, but closer inspection reveals some less expected offerings. Where possible, Anthony Banks likes to support newer design companies

and gives as much emphasis to Kim Greenaway's white ceramics, Isabel Stanley's table lights and tableware from Bookan and base d as he does to international suppliers like De Sede, Magis, Santa + Cole, Room, Naos, Oluce, Fabbian, Lexon or Targetti. The helpful and approachable staff are keen to point out that what you see is only a fraction of the options. Due to lack of space, Right Angle is unable to show a huge amount of furniture, but staff will happily guide customers through supplier catalogues to illustrate the breadth of products that can be ordered.

Right Angle also has a shop in Paris (26 rue Mayet, 75006. +33 1 45 44 99 01), which showcases a similarly funky and individual range. Anthony Banks is keen to expand his Blackheath premises and increase his street presence. In the meantime, pop by and see what takes your fancy.

RJM FURNITURE

RJM Furniture
203 Kentish Town Road
London NW5 2JU
020 7428 9761
Tube: Kentish Town
Open: Mon – Fri 10 – 6:30
Sat 11 – 5:30
Sun 12 – 5

Gainsborough Studios
1 Poole Street
London N1 5EA
020 7428 9761
Tube:Old Street
Open: Mon – Fri 10 – 6:30
Sat 10:30 – 5:30
Sun 12 – 5

16 Wigmore Street
London W1U 2RF
020 7428 9761
Tube: Oxford Circus or Bond Street
Open: Mon – Fri 10 – 6:30
Sat 10:30 – 5:30
Sun 12 – 5

www.rjmfurniture.com

DESIGNERS INCLUDE:
Alivar
Artemide
Fiam
Flexform
Flos
Mobileffe
Moroso
SCP
Tagliabue
Tisettanta
Walter Knoll
Zanotta

SERVICES:
Contract Division
Interior Advice

CLOSE TO:
(Wigmore Street):
Key London
Mint
Noel Hennessy
Furniture
Skandium

the potential of his Kentish Town retail space situated on a main artery between the West End and the richer north London suburbs, and went about setting up RJM Furniture, launched in spring 2001. Occupying a slick and spacious 15,000 sq ft showroom across two floors, the store has already exceeded predetermined sales targets. RJM's large selection of mainly Italian furniture and lighting, with some accessories, appeals to those who want quality lasting design and don't mind paying the price for it.

The open-plan floor space has a range of ever-changing items to appeal to varying tastes, be it a rather garish Edra Flip sofa in pink PVC or a gently curvaceous tan leather Balzac armchair by Matthew Hilton for SCP. RJM's supplier list certainly reads well, with pieces from companies such as Alivar, Artemide (p 24), Fiam, Flos, Flexform, Mobileffe, Tisettanta, Zanotta, De Sede, Walter Knoll, Stelton, Moroso, Tagliabue and Vitra. While the clean uncluttered displays speak for themselves, helpful and knowledgeable staff are always nearby to handle any enquiries. Should you require more than a single piece but feel daunted by the prospect, you can make use of RJM's design and refurbishment service.

Driving or walking past the shop, you can't fail to be impressed by its splendour on an otherwise grimy high street. Don't feel nervous about entering – professional attentive service goes a long way to reassure you about any extravagant purchases.

THE ROOM
STORE

DESIGNERS INCLUDE:
Alessi
B&B Italia
Charles and Ray Eames
Gandia Blasco
Global
iittala
Kartell
Le Corbusier
Leonardo
LSA International
Maxalto
Rosendahl
Sancal
SCP
Teemo
Vitra
Zack

SERVICES:
Gift Vouchers
Gift Wrapping
Interior Advice
Wedding List

The Room Store
Grand Hall
Albert Dock
Liverpool L3 4AA
0151 708 0000
www.theroomstore.co.uk
Open: Mon – Sat 10 – 5:30
Sun 11 – 5

Albert Dock is one of Liverpool's best-known attractions on the city's famous waterfront. It comprises the UK's single largest group of Grade 1 listed buildings, the dock houses restaurants, bars and small retailers as well as Tate Liverpool. In April 2002, Jane Wade-Smith opened The Room Store in one of these immense warehouse spaces, selling a large collection of contemporary furniture, lighting, tableware and kitchenware.

Entering the double-height glass-fronted shop, you first encounter a selection of affordable items, such as glasses, vases, crockery and cutlery from well-known companies like Leonardo, LSA International, iittala, Rosendahl, Alessi, Global and Zack. Not all of the items in the ground floor space are of a modern design aesthetic due to the need to appeal to the wide variety of visitors.

Climbing the stairs to the next floor you can take in the lighting displays on your right and an overhead view of the ground floor on your left before entering the furniture section. This is a much darker space with low arched ceilings and exposed brick walls and floor. It forms an interesting open-plan old-industrial warehouse backdrop for a selection of

iconic twentieth-century designs from the likes of Le Corbusier, and Charles and Ray Eames, as well as more contemporary offerings from SCP, Vitra, B&B Italia, Maxalto, Sancal, Kartell, Teemo and Gandia Blasco. In this fantastic room with its low windows that look out over the waterfront, you can find modern additions for living, dining and bedrooms.

Achieving good sales figures from the outset, the already vast retail space is set to expand to incorporate even more choice for the growing customer base. Hopefully, this will lead to the introduction of some newer edgier products to really capture the imagination. But The Room Store must still remain consumer-friendly to continue pulling in a steady flow of business. Jane Wade-Smith's store should be congratulated for enticing the everyday shopper into the exciting realm of contemporary design.

ROOST

Roost
26 Kensington Gardens
Brighton BN1 4AL
01273 625 223
Open: Mon – Fri 10 – 5:30
Sat 10 – 6
Sun 12 – 4:30

The maze of streets that makes up the infamous Brighton Laines is home to an eclectic array of shops catering for the city's lively inhabitants. Roost, founded by Claire Gilliver and Lucien Hewetson in 1996, is situated in the heart of the North Laines on an ever-bustling pedestrianized thoroughfare. The clean, professional appearance of this shop succeeds in attracting a lot of passing trade, lured through the doors by the warm glow generated by a growing selection of lighting.

Once through the doors, customers are greeted by a fantastic collection of international design objects, not to mention friendly and helpful staff.

Although mainly smaller products are on sale due to the size restrictions of the premises, the range of carefully selected pieces is impressive. Roost has clearly considered the market in Brighton and features designs suitable for all budgets, with very little exceeding the £500 mark. Accessories and tableware come from the likes of Driade, Stelton, Inflate, Tonfisk, Zack, Bodum, Room Interior Products, Hub, Marc Boase, Julie Goodwin, Susan Pryke and Karen Smith. There is lighting from Le Klint (pictured), Tom Dixon, David Design, Suck UK (p 288), Unique, One Foot Taller and new Danish designer Sofie Refer. At the back of the shop there is just enough space for some furniture, including recently introduced pieces from Vitra. Claire Gilliver's favourite new additions to the store are the vibrant, graphic fabrics from Finnish textile superstars Marimekko.

An individual selection coupled with a digestible quantity of products makes Roost a perfect one-stop shop for interiors.

DESIGNERS INCLUDE:
Bodum
David Design
Driade
Hub
Inflate
Julie Goodwin
Karen Smith
Le Klint
Marc Boase
Marimekko
One Foot Taller
Sofie Refer
Susan Pryke
Room Interior Products
Stelton
Suck UK
Tom Dixon
Tonfisk
Unique
Vitra
Zack

SERVICES:
Contract Division
Gift Vouchers
Wedding List

CLOSE TO:
Caz Systems
Mojoe

199

Sarf
99 St John's Hill
London SW11 1SY
020 7228 0005
www.sarf.co.uk
Train: Clapham Junction
Open: Mon & Tues 12–6:30
Wed–Sat 10:30–6:30
Sun 12–5

SARF

DESIGNERS INCLUDE:
Artemide
Box Design
Engelbrechts
Flos
Frighetto
Gekko
Harkin
Kartell
Loop House
Marc Boase
Nelson
Nic Wood
Oluce
Peppermint
Tom Kirk
Zanotta

SERVICES:
Contract Division
Interior Design
Wedding List

Brothers Darren and Brendan Richardson used to work in the City as brokers before deciding to change tack in 2001 and open a shop selling what they love most – furniture, lighting and interior products. They have swapped long days trading on the Square Mile for equally long days honing their skills to the new task of selling contemporary design objects from modest-sized premises up the road from 'sarf' London's Clapham Junction.

Avoiding over-exposed 'classics', Darren and Brendan Richardson instead choose to stock the contemporary creations that they love. While applying their commercial expertise to the difficult job of selecting suitable items for the retail market, it is clear that they thoroughly enjoy their new profession.

On a tree-lined stretch of St John's Hill you could easily miss the store if driving past. The small shop front fortunately benefits from large windows that allow in enough natural light to illuminate the room-sets within. As well as selling furniture and lighting from the larger European brands such as Zanotta, Kartell, Frighetto, Flos, Artemide and Oluce, Sarf also has an array of designs from Engelbrechts and Box Design. UK talents feature too – ceramics from Marc Boase, lighting from Gekko, Nelson and Tom Kirk, pewterware from Nic Wood, stacking shelving units from Peppermint, faux-fur cushions and throws from Harkin and colourful rugs from Loop House.

Supplying an array of colourful eye-catching pieces and practical designs for domestic settings, Sarf is a welcome addition to this area of London. The logical next step would be for the brothers to open a 'norf' London counterpart.

DESIGNERS INCLUDE:
Alvar Aalto
Erik Magnussen
Eva Solo
iittala
Kosta Boda
Jørgen Gammelgaard
Poul Kjaerholm
Bruno Mathsson
Menu
Niels Møller
Orrefors
Pandul
Rosendahl
Stelton
Hans Wegner

SERVICES:
Bespoke Orders
Contract Division
Gift Wrapping
Interior Advice
Wedding List

Schiang
58 Holywell Hill
St Albans
Hertfordshire AL1 1BX
08702 202 055
www.schiang.com
Open: Wed – Sat 9:30 – 5:30
Sun 11 – 4

Before moving out to St Albans in 2001, Matthew Rhodes operated his business under the name of Cale Associates, selling timeless furniture from Danish and Swedish design masters from a trade showroom on London's Portobello Road. Holding the UK agency rights since the mid-1980s to a vast collection of designs from Hans Wegner, Bruno Mathsson, Jørgen Gammelgaard and Poul Kjaerholm, he had always dealt with contract clients away from the public realm. Relocating to the historic city of St Albans was his opportunity to open a retail outlet combining furniture with complementary Scandinavian lighting and accessories.

Schiang is housed in a sixteenth-century building on a busy hill leading into the city centre. Quirky walls and crooked ceilings provide an unusual yet somehow suitable backdrop for the timeless creations displayed within. Looking at designs that have been in production since the 1940s and 1950s – Hans Wegner's classic Wishbone Chair (pictured) or the curvaceous form that

is Bruno Mathsson's Mina armchair – makes you wonder who can rival the high quality of such pieces, still hand-assembled at the original factories in Denmark and Sweden. Further items are available from Alvar Aalto, Erik Magnussen and Niels Møller with task, wall, pendant and floor lights from Pandul illuminating the displays. There are plenty of glass creations from iittala, Kosta Boda and Orrefors, tableware accessories from Menu, Eva Solo and Rosendahl, as well as classic flawless stainless-steel designs from Stelton. Matthew Rhodes sells what he loves, and a chat with him quickly communicates his passion for and knowledge of the designs he trumpets. His location out of London hasn't hindered sales as many people make the effort to travel to the store. But for anyone unable to visit, Schiang's website contains comprehensive information about the designs on sale.

SCP
135 – 139 Curtain Road
London EC2A 3BX
020 7739 1869
www.scp.co.uk
Tube: Old Street
Open: Mon – Sat 9:30 – 6
Sun 11 – 5
Concession in Selfridges, London and
Manchester Trafford Centre (p 208)

World-renowned SCP was founded by Sheridan Coakley, a top retailer of contemporary design and manufacturer of an ever-increasing selection of furniture. He has established close working relationships with a number of successful UK designers, such as Jasper Morrison, Matthew Hilton, Terence Woodgate, Michael Marriott, Andrew

Stafford and Michael Sodeau, in his bid to put their creations into production and place them on the international design market. Despite nurturing new UK design talent, Sheridan Coakley has not succumbed to fashionable whims. Instead, he commissions products that embody clarity and simplicity of form, and that are made to a high quality to stand the test of time.

The SCP store in the heart of London's Shoreditch triangle is the company's creative pulse where its own furniture ranges are married with designs from other suppliers. An enticing selection of furniture, lighting, ceramics, glassware, tableware and textiles embodies SCP's core values of resourcefulness and ingenuity. The buyers have an eye for well-made classic designs that simply

DESIGNERS INCLUDE:
Artek
Artemide
Cappellini
Cor Unum
Flos
Fontana Arte
Fritz Hansen
iittala
Knoll
Le Klint
Louis Poulsen
Luceplan
Mandarina Duck
Pia Wallen
Rosenthal
Salviati
SCP
Stelton
Thonet
Vitra

SERVICES:
Contract Division
Wedding List

CLOSE TO:
Morris & Co
Two Columbia Road

ooze desirability, choosing products that will surely be impulse buys and others that are destined to be carefully considered long-term investments. On the ground floor are smaller items such as ceramics from Cor Unum, glassware from Salviati, china from Rosenthal, tableware from iittala, stainless-steel pieces from Stelton, bags from Mandarina Duck, throws from Pia Wallen and a myriad of design books. Gracing one corner is a good choice of lighting from major suppliers – Artemide, Flos, Louis Poulsen, Fontana Arte, Luceplan and Le Klint.

Climb the stairs for furniture from Knoll, Vitra, Artek, Fritz Hansen and Thonet, as well as extensive choices from the SCP range, all complemented by select creations from Cappellini and other brands. Touring the store is always a

delight but customers can easily go unnoticed by the busy staff.

In London's West End or in Manchester's Trafford Centre, pop into the SCP concession at Selfridges, where the emphasis is entirely on retail sales – unlike the east London flagship store, which also tackles the business-contract market. Whichever premises you visit, SCP will leave you with a lasting impression.

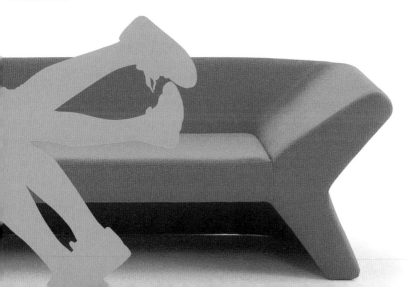

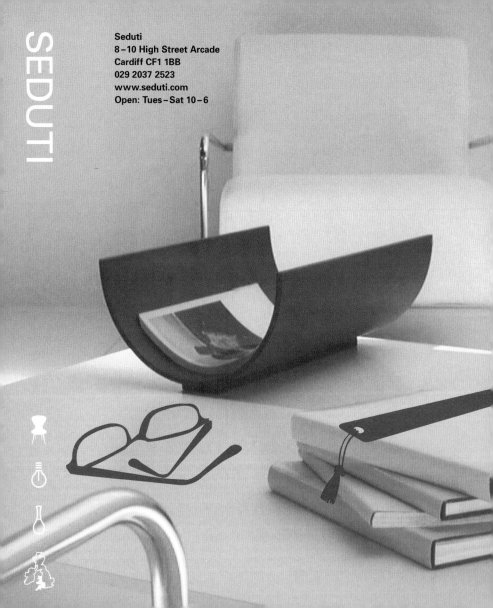

Seduti
8–10 High Street Arcade
Cardiff CF1 1BB
029 2037 2523
www.seduti.com
Open: Tues–Sat 10–6

SEDUTI

DESIGNERS INCLUDE:
Alivar
Cappellini
Fiam
Flos
Kevin Bankhead
Kristalia
Normann
Penta
Seven Salotti

SERVICES:
Bespoke Orders
Contract Division
Gift Vouchers
Gift Wrapping
Interior Design
Wedding List

CLOSE TO:
Back2myplace
Momentum

Seduti was opened by Lorna Oakley in Cardiff's High Street Arcade in October 2001. Knowing what appeals to Cardiff and South Wales residents, she has introduced muted, neutral-toned furniture into her store, mixed with some clever lighting and a few accessories. Rather than buy into the more off-beat aesthetic often associated with contemporary design, Seduti offers a slightly safer modern look with clean-lined forms and quality craftsmanship.

As the Welsh public have only recently started coming around to the possibilities of modern design in their homes, Lorna Oakley knows that her business must offer a complete interior design service to make any interior transitions hassle-free for clients, regardless of the size of the job.

In the large shop windows is a changing array of furniture pieces and lighting from the likes of Alivar, Fiam, Flos, Kristalia, Seven Salotti, Normann and local talent Kevin Bankhead. The shop also has a basement that acts as space for changing room-sets and exhibitions. Local artwork graces the walls and gives context to a display of Fiam glass tables, lighting from Penta, Starck-designed stools and Cappellini dining chairs. You can choose many other pieces from the product database, too. Lorna Oakley and her staff are always there to help, making parting with your cash a strangely enjoyable prospect.

SELFRIDGES

Selfridges
400 Oxford Street
London W1A 1AB
Tube: Bond Street
Open: Mon – Fri 10 – 8
Sat 9:30 – 8
Sun 12 – 6

1 Exchange Square
Manchester M3 1BD
Open: Mon – Fri 10 – 8
Thurs til 9
Sat 9 – 8
Sun 12 – 6

No 1 The Dome
The Trafford Centre
Manchester M17 8DA
Open: Mon – Fri 10 – 9
Sat 9 – 7
Sun 12 – 6

08708 377 377
www.selfridges.co.uk

DESIGNERS INCLUDE:
Alessi
Artomatic
Cappellini
Driade
Eat My Handbag Bitch
Kartell
Lounge
Marimekko
Ogier
SCP
Skandium

SERVICES:
Gift Vouchers
Gift Wrapping
Wedding List

CLOSE TO:
Alessi
Key London
Mint
Skandium

In the battle of the department stores, nobody can argue against the brilliance of Selfridges in consistently maintaining its contemporary appearance over the years. Headed up by the extraordinary vision of chief executive Vittorio Radice since 1996, Selfridges never grows complacent with its success but, instead, manages to continually impress. With so many different areas inside the store to awaken the senses, Selfridges selects the best concession brands that collectively create a sense of occasion for its 21 million annual customers.

Contemporary architecture and design are essential components of Vittorio Radice's philosophy to create a vibrant atmosphere throughout the store. And it works – more than fifty per cent of visitors leave having bought something, even if they entered with no intention of purchasing. Selfridges has no own-brand goods – its brand 'is a place not a product'.

Selfridges' fashion departments have always been strong, but it is only in the past few years that it has fully embraced contemporary furniture and design. Starting with an SCP concession on the fourth floor (p 204), the London store has since introduced Driade, Kartell and Cappellini on the same floor, as well as Skandium (p 212), Marimekko, Alessi (p 12), Eat My Handbag Bitch (p 84), Artomatic, Lounge and, more recently, Ogier in the basement. Selected to avoid clashes, each of these concessions retains its own distinctive style and product integrity while collectively offering a variety of interior choices from affordable tableware to high-end furniture.

Selfridges' constant ability to attract a huge number of shoppers is amazing. Part of its success must be due to the sheer scale of the building – this immense emporium seems to offer a new shopping experience on every visit. With an ambitious expansion scheme unfolding in the UK that already incorporates two stores in Manchester and a Future Systems-designed centrepiece in Birmingham's Bullring (pictured), Selfridges is rapidly establishing itself as a business with no limits.

SHANNON

Shannon
68 Walcot Street
Bath BA1 5BD
01225 424 222
www.shannon-uk.com
Open: Mon – Sat 9:30 – 5:30

Shannon is situated in the artisan quarter of the picturesque and historical city of Bath, on a street dominated by specialist craft and antique shops. Owner Sue Shannon wanted to stand out from the rest when she opened her small store in April 2000, selling a comprehensive selection of classic and contemporary Scandinavian furniture, lighting and accessories. The increasingly popular Nordic style has appealed strongly to West Country residents who no longer have to travel to London to find it.

In a city dominated by traditional exteriors, you wouldn't necessarily expect the clean-lined aesthetic of Scandinavian interiors to be popular. But the understated beauty of furniture

DESIGNERS INCLUDE:
Alvar Aalto
Arne Jacobsen
Boda Nova
Bruno Mathsson
Eva Solo
Hans Wegner
iittala
Le Klint
Louis Poulsen
Menu
Pandul
PP Møbler
Poul Kjaerholm
Rosendahl
Stelton

SERVICES:
Contract Division
Gift Wrapping
Interior Advice

from designers such as Hans Wegner, Bruno Mathsson, Arne Jacobsen, Alvar Aalto and Poul Kjaerholm has captured the attention of the design world since the 1950s. Still in full production, the designs appeal just as strongly to today's customers – the forms so iconic as to have stood the test of time. The quality of the Wegner chairs produced by PP Møbler, is second to none, with precision wood bending and the silky smooth finish a feat in manufacturing prowess. As you would expect, such pieces don't come cheap, and so Sue Shannon has been sure to stock some more accessible items, including ceramics, glassware and tableware from brands such as iittala,

Stelton, Menu, Rosendahl, Boda Nova and Eva Solo. Believe it or not, despite the small shop space, lighting also plays its part here. No Scandinavian design shop would be complete without stunning creations from Louis Poulsen, Pandul and Le Klint.

As with many small shops, it is not possible to showcase all of the offerings from the many suppliers. For this reason, it is worth speaking to the owner as her enthusiasm and knowledge of the market are an inspiration. Her attention to customer relations will ensure you receive the advice that you need. With customers travelling from far and wide, Sue Shannon has successfully created a business that runs parallel with her passion.

SKANDIUM

DESIGNERS INCLUDE:
Arne Jacobsen
Alvar Aalto
Björn Dahlström
Carina Seth-Andersson
Claesson Koivisto Rune
David Design
Eero Aarnio
Hans Wegner
Harri Koskinen
Lena Bergström
Pia Wallen
Poul Kjaerholm
Poul Henningsen
Tapio Wirkkala
Thomas Sandell
Timo Sarpaneva
Tonfisk
Verner Panton

SERVICES:
Contract Division
Gift Vouchers
Gift Wrapping
Interior Advice
Wedding List

CLOSE TO:
Key London
Mint
Noel Hennessy
Furniture
RJM Furniture
(Wigmore Street)
Selfridges

Skandium
72 Wigmore Street
London W1U 2SG
020 7935 2077
www.skandium.com
Tube: Bond Street
Open: Mon–Sat 10–6:30
Sun 12–5

Concession in Selfridges, London and Manchester Trafford Centre (p 208)

It is hard to believe that Skandium first opened its doors as recently as September 1999 because the company has evolved at an impressive rate. This is due mainly to the energy of owners Christopher Seidenfaden, Chrystina Schmidt and Magnus Englund, who have consistently applied their knowledge of the Scandinavian design market with a clear and directional approach. No longer just based on London's Wigmore Street, Skandium now runs a successful concession in Selfridges in London and Manchester. While still welcoming the general public, the original store is now the central operating ground for its contract business.

You can't miss the floor-to-ceiling glass shop front of the London W1 store. The curved pine wall and painted wooden floors provide an unobtrusive backdrop for the beautiful furniture, lighting, ceramics, glassware, tableware and fabrics displayed tidily within. Skandium operates simple buying criteria – either

the designer or the manufacturer of the designs must be Scandinavian.

Nordic nations have developed a reputation for contributing to the forefront of contemporary design over many decades, with talents like Arne Jacobsen, Alvar Aalto, Hans Wegner, Poul Kjaerholm, Poul Henningsen, Verner Panton, Eero Aarnio, Timo Sarpaneva and Tapio Wirkkala. So it is no surprise that Skandium aims to celebrate and sustain this global recognition. The company also showcases new designs from talents such as Björn Dahlström, Lena Bergström, Thomas Sandell, Tonfisk, David Design, Claesson Koivisto Rune, Harri Koskinen, Pia Wallen and Carina Seth-Andersson. If these names mean nothing to you, why not pay the shop a visit? You will, no doubt, succumb to the sheer beauty of the selection – with cool music, efficient service and helpful staff adding those crucial final touches.

SNOWHOME

DESIGNERS INCLUDE:
Alessi
Black + Blum
Eurolounge
Flos
Foscarini
iittala
Innermost
Isokon Plus
Keramica
LSA International
Magis
Mathmos
Propaganda
Scabetti
Suck UK
Umbra
Vitra
Worldwide Co

SERVICES:
Contract Division
Gift Vouchers
Wedding List

Snowhome
38 Gillygate
York YO31 7EQ
01904 671 155
www.snow-home.co.uk
Open: Mon – Sat 10 – 5

Over the past few years, only the UK's major post-industrial cities have witnessed significant investment in modernization, regeneration and development. Smaller cities, such as picturesque York are tourist attractions, and their heritage and traditions have not really called for change. But attitudes are changing, with the introduction of more and more stylish independent retailers, bars, cafés and restaurants. Snowhome, opened in York in summer 2001, is one of these much-needed additions – a tiny shop selling well-displayed contemporary homeware for the city's increasingly modern, young inhabitants.

When Angus McArthur moved to York, he felt cut off from contemporary design. Having trained at the Royal College of Art in London, it seemed only logical to open a shop supplying design-led goods. All too aware that a new business of this sort could not take huge risks, he set up in small premises on a busy central road selling mainly affordable tableware items from the likes of Innermost, Black + Blum, Mathmos,

Keramica, Suck UK (p 288), Umbra, Worldwide Co, Propaganda, LSA International, iittala and Scabetti.

As Snowhome's reputation has grown, so, too, has Angus McArthur's confidence, and he has introduced a small selection of furniture and lighting from Kartell, Vitra, Eurolounge, Isokon Plus, Magis, Foscarini and Flos. Also selling some iconic Alessi pieces, Snowhome has managed to select good design that isn't exclusive or prohibitively expensive. It has succeeded in creating a business that opens up modern design products to a wider audience who might not usually be exposed to it. My feeling is that other similar-sized cities could benefit from a store like Snowhome to reinforce the message that design-led products needn't cost a fortune and are available to all.

Suburbia
17 Regent Street
Clifton
Bristol BS8 4HW
0117 974 3880
Open: Tues – Sat 10 – 6

DESIGNERS INCLUDE:
Eurolounge
iittala
Inflate
Innermost
Kartell
Koziol
LSA International
Magis
Mathmos
Room Interior Products

The ever-friendly and enthusiastic owner of Suburbia, Sue Williams, opened her design shop in the rather quaint environs of Bristol's Clifton Village in 1999 – a bold move, some may say, to introduce contemporary design to a city that had previously never fully embraced it. A few years on, and with the benefit of hindsight, Sue admits that it was a risk to open a totally new retail venture in an area otherwise dominated by gift shops and tourists. Approaching the market gently, Suburbia's appearance on Regent Street has remained low key so as not to frighten off or intimidate cautious Bristol customers. But even Jasper Morrison's candy-coloured Air Chair for Magis has not deterred local people, who continue to come back for more items to grace their increasingly modern homes.

Sue Williams is a fan of mass-production and her buying decisions reflect this. Affordable pricing goes hand-in-hand with such products, so you can rest assured that you won't be too horrified when you pick up the bill. Sue's philosophy is that good avant-garde design needn't break the bank, and her growing customer base clearly agrees. A digestible quantity of furniture, lighting and accessories are displayed in the small shop space in a welcoming way that doesn't put you off touching any prospective purchases. With products from accessible companies such as Kartell, Magis (pictured), Inflate, Eurolounge, iittala, LSA International, Room, Mathmos, Koziol and Innermost, it is no surprise that shop sales continue to increase. I would not be surprised if expansion were soon on the cards.

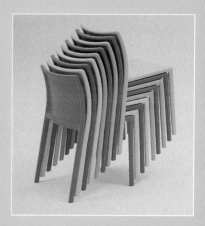

TANGRAM

Tangram
33 – 37 Jeffrey Street
Edinburgh EH1 1DH
0131 556 6551
www.tangramfurnishers.co.uk
Open: Tues – Fri 10 – 5:30
Sat 10 – 5

Husband and wife duo Eleanor and Julian Darwell-Stone started their furniture retail business in 1994, and in 2000, the company expanded into larger premises on the hill overlooking the city's mainline station. The light and airy space on two floors is home to a carefully selected choice of high-quality modern furniture and lighting designs from a refreshing mix of suppliers. While stocking big boys like B&B Italia, Artifort, Baleri Italia, Driade, Lammhults, MDF Italia, Montis and Vitra, the showroom also plays host to lesser-exposed brands such as Stua, Gloria, Piiroinen, Punt Mobles, Jesper Holm, Amat, Horm and Paola Lenti.

Understandably, these supplier names may well mean nothing to you, but the overall feeling of the collection at Tangram is of understated elegance. Apart from the occasional quirky and humorous lighting item from Ingo Maurer, the shop displays a selection of timeless designs. For anyone contemplating the transition to contemporary living, Tangram is the place to purchase pieces that will soften your fall. Not preoccupied with a quick sale, the friendly staff are more than happy to give you their time and share their knowledge to ensure that you leave with a purchase most suited to your requirements and taste.

As I wandered around the spacious room-set displays, I felt that the staff really cared about their customers, which gives added confidence when it comes to handing over the credit card. Rest assured that orders will be processed efficiently and delivered with minimum hassle, making for a streamlined purchase.

DESIGNERS INCLUDE:

Amat
Artifort
B&B Italia
Baleri Italia
Driade
Gloria
Horm
Ingo Maurer
Jesper Holm
Lammhults
MDF Italia
Montis
Paola Lenti
Piiroinen
Punt Mobles
Stua
Vitra

SERVICES:

Contract Division
Interior Advice

CLOSE TO:
Concrete Butterfly

TEMPTER

Tempter
12a Nelson Street
Newcastle upon Tyne
NE1 5AW
0191 230 2251
www.tempterinteriors.com
Open: Mon – Sat 10 – 5:30
Thurs til 8
Sun 11 – 5

It was in January 2002 that the entrepreneurial brother and sister duo Sara and Mark Bawden opened their own contemporary design store in Newcastle city centre. Until then, the city had been devoid of any store of this sort, so the owners were confident that their new venture would breathe fresh life into the previously staid interiors market. The store, located in the heart of the central shopping area, was originally two floors of a former building society. Sara and Mark have transformed the space into a fantastic modern design showroom.

The selection at Tempter combines established brand suppliers with lesser-known artists and designers, creating a fusion of styles, materials and price points. The choice on display has been well edited to avoid clutter, allowing the unobtrusive chairs, sofas, sideboards and tables from Seven Salotti, Kristalia, Alivar, Tagliabue, and Isokon Plus to truly shine. Accompanying these larger items are interesting individually chosen accessories, ceramics and glassware to attract impulse buyers. On my visit, various designs caught my eye, such as a line of quirky Egg, Sponge and Foam

vases by Marcel Wanders, a blown-glass Cherub table lamp from Ochre and a peculiar tall cone-shaped ashtray by Ross Lovegrove for Driade. Beautifully proportioned white ceramics from Bodo Sperlein, glass table lighting by Gitta Gschwendtner, quirky CD rack towers from Sponge and graphic cushions from Double Helix are just some of the pieces on offer from talented UK designers. The owners are keen to introduce fresh pieces on a regular basis, creating a different experience for customers on each visit. A decent turnover of large artworks from local talents contributes to this objective, as well as livening up the otherwise plain white walls.

It is difficult to pin-point exactly what it is that gives Tempter a different feel from other design shops. Perhaps it is the owners' ability to fill the space with quality rather than quantity, or the careful blend of well-known designs and newer choices. Whatever the case, it is a fantastic contemporary design retail outfit.

DESIGNERS INCLUDE:
Alivar
Bodo Sperlein
Double Helix
Driade
Gitta Gschwendtner
Isokon Plus
Kristalia
Marcel Wanders
Ochre
Ross Lovegrove
Seven Salotti
Sponge
Tagliabue

SERVICES:
Gift Vouchers
Gift Wrapping
Interior Design
Wedding List

THEMES & VARIATIONS

Themes & Variations
231 Westbourne Grove
London W11 2SE
020 7727 5531
www.themesandvariations.co.uk
Tube: Notting Hill Gate
Open: Mon–Fri 10–1 & 2–6
Sat 10–6

Themes & Variations was opened by Liliane Fawcett on Notting Hill's Westbourne Grove in 1985, where she has since established a reputation as one of the leading specialists in post-war decorative arts and furniture. What makes this spacious design gallery unique is the ever-changing display of contemporary creations mixed in with older pieces, which cleverly avoids the gallery being bracketed within any one particular style or era. This ambiguity is an intriguing feature and one that obviously appeals to loyal customers in search of unusual or rare collectibles for the home.

If you are increasingly fed up with the continual bombardment of the same brands and designers, then Themes & Variations is for you. Lured through the open door by the select objects in the window displays, you gratefully escape the endless fashion boutiques that have started to dominate Westbourne Grove

DESIGNERS INCLUDE:
Benedetta Mori
Ulbadini
Carl Hahn
Flavio Poli
Ingo Maurer
Hans Wegner
Mario Pinzoni
Piero Fornasetti
Seguso Vetri d'Arte
Vittorio Rigattieri

SERVICES:
Sourcing

CLOSE TO:
Bowles and Linares
Flow
Mission
Vessel

in recent years. The display of items within is suitably refined and uncluttered, with each piece given equal pride of place to capture customers' attention. On my visit I was met by an ornately decorated sideboard by Piero Fornasetti positioned near some gorgeous low-level armchairs by Hans Wegner. Gracing the elegant shelving displays were various mid-twentieth-century vibrant Murano glass designs by the progressive Italian designers Flavio Poli, Mario Pinzoni and Vittorio Rigattieri for Seguso Vetri d'Arte. Working in harmony with these older objects are fragile Japanese Samurai paper light sculptures by

Ingo Maurer, graphic wire mesh animal figures by Benedetta Mori Ulbadini and solid sycamore stools by Carl Hahn. Obtaining items from around the world, in particular Italy and Scandinavia, Themes & Variations is able to source particular pieces from a network of international contacts.

The rare finds provide a feast for the senses as you are introduced to an unpredictable mix of decorative arts and designs combining various styles, eras and material finishes. Liliane Fawcett simply buys what she loves, which is reflected in this most individual of design galleries.

TOM TOM

Tom Tom
42 New Compton Street
London WC2H 8DA
020 7240 7909
www.tomtomshop.co.uk
Tube: Tottenham Court Road
Open: Tues–Fri 12–7
Sat 11–6

Tom Tom was opened in 1993 by Tommy Roberts in premises just around the corner from Denmark Street, the street of rock'n'roll off London's Charing Cross Road. It's the ideal location for this retailer of original twentieth-century furniture, lighting and artwork, which attracts many rock'n'roll clients looking for original and often iconic additions to their extravagant homes. Discreetly distant from the main throng of busy West End shoppers, Tom Tom enjoys a gentle stream of customers who are interested in interior products designed between the 1940s and 1980s. Managing the flow of changing stock across the two floors of this small shop is Gary Mitchell, who has increased expenditure over the past two years, introducing more unusual limited

DESIGNERS INCLUDE:
Arne Jacobsen
Charles and Ray Eames
Eero Aarnio
Ernest Race
Gaetano Pesce
Hans Wegner
Harry Bertoia
Olivier Mourgue
Robin Day
Verner Panton

SERVICES:
Sourcing

cdition items to the displays. On my visit, displayed with pride of place in the window, was a highly desirable, status-driven Rolls Royce coffee table designed by Ringo Starr and Robin Cruickshank, one of an edition of only three. Numbered prints from the likes of Bridget Riley, Gilbert & George, and Andy Warhol lined the walls, overlooking celebrated furniture designs from prolific talents like Verner Panton, Eero Aarnio, Gaetano Pesce, Ernest Race, Charles and Ray Eames, Arne Jacobsen, Robin Day, Hans Wegner, Olivier Mourgue and Harry Bertoia.

The shop exudes a cheerful appearance with its lighting displays and colourful artwork, cheering up even the greyest of London days. The staff are friendly and knowledgeable and, thankfully, leave you alone to browse the selection of interior treats. Needless to say, should you be seeking a particular item, Tom Tom will happily try to source it for you, depending on market availability. With a variety of styles and design eras on display, there will inevitably be some pieces you love and some you hate, creating an intriguing balance that inspires regular visits.

TONY WALKER INTERIORS

Tony Walker Interiors
Whitehall Court
14 Telford Road
Edinburgh EH4 2BD
0131 343 6151
Open: Mon–Fri 9–5:30
Sat 9–4:30

70 Ingram Street
Glasgow G1 1EX
0141 574 1340
Tube: Buchanan Street
Open: Mon–Fri 9:30–5:30
Sat 10–4
Sun 12–4

www.tonywalkerinteriors.com

Tony Walker established his company in 1973, and it has grown steadily to become one of Scotland's largest suppliers of top-quality contemporary furniture for home and business interiors. Occupying showrooms and offices in Edinburgh and a London office for Business Interiors (020 7737 7704), Tony Walker has significant market presence, which increased even more in autumn 2002 with the opening of the Glasgow showroom (pictured) in the heart of the Merchant City. Displayed across the two floors of this 3,300 sq ft store is a sizeable range of contemporary furniture, fabrics, lighting and accessories for home and business. The establishment of strong relationships with reputable European suppliers over the years has been reinforced by Tony Walker's deep understanding of design. He possesses clear ideas of what constitutes good design – quality, appearance, flair, comfort and, above all, functionality. He has built his reputation around these key attributes by supplying numerous projects with products from the likes of Cassina, Desalto, Fritz Hansen, Mobileffe, Rolf Benz, Vitra, Interlübke, Hitch Mylius, Kartell, Cor, and Artemide.

While the products are clearly of core importance, the staff place huge emphasis on the efficient provision of a professional service to take the sweat out of the daunting task of an interior overhaul. On-hand designers offer a complimentary design service for home interiors, as well as a comprehensive range of logistical services for business clients.

The furniture displays are lifted by a few choice accessory pieces and softened with a selection of fabrics from Anna French, Bute, Kvadrat and Osborne & Little, to name but a few. The range of products combines iconic creations with understated modern pieces, livened up by various vibrant contemporary items. Welcoming contract clients as well as retail and domestic ones, Tony Walker Interiors has a big-business atmosphere that could prove intimidating for some customers. Dispel your insecurities and you will experience friendly and informative service in the company of gorgeous European designs.

DESIGNERS INCLUDE:
Anna French
Artemide
Bute
Cassina
Cor
Desalto
Fritz Hansen
Hitch Mylius
Interlübke
Kartell
Kvadrat
Mobileffe
Osborne & Little
Rolf Benz
Vitra

SERVICES:
Contract Division
Interior Design

CLOSE TO
(GLASGOW):
Dallas + Dallas
Inhouse

227

TWENTY
TWENTY ONE

DESIGNERS INCLUDE:
Barber Osgerby
Bouroullec brothers
Charles and Ray Eames
Claesson Koivisto Rune
Jasper Morrison
Konstantin Cricick
Gio Ponti
Michael Sodeau
Michael Young
Robin Day
Ron Arad
Ronan and Erwan

SERVICES:
Bespoke Orders
Contract Division
Wedding List

CLOSE TO:
Area Squared Design
Aria
Fandango
Living Space

Twentytwentyone
274 Upper Street
London N1 2UA
020 7288 1996
Tube: Angel or Highbury & Islington

18c River Street
London EC1R 1XN
020 7837 1900
Tube: Angel
Open: Mon – Fri 10 – 6
Sat 10 – 5:30

www.twentytwentyone.com

Enterprising duo Simon Alderson and Tony Cunningham started out in the business of selling twentieth-century originals from a converted stable in Camden Town, rather unimaginatively called Twentieth Century Design. In 1996, they decided to open a shop in Islington where they continued to trade a successful turnover of iconic design objects. But the increase in fantastic new creations within the contemporary design world caught their attention and, eventually, they changed their name to Twentytwentyone to reflect this new influence on their collection.

The business has been fine-tuned over the past five years, gaining a reputation as one of London's best design retailers. The tiny Upper Street premises do not allow the shop to showcase huge quantities of products, meaning the selection of furniture, lighting and accessories on display is always carefully edited. The successful combinion of original pieces and new designs with impeccable taste means you'll want to buy everything in this Brinkworth-designed store. Changing displays of stunning designs are chosen from the likes of Claesson Koivisto Rune, Michael Young, Ron Arad, Jasper Morrison, Robin Day, Gio Ponti, Barber Osgerby, the Bouroullec brothers, Michael Sodeau, Charles and Ray Eames, the Azumis and Konstantin Cricick. The Twentytwentyone team should be aware that its head-turning window display is a hazard to all passing traffic, as I discovered to my embarrassment when I drove into the back of a car having been distracted by the gorgeous offerings within!

Staff are well informed about items on sale, and if a particular piece is missing from the Upper Street store, they will take you to larger warehouse premises 10 minutes' walk away on residential River Street. Here you will find a more comprehensive array of larger items of furniture from the huge supplier list. Operating a strong contract division from this head office, as well as manufacturing its own collection of furniture and acting as UK agent for Swedish companies David Design and Snowcrash, the Twentytwentyone team have got their work cut out and can now only progress from strength to strength.

TWO COLUMBIA ROAD

DESIGNERS INCLUDE:
Arne Jacobsen
Charles and Ray Eames
Eero Saarinen
Joe Colombo
Mies van der Rohe
Pierre Paulin
Poul Kjaerholm
Verner Panton

SERVICES:
Sourcing

CLOSE TO:
Morris & Co
SCP

Two Columbia Road

2 Columbia Road
London E2 7NN
020 7729 9933
www.twocolumbiaroad.com
Tube: Old Street
Open: Tues – Fri 12 – 7
Sat 12 – 6
Sun 10 – 3

Driving down London's Hackney Road one evening, I first spotted Two Columbia Road – it's hard to miss the well-lit shop window displays on this prominent corner spot. Returning during the day, I was able to meet owner Keith Roberts and browse the changing displays of twentieth-century furniture, lighting, prints and complementary glassware and ceramics. Like all shops dealing in originals, Two Columbia Road is always going to feel different on each visit, depending on what the latest delivery contained. Items are continually sourced from various countries across Europe, resulting in an unpredictable yet interesting diversity of styles.

On my visit, the shop had just received a delivery from Denmark, including beautifully crafted rosewood and teak desks and sideboards. Positioned next to these were a pair of perfectly proportioned Poul Kjaerholm chairs, illuminated strategically by an elegant Joe Colombo Coupé floor lamp. The mixture of styles from various eras and the combination of iconic designs next to lesser-known generic creations mean that customers should succeed in finding a piece that will appeal to their own particular interior taste.

A number of better-known designs are usually available from twentieth-century pioneers such as Verner Panton, Pierre Paulin, Eero Saarinen, Charles & Ray Eames, Arne Jacobsen and Mies van der Rohe, but it is always worth asking the staff if you are trying to find something in particular. With limited floor space in the shop, they may well have your request held in storage or be able to source the item from elsewhere. Staff are never willing to compromise on quality, so customers can rest assured that all of the pieces they purchase are carefully checked for damage and restored accordingly before being delivered.

With stock frequently coming and going, try checking out the website for the latest offerings – by subscribing to the mailing list you can be regularly notified of new additions via email. If the internet isn't your game, then simply visit the store and snap up a collectible.

DESIGNERS INCLUDE:
Alivar
Artemide
De Sede
Driade
Fiam
Flos
Foscarini
Jesse
Kartell
Kristalia
Magis
MDF Italia
Montis
Naos
Oluce
Rolf Benz
Seven Salotti
Tagliabue
Tonelli
Vitra

SERVICES:
Bespoke Orders
Gift Vouchers
Gift Wrapping
Interior Design
Wedding List

Unique Interiors
252–256 Whitegate Drive
Blackpool FY3 9JW
01253 698 989
www.uniqueinteriors.co.uk
Open: Mon–Fri 10–6
Sat 10–5

Of all the cities in the UK, Blackpool is not one in which I would expect to find a contemporary design store. The town centre lives up to all its stereotypes, with fruit machines, games arcades, roller coasters and candy floss playing a significant role. Away from the seafront madness in a more subdued residential area is Unique Interiors, set up by husband and wife duo Glynne and Sue Gerrard in 1997. When they first opened, the couple supplied an altogether different style of furniture, but, over the years, they have gradually fine-tuned the collection towards an increasingly popular modern aesthetic.

As the business has grown, so, too, has the size of the premises. Initially occupying a limited corner unit, Unique Interiors expanded into the shop next door before creating another floor upstairs in autumn 2002. Instead of opting for a bold and brash modern style,

pieces have been selected from a range of high-quality suppliers such as Alivar, De Sede (pictured), Driade, Fiam, Kristalia, Naos, Montis, Seven Salotti, Tonelli, Jesse, MDF Italia, Rolf Benz and Tagliabue. Recently some lively choices have been included from Kartell, Magis and Vitra as a response to clients requesting more variety. With lighting companies like Flos, Oluce, Artemide and Foscarini adding to the significant list of suppliers, the owners are all too aware that it is impossible to showcase every available design in their shop. Frustrated by this restriction, Glynne Gerrard masterminded a Powerpoint presentation of all of the various furniture and lighting options available to customers. Projected onto one of the white walls, customers can sit on a comfy sofa and watch the choices unfold. Using electronic cataloguing has got to be the way forward to provide customers with an overview before narrowing in on the final choice.

On most visits you are likely to be welcomed by one of the friendly owners, who ensure that high levels of service are maintained. Attracting customers from a large catchment area, it is encouraging to see Unique Interiors carving a niche in this area of the country.

UNTO THIS LAST

Unto This Last
230 Brick Lane
London E2 7EB
www.untothislast.co.uk
Tube: Shoreditch or Old Street
Open: Sun 10–6

DESIGNERS INCLUDE:
all own brand

SERVICES:
Bespoke Orders

CLOSE TO:
Eat My Handbag Bitch
Overdose On Design

Located just a stone's throw north of Bethnal Green Road on East London's infamous Brick Lane is Unto This Last, a unique venture launched by amicable Frenchman Olivier Geoffrey in January 2001. An admirer of the cost-efficiency structures employed by own-brand mass-production giants IKEA and Habitat, Geoffrey aims to produce contemporary furniture, lighting and accessories at reasonable prices while supplying small locally driven market demand.

Using software-based CNC cutting technology to produce its range from various sheet materials, Unto This Last designs are inspired by the manufacturing process, using the precision of the latest 3-D modelling software programmes to ensure that prototyping expense and waste is kept to a minimum. To most customers' surprise, every component is produced in the basement, recreating the atmosphere and convenience of a local craftsman's shop.

These 'digital craftsmen' are open only on Sundays to coincide with Brick Lane Market and Columbia Road Flower Market. On entering the wonderful old textural interior, you are immediately struck by the purity of the contemporary selection against this unique retail backdrop. Some pieces are available to purchase off the shelf, but most items on display need to be ordered for collection the following week. Supplying local demand doesn't require spending large sums on marketing, while production to order avoids investment in unsold surplus stock. Controlling the market directly in the form of manufacturer as retailer cuts out any middlemen, keeping prices low for customers. As every piece is made to order, customers can request certain sizes and colours to suit specific requirements.

For a fulfilling visit to Unto This Last, you need to understand the visionary business model that Olivier Geoffrey is still in the early days of developing. Be sure talk to him or his staff to learn more about their approach. Expect to see Unto This Last utilize this concept in more locations, as both investors and consumers catch onto the possibilities of this new business model.

UTILITY

Utility
85 Bold Street
Liverpool L1 4HF
0151 707 9919

86 Bold Street
Liverpool L1 4HY
0151 708 4192
Open: Mon – Fri 10 – 6
Sat 9 – 6

www.utilityretail.co.uk

The first Utility store was opened at 85 Bold Street in 1999 by Richard Mawdsley, Richard Skelton and Kate Cowie, selling mainly small design-led accessories. In the central core of the floor space, select chairs and stools were on display, but the size of the store restricted the expansion of the furniture element. Just as the directors were discussing moving to larger premises, a retail unit became available across the road. Seizing this opportunity, they opened the new division of Utility in August 2002 at number 86, benefiting immediately from the steady flow of customers shopping on Liverpool's Bold Street.

The original shop has become more gift orientated, and the new store is responsible for contemporary furniture, lighting and accessories. Witnessing Liverpudlians' change of attitude to interior design over the past few years has given the owners of Utility the confidence to introduce exciting new suppliers to their list. Vibrant chair, stool and table designs from Kartell, with reasonable price tags, are a big hit in the window display and work well to attract passing customers. Other recognizable brands, such as Magis, Vitra, Fritz Hansen and Knoll, grace the space, as well as less obtrusive wood and glass designs from Artek, Punt Mobles, Fiam and Mobles 114. The store is keen to stock pieces from suppliers who produce work from iconic twentieth-century designers like Charles & Ray Eames, Arne Jacobsen, Alvar Aalto and Harry Bertoia and 'it' creators like Jasper Morrison, Ron Arad, Philippe Starck and Marc Newson. Consequently, the newest, lesser-known design talents are not allocated much shelf space. Most tableware is supplied by Alessi, LSA International, Keramica, Rosendahl, iittala and Zack. But a shop shouldn't be judged purely on brands but rather on the actual products themselves. Selecting an altogether commercial collection, Utility has succeeded in attracting a wide audience to contemporary design. Great street presence, well-displayed products, gentle music, plus friendly and helpful staff contribute to a welcoming environment that will no doubt sustain its present appeal.

DESIGNERS INCLUDE:
Alessi
Alvar Aalto
Arne Jacobsen
Artek
Charles and Ray Eames
Fiam
Fritz Hansen
Harry Bertoia
iittala
Jasper Morrison
Kartell
Keramica
Knoll
LSA International
Magis
Marc Newson
Mobles 114
Ron Arad
Rosendahl
Philippe Starck
Punt Mobles
Vitra
Zack

SERVICES:
Bespoke Orders
Contract Division
Gift Vouchers
Gift Wrapping
Wedding List

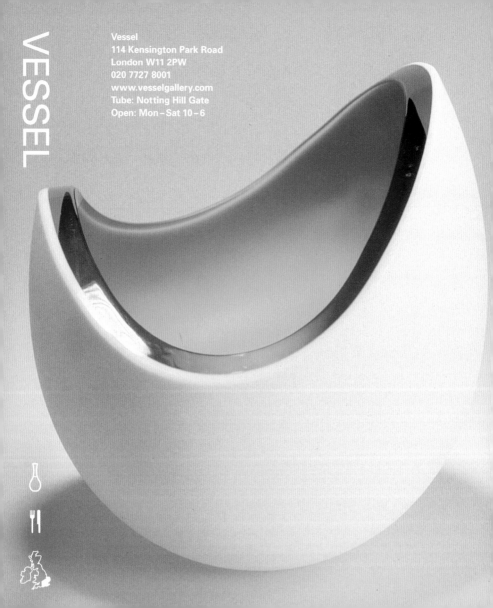

Vessel
114 Kensington Park Road
London W11 2PW
020 7727 8001
www.vesselgallery.com
Tube: Notting Hill Gate
Open: Mon – Sat 10 – 6

VESSEL

DESIGNERS INCLUDE:
Amy Cushing
Arcade
De Vecchi
Driade
Fontana Arte
Hannah Dipper
iittala
Isabel Hamm
Kosta Boda
Lena Bergström
Nymphenburg
Orrefors
Rina Menardi
Rosenthal
Salviati
Stelton
Venini

SERVICES:
Bespoke Orders
Contract Division
Gift Vouchers
Gift Wrapping
Interior Advice
Wedding List

CLOSE TO:
Flow
Themes & Variations

Until Vessel opened in spring 1999, where did people go for one-stop table accessories in London? The main option was to trawl through department stores, only to find a confused and fussy selection of glassware and ceramics. Vessel's owners Nadia Demetriou Ladas and Angel Monzon saw the gap in the market. Their store in Notting Hill sells beautiful contemporary tableware to customers wanting to add visual and functional beauty to increasingly modern home interiors. In the few years since it opened, Vessel has achieved the recognition and reputation it deserves.

Spread across two floors is an extensive collection of awe-inspiring objects, ranging from understated production crockery sets to vibrant one-off Murano glass vases. Continually sourcing novel modern glass, ceramic and silverware 'vessels' from around the world is no easy feat. Since launching Vessel, Nadia Demetriou Ladas and Angel Monzon have held regular evolving exhibitions in the basement space and developed a close relationship with many suppliers by showcasing exclusive new pieces from the like of Salviati, Orrefors, Nymphenburg and Rosenthal. The interior, designed by Angel Monzon, with its white walls, slate floor and glass and elm display shelving, provides a serene and unobtrusive backdrop to allow the likes of Lena Bergström's sensuous vibrant glass creations

(pictured) to truly shine. It is refreshing to witness the combination of designs from larger established companies like iittala, Stelton, Venini, De Vecchi, Kosta Boda, Fontana Arte, Arcade and Driade with smaller independent designers, some from the UK, including Isabel Hamm, Amy Cushing, Hannah Dipper (p 268) and Rina Menardi.

At Vessel, quality is an attribute possessed by all the pieces on display, but it isn't always cheap. Nevertheless, the owners are careful to also stock affordable objects so that the gallery appeals to both impulse buyers and serious collectors. For assistance with difficult decision-making, ask the friendly, knowledgeable and well-presented staff, who take pride in maintaining the vision and high standards that have become associated with this West London success story.

VIADUCT

Viaduct
1 – 10 Summer's Street
London EC1R 5BD
020 7278 8456
www.viaduct.co.uk
Tube: Chancery Lane or Farringdon
Open: Mon – Fri 9:30 – 6
Sat 10:30 – 4

UK AGENT FOR:
Driade
E15
Maarten Van Severen
MDF Italia
Montis
Pallucco Italia
x0
Zeus

DESIGNERS INCLUDE:
Alivar
B&B Italia
Baleri Italia
Cappellini
Crassevig
Edra
Fritz Hansen
Hitch Mylius
Lammhults
Magis
Vitra

SERVICES:
Contract Division

CLOSE TO:
Applied Arts Agency
Inflate
Lowe Interiors
Mac London

Architecturally trained James Mair founded Viaduct in 1988 with the aim of introducing exciting, high quality, contemporary European design to the British market. His passion and hard work have been rewarded and Viaduct is now UK agent for major companies Driade, E15, Maarten Van Severen, MDF Italia, Montis, Pallucco, XO and Zeus.

Viaduct's showroom is housed in a sizeable 1930s converted print house over two floors that benefit from plenty of natural light. On your first visit, you can be excused for feeling slightly intimidated as it is a trade showroom occupied by hard-working staff in the open-plan offices upstairs. Venture in, however, and you will soon be greeted by a friendly face and offered all the assistance you need.

There is enough space to display a large collection of constantly changing items from well-known international design names. Start talking to your knowledgeable assistant and you'll soon realize that Viaduct is capable of offering a considerably larger choice. In addition to the companies represented, Viaduct also has access to other key European furniture and lighting producers, such as Cappellini, B&B Italia, Fritz Hansen, Alivar, Baleri Italia, Hitch Mylius, Magis, Lammhults, Crassevig,

Vitra and Edra. Essentially what this boils down to is unrivalled product diversity for your every need, be it one piece or a complete interior overhaul. Although Viaduct caters mainly for the contract market, it offers retail clients a furniture design consultancy service to advise on spatial planning, furniture selection, colour and dimension.

You can't help but be impressed by the sales team, whose experience, coupled with their enthusiasm, makes the daunting task of choosing the right item that much easier and more enjoyable. To my satisfaction, I always come away from Viaduct feeling that I've learnt something new about the ever-changing design industry.

VITRA

Vitra
30 Clerkenwell Road
London EC1M 5PG
020 7608 6200
Tube: Barbican
Open: Mon – Thurs 9 – 5:30
Fri 9 – 5

First Floor
The Lighthouse
11 Mitchell Lane
Glasgow G1 3LX
0141 221 3453
Open: Mon – Fri 10:30 – 5

www.vitra.com

Vitra was founded in 1950 and has since established a global reputation as one of the best manufacturers of high-quality furniture and furnishing systems for both domestic and office environments. Continually experimenting with new ideas with renowned designers, the company strives to integrate 'comfort, technology, ergonomics, ecology, economics, and aesthetics' into every product it releases. Vitra boasts a huge range of furniture from design masters like Antonio Citterio, Charles and Ray Eames, Ettore Sottsass, Frank Gehry, Gaetano Pesce, Jean Prouvé (pictured), Jasper Morrison, Maarten Van Severen, Mario Bellini, Philippe Starck, Ron Arad, and Verner Panton, which contributes to the company's annual sales of nearly €300 million.

The collections can be viewed at Vitra's David Chipperfield-designed London showroom in Clerkenwell, which was launched in autumn 1999. Since opening, the company has increasingly tailored the showroom displays towards practical office systems for the contract market – in particular architects, interior designers and specifiers. Vitra aims to attract the trade rather than the general public, which explains the intimidating business-orientated atmosphere of the showroom. Greeted by a receptionist, you are asked to sign in before continuing on to the two-floored show space. Here you will encounter rather sterile displays of finely calculated design. Normally I wouldn't feature trade showrooms but, with so many strong iconic designs and an interesting company history and philosophy, it is worth experiencing Vitra without the exterior influence of items from other companies. As well as the London outlet, there's the newer Scottish showroom, which shares space with Form as part of the Lighthouse in Glasgow (p 96), or ring for details of your nearest Vitra dealer. This is a pioneering global company that is set to keep growing and become even more influential.

DESIGNERS INCLUDE:
Antonio Citterio
Charles and Ray Eames
Ettore Sottsass
Frank Gehry
Gaetano Pesce
Jasper Morrison
Jean Prouvé
Maarten Van Severen
Mario Bellini
Philippe Starck
Ron Arad
Verner Panton

SERVICES:
Contract Division

CLOSE TO:
Flin Flon
Her House

243

THE WEDGE

DESIGNERS INCLUDE:
Angelica Gustafsson
Driade
Ed Carpenter
El Ultimo Grito
Extremorigin
Flos
iittala
Magis
Rainer Spehl

SERVICES:
Bespoke Orders
Interior Advice

The Wedge
9 Catherine Hill
Frome
Somerset BA11 1BY
01373 472 077
Open: Mon – Sat 10 – 6

Celebrating beautiful modern interior objects in her intimate wedge-shaped store in Somerset is Eleanor Thompson, whose enthusiasm for design prompted her to open the shop in October 2002. The response from locals has been extremely positive – at last they no longer have to travel to major cities to find contemporary additions for their homes. Occupying only 320 sq ft of display space, much of the range is dominated by smaller items, with a particular onus on Eleanor Thompson's love of lights.

Having worked at *World of Interiors* magazine, Eleanor Thompson decided to abandon her hectic, city lifestyle and open her own shop selling everything she loves most, as well as her own-design hand-blocked fabrics. She is the first to admit that her knowledge of design isn't deeply grounded, and her buying criteria remain refreshingly naïve as she simply stocks contemporary objects that excite her senses. Offended by expensive pieces that are badly made, the charismatic owner is careful to order designs of quality that are beautiful, clever and possess a justifiable price tag.

The eclectic mix seamlessly combines gorgeous items from global brands, such as Driade's plastic vases, iittala's glass and kitchenware, Magis' gas injection-moulded chairs and tables, and certain lighting from Flos, with other items from independent names like Angelica Gustafsson, Ed Carpenter, Rainer Spehl, Extremorigin and El Ultimo Grito, as well as various artists. An ever-morphing array of unpredictable offerings means you are likely to spot many items that you would buy for yourself or as gifts. There is also a design consultation service for domestic and commercial clients.

The scarlet-painted exterior adds colour to the street and successfully draws in customers. A beautiful Danish Morsø stove warms the space and immediately makes you feel welcome. The friendly and personable owner has contributed to the UK's growing love of design in a town that wouldn't expect such additions. I can only congratulate her on such a venture.

WHIPPET

Whippet
190 Upper Richmond Road West
London SW14 8AN
020 8878 3141
Train: Mortlake
Open: Tues – Sat 10:30 – 6

The eccentric owner of Whippet, Vincent Wainwright, opened his first design-orientated shop near Crystal Palace in south-east London in 1997. He then saw a gap in the market for a similar shop in the affluent area between Barnes and Richmond. Juggling two stores, he decided to cease trading in Crystal Palace and focus his attention on the Upper Richmond Road store.

On opening in 2000, the store had a very clean, uncluttered display of select ceramic, glass and tableware pieces, accompanied by a few unusual gimmicky items. Perhaps the realities of the local customer base set in because the store

DESIGNERS INCLUDE:
Arabia
Arzberg
Hackman
iittala
Lindshammer
LSA International
Rörstrand
Soendergaard Design

SERVICES:
Interior Advice
Gift Vouchers
Gift Wrapping
Wedding List

has recently taken on a cluttered feel to accommodate significantly more gift market items. Increasingly attracting 'those who lunch', the selection is geared towards female customers in search of a small contemporary addition to the home.

Occupying only a limited space with plenty in it, Whippet has sidestepped any risk of creating an intimidating environment. Instead, customers are happy browsing the Scandinavian-influenced offerings, such as colourful glassware from LSA International and the iittala brand, ceramics from Arabia, and Rörstrand (pictured) and cutlery from Hackman. Pieces are also sourced from a

few lesser-exposed Swedish companies, such as Soendergaard Design and Lindshammar glass. Something that caught my attention was the array of crockery from Arzberg (pictured), who produce clean-lined tableware with understated splashes of colour.

Vincent Wainwright's much-loved canine partner is the face behind the shop name and is usually in store to greet customers, helping to turn a visit into an enjoyable experience. Selling a few pieces of furniture and select lighting amid the smaller items, Whippet is a good place to find a stylish gift or an addition to your interior that is unlikely to break the bank.

DESIGNERS INCLUDE:
Arper
B&B Italia
Fiam
Flexform
Kristalia
Label
Maxalto
Mobileffe
Molteni & C
Naos
Tonelli

SERVICES:
Bespoke Orders
Contract Division
Interior Design

CLOSE TO
Fusion

XU
55 Cornwall Street
Birmingham B3 2DH
0871 872 4012
Open: Mon – Fri 10 – 6
Thurs til 7
Sat 10 – 5:30
www.xux.co.uk

Interior designer Su Satchwell has been in the business for nearly fifteen years, creating gorgeous interior solutions for satisfied customers. In autumn 1999, she opened her first design store in Leamington Spa, selling a mix of contemporary furniture and lighting, accessories and artwork. Avoiding the sterility of a lot of showrooms, she has introduced a rounded lifestyle concept to her retail premises by creating a tactile and seductive environment.

As a number of her customers were travelling from Birmingham, the owner decided to open a store in the Midland's capital in November 2001, here she has since successfully tapped into the growing local market for contemporary modern interiors. In fact, business here proved to be so strong that in February 2003, the owner chose to merge the original Leamington Spa store into her newer flagship Birmingham showroom. These corner premises benefit from plenty of natural light. As you enter the large white-walled shop, you are immediately greeted by one of the friendly staff. The slate-tiled floor showcases high-quality, sharp-lined yet unobtrusive sofas from the likes

of B&B Italia, Molteni & C, Maxalto, Seven Salotti and Flexform. While encouraging uncluttered, simpler living spaces without falling into the bracket of minimalism, XU also promotes sumptuous rugs, tactile cushions and cosy throws to soften the look. As well as sofas, there are plenty of chair variations from other brands such as Kristalia, Label, Tagliabue and Arper, not to mention clever adjustable dining tables from market leaders Naos, Tonelli and Fiam, and storage from Mobileffe.

In wanting to add context to the realities of most home interiors, XU is not afraid to combine some older one-off antique pieces with the new offerings, and uses natural plants, smells and cool sounds to enhance the senses. In an interior design office at the rear of the showroom, designers work on complete residential schemes or smaller individual bespoke pieces. Sourcing designs from around the world, XU provides a professional and friendly service that will appeal to those wanting to embrace the possibilities of refined modern living.

ALEXANDER TAYLOR DESIGN
ROSE COBB BRENDA FEE HAN
ANNE KYYRÖ QUINN DOISTRI
PHÖRM DESIGNERS STUDIO
HANNAH DIPPER MARTINO G
ROSE COBB DOISTRINTA HUG
DIAPO TWO CREATE SUCK U
ALEXANDER TAYLOR DESIGN
MARKO POLO DESIGNS FUS
FOUNDATION 33 HUGO ECCL
DOISTRINTA TWO CREATE BR
STUDIO PLATFORM MARKO
DIAPO ANNE KYYRÖ QUINN

UCK UK FUSION DOISTRINTA
AH DIPPER BLUE MARMALADE
A PROCTER:RIHL KAYA HOANG
ATFORM MARTINO GAMPER
PER PHÖRM FOUNDATION 33
ECCLES JONATHAN WOOLLEY
ANNAH DIPPER PROCTER:RIHL
SE COBB ANNE KYYRÖ QUINN
STUDIO PLATFORM PHÖRM
EXCLUSIVE PRODUCTS DIAPO
DA FEE JONATHAN WOOLLEY
O DESIGNS FUSION SUCK UK
E MARMALADE KAYA HOANG

Alexander Taylor Design
www.alexandertaylor.com

Alexander Taylor launched independently onto the UK design scene in August 2002. While studying Furniture and Product Design at Nottingham Trent University, he developed a sophisticated understanding of materials and construction techniques by relentless experimentation in the college workshop. After graduation, he spent more than a year working part time with Procter:Rihl (see p282) and designing kitchens at Tsunami and Zeyko.

On an installation job he had a chance meeting with one of the directors of McDonnell Associates, a London architecture practice, and was invited to design a furniture range to complement the company's architectural work. Much of his work was showcased at the company's stand at the 100% Design trade fair in 2001 – his super-cool creations in Perspex, plywood and steel earning him considerable acclaim from the design world.

Building up contacts, experience and exposure, Alexander decided to branch out alone, despite the challenges ahead in the famously cut-throat design industry. His clean-lined and rather slick yet unobtrusive style was snapped up by UK agent and producer Thorsten van Elten. One of his first commissions was an elegant floor and table lamp, launched in September 2002 at 100% Design.

The calm yet confident personal characteristics of this designer translate across into much of his work. First and foremost, he trumpets elegance of form,

working with appealing proportions and the fluidity of lines in the initial design stages. He enjoys the interplay of lines working with and against each other, breaking soft, nature-inspired curves with hard, manmade edges. His main body of work deals with the manipulation of flat sheet materials by cutting and forming beautiful new functional designs.

The Butterfly coffee table (pictured here in Perspex) was designed around the technologies of laser and computer controlled (CNC) cutting. The design scheme was entered into the configuring software that delivers the data to the laser-cutting machine for production. The beautiful, ethereal result (shown in clear, tinted and frosted acrylic) can be produced in a variety of colour configurations, as well as in aluminium or laminated plywood using a similar software-based production process. The digital drawings can be manipulated for larger or smaller variations of the design, making it an ideal candidate for individual commissions.

While remaining enamoured by the latest technologies, Alexander Taylor is adamant that he won't be pigeon-holed in the industry by his techniques and material usage. In addition to his own brand, he wants to be seen and known for maintaining his design integrity across a range of products with different technical approaches, materials and functions. Undoubtedly Alexander Taylor will continue to create uncompromising, good-looking objects that will attract both public and industry alike.

AWARDS:
FX finalist with
Clearcut chair for
McDonnell Associates,
London, 2001

DESIGN EVENTS:
Clearcut 2002,
Zone Creations,
Parsons Green,
London (Sept 2002)
**100% Design,
Earls Court,
London (Sept 2002)**
Inside – Outside,
La Pelota, Milan,
Italy (April 2002)
**Contemporary
Decorative Arts,
Sothebys, London
(February 2002)**
100% Design,
Earls Court,
London (Sept 2001)

UK RETAILERS:
Contact Alexander
Taylor studio
for stockists

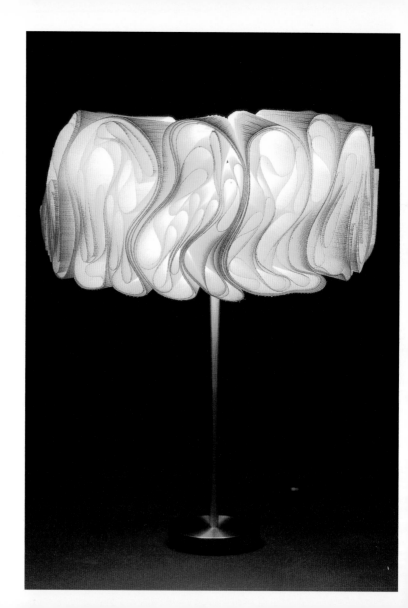

AWARDS:
Finalist for John Little
Management Marketing
Award, Chelsea
Crafts Fair (2002)
**Winner of 3M
sponsorship prize,
Birmingham
Spring Fair (2002)**
Design Nation's 100%
Design Exhibition
Bursary (2001)
**Light Magazine's Best
New Product On Show
Award, Birmingham
Lighting Show (2001)**
Crafts Council
Setting-up Grant (2000)

DESIGN EVENTS:
Chelsea Crafts Fair,
London (Oct 2001 & 2002)
**100% Design, London
(Sept 2001 & 2002)**
ICFF, Jacob Javitts
Center, New York,
USA (May 2002)
**Salone Satellite, Milan
Furniture Fair, Milan,
Italy (Apr 2002)**
Fabricated Show,
Spring Fair, NEC,
Birmingham (Feb 2002)
**Illuminated, exhibition
touring USA (2001)**
Designers Block,
St Pancras Chambers,
London (Oct 2000)

UK RETAILERS:
The Conran Shop,
London
**Crafts Council Gallery
Shop, London**
Dallas + Dallas,
Glasgow
Heal's, London
Purves & Purves,
London
**Tony Walker Interiors,
Edinburgh**

Anne Kyyrö Quinn
www.annekyyroquinn.com

Born and raised in Finland, Anne Kyyrö Quinn moved to England in 1988 and worked for several years before starting a BA course in Textile and Furnishing Design and Manufacture at London Guildhall University. She finished her degree in 1998, having enjoyed three years of handmade material manipulation and experimentation.

Applying the simple purity of her homeland's design aesthetic, Anne Kyyrö Quinn quickly realized the commercial applications of her work, selling her designs while continuing her studies with a Masters in Art, Design and Visual Culture. Graduating in 2001, she sensibly adapted her time-consuming handcrafted designs for manufacture.

Steve Jones, director of Innermost, spotted her BA final project, the Cable Lamp, which he consequently helped develop, manufacture and add to his collection. The slender light, available in various sizes as a floor or pendant light, introduced a new way of constructing a textile using felt reinforced with steel inserts. The result is an elegant design that efficiently employs industrial materials and processes to create a soft ambient glow for the modern interior.

Since then, Anne Kyyrö Quinn has built up a collection of cushions, throws, table runners, blinds, lamps and stools that has received international praise at trade fairs worldwide. She is interested in manipulating readily available flat textiles to create structural three-dimensional forms and tactile surface beauty. She applies a graphic eye to pattern, considering the relationship of colours, textures, lines and shadows. As her collection suggests, Anne steers clear of the intricate and fussy detailing – lace, tassels and frills. Instead, she creates surface patterns by applying additional folded and looped material to create a tactile, relief-like effect. She strives for beauty in her designs coupled with purity of form, hoping that they will have timeless appeal.

Anne positions herself firmly in the contemporary design world as she continues to successfully expand her interior collection, which attracts international sales and press coverage.

All too aware how easy it is to become bracketed by the industry for the use of a particular style, material or aesthetic, Anne chose to design her product for *Design UK 2* using a material commonly employed in 1970s office blinds. Continuing her quest to use existing industrial textiles, the Ruffle light (pictured) gives new life to the material's dated application by transforming the textured pre-cut strips into an organic light-diffusing shade.

Apart from her designs for Innermost, all of Anne Kyyrö Quinn's felt creations are hand-stitched in the UK by a textile-manufacturing business in Lancashire that also undertakes her commission work. With her collection already well received, the designer is keen to expand her business to the next stage. Eventually she has visions of opening her own shop to sell her collection alongside complementary creations from talented new designers. Watch this space…

BLUE MARMALADE

Blue Marmalade
www.bluemarmalade.co.uk

Blue Marmalade, comprising Namon Gaston and Trent Jennings, is a new partnership. These Edinburgh-based designers joined forces in June 2002, officially launching their company Blue Marmalade shortly afterwards.

Namon Gaston and Trent Jennings, who graduated in furniture design from Edinburgh College of Art in 2001, are master-manipulators of polypropylene. This material has been used in some tacky products in the past, but these are a world apart. The designs are made by cutting, folding and manipulating polypropylene to create strong furniture and product designs without fixings or glues.

Blue Marmalade has a practical approach to every product they design. Take the i.b.pop chair (pictured), which was designed exclusively for *Design UK 2*. The elegant curvaceous form is made from 6mm polypropylene that has been cut and scored from a standard industrial-sized sheet, although it took dozens of 'generation' prototypes to achieve the perfect finale. The chair is delivered flat-packed and assembled without adhesives; it is held together by three clips that slot from the seat into the side panels.

The process doesn't end there, though. Very aware of their environmental responsibilities in today's throw-away culture, they recycle off-cuts from the polypropylene sheets into new sheets, and then dye them black to hide any slight colour imperfections from the process. They then produce a second-generation black version of the chair.

Blue Marmalade's design process always begins with a sheet material. With the help of a few sketches, the designers start to build miniature mock-up models that provide immediate feedback on the success or failure of the form, its ease of construction and structural strength. Once perfected, the dimensions are transferred to computer drawings to provide the software-guided CNC cutting machine with the necessary data to undertake production. The Polyrap Bin (pictured) is another product developed using the same process as the chair but it is made from thinner sheet polypropylene that has been scored to form a rigid folding structure boasting only 4 per cent material wastage when die-cut from a standard sheet.

Namon Gaston and Trent Jennings are constantly experimenting with new ideas, techniques and materials. They have recently identified the strength and recyclable nature of cardboard as having huge potential.

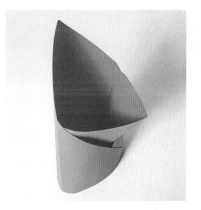

Brenda Fee
www.brendafee.com

When you see Brenda Fee's ceramic work and witness her passion for its creation, it's hard to believe that she once worked as an administrator at a solicitors' office, dental practice and credit-card company.

Once her children had completed school, Brenda Fee re-evaluated her career. She had always loved working with clay, so embarked on an evening access course before starting a degree in Tableware at the University of Central Lancashire in Preston in 1998. The course taught craft and design in equal measure, but Brenda Fee quickly identified that she favoured the latter, and she spent three years working independently on design experimentation.

This proved to be a liberating period. She translated her love of sculpture into functional designs, taking the fluidity of fabric as the source of inspiration for her flowing, wave-like platters (pictured). Sketches and drawings play a part in her work, but she prefers to direct her creativity straight into the manipulation of the clay, carving it away until it meets her idea of visual perfection.

Brenda Fee aims to enhance the experience of dining by introducing both visual and tactile treats to the dinner table. Her platters capture a moment in time, from the flow of fabric or the movement of water, and solidify it in the form of earthenware or porcelain. Intuition plays a significant role in her quest to find forms that articulate and exemplify the interaction with the food served. She aims

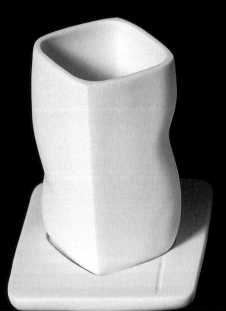

DESIGN EVENTS:
Ceramic
Contemporaries 4,
organized by NACHE,
1 year touring
exhibition 2002–2003
Design UK
Designer Showcase,
Designersblock,
Bermondsey,
London (Sept 2001)
New Designers,
Islington, London
(July 2001)

UK RETAILERS:
Contact Brenda Fee
studio for stockists

to create a flow of energy across a table and works on connecting this movement through her separate pieces.

Her existing range possesses distinct sculptural qualities. Light plays on the soft and silky-smooth surface finish, lending the pieces a continually changing beauty and elegance. On some of her designs, she has introduced fabric-inspired surface textures that act in harmony with the fluid forms, while adding contrast to the normally smooth finish.

Brenda Fee's studio was completed in June 2002 within the Watermark workshop development in Preston, which has given her the freedom to try out new ideas. Her sake/liqueur cups (pictured), designed exclusively for *Design UK 2*, are the result of a desire to work on a smaller scale. She has also introduced

the idea of carving thin lines into the porcelain to link the separate elements together, such as the cup and saucer. In addition, she has begun to incorporate elements of colour in her predominantly white range, and has expressed interest in the textured and contrasting qualities of concrete.

Brenda Fee enjoys working alone in her studio, where she oversees the whole design and production process to ensure the highest standards of quality.

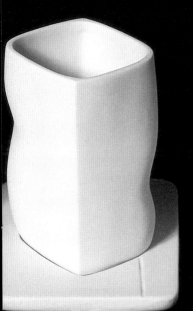
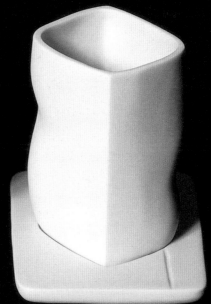

DESIGN EVENTS:
PROTOTYPE UK,
Designersblock 2002,
South Bank, London
(Sept 2002)
**Design UK in NYC,
Terminal NYC, Soho,
New York, USA
(May 2002)**
Designersblock,
Spazio Consolo,
Milan, Italy (Apr 2002)
**Designersblock 2001,
Bermondsey, London
(Sept 2001)**
Salone Del Mobile,
Milan, Italy (Apr 2001)
**East London Design
Show, Shoreditch,
London (June 2000)**
Quality Britain, British
Trade International,
Manila, Philippines
(Mar 2000)

UK RETAILERS:
Lowe Interiors, London
**Contact Diapo studio
for additional stockists**

Diapo
www.diapo.co.uk

Nathan Abbey set up Diapo, his furniture and interior design studio, in London's East End in early 2000, a year after graduating from Camberwell College of Art in Applied Art: 3-D Design.

He immediately set his mind to designing a furniture collection, using his specialist skills in metalwork. His first collection, working with mainly steel and glass, was called Low & Afloat. It introduced fluid lines using traditional metalworking skills as a way of controlling the material without heavy machinery. The collection comprises tables and chairs, and exploits the inherent strength of metals in combination with fragile floating glass surfaces. The juxtaposition of the strength of steel and the transparency of glass gives a sense of visual tension to the collection. Inspired by the engineering involved in bridge design, Nathan Abbey challenges the conventional appearance of a table with his geometrically driven Pont Neuf centrepiece low table.

Diapo has also been responsible for a number of fashionable bars in London's Soho, such as Alphabet, Lab and Amber. With such large-scale commissions, the studio could no longer be run single-handedly, so Nathan Abbey employed David Lai with his technical engineering skills. He has since become a partner in the company. Much of the studio's work now involves the design of spaces as well as the objects that go in them, and the duo are very conscious of the relationship between furniture and its environment.

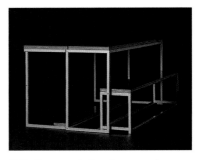

Collections are designed on a yearly basis. The Expression 2002 range dealt with flexibility and multifunctionalism. In contrast to Low & Afloat, all of the pieces took on a more linear approach, dealing with the juxtaposition of different structural planes.

The Duo mobile dining table and breakfast bar (pictured) is Diapo's exclusive design for *Design UK 2*. Part of the Expression collection, the module consists of three tubular aluminium base structures with varnished plywood surfaces that can be used separately or locked together as a dining table or space-saving breakfast bar/shelving unit. Unlike other multifunctional furniture, this module refrains from being overly clever and combines practicality with timeless geometric structural form.

Nathan Abbey's use of materials tends to steer towards metalwork. However, he is always keen to explore new materials and processes, but only when he believes it necessary. He loves the ageing properties of metals, woods and leather but will always fine-tune the structure and comfort elements of a design before assigning materials.

Doistrinta
www.doistrinta.co.uk

Most of us really only encounter cork as inexpensive bathroom flooring or when opening a bottle of wine. But designers Miguel Cunha and Simon Mount of Doistrinta have identified the versatility of this natural resource as an exciting new material in furniture design, and are responsible for changing preconceptions about its possible applications.

Born and bred in Portugal, Miguel Cunha was already familiar with cork, which is produced locally. After studying town planning and working in architecture, he decided that his future lay with furniture design. So he moved to London to study the subject at London Guildhall University, graduating in 2000.

Simon Mount worked on his own model-making, prototyping and batch production business called D3 until he spotted Miguel's work with cork at New Designers exhibition at the Business Design Centre in London's Islington in July 2000. He was captivated by Miguel's use of a seemingly dated material and, on further discussion, he realized that they shared a similar enthusiasm and design vision. Over the following year, the duo set up Doistrinta and officially launched it at the One Year On exhibition as part of New Designers in 2001.

The designers decided to use cork as their signature material because they had identified little competition within the industry and they also recognized an opportunity to explore the properties of cork for use in commercial furniture design. As expected, the development process was a steep learning curve as they tried out relatively uncharted manipulations. They quickly realized that cork had not really been applied to new industrial processes. With the support of the cork producer Amorim UK, however, they experimented with a continual supply of various cork composites.

Cork comes from the outer bark of the southern European oak tree, which naturally discards its outer skin, rather like a snake. Removing the bark doesn't damage the tree but renews growth, making it an environmentally and ecologically friendly material. The duo were faced with the task of convincing others that cork was an appealing form of upholstery for furniture. You need only sit on their 'Clumsy' chair (pictured), developed exclusively for *Design UK 2*, to experience the warm, tactile nature of the material. They have cleverly developed a way to join the cork 'upholstery' to the plywood at the same time as they form the chair shape. This makes the chair easier to produce and an attractive prospect to potential manufacturers. To soften the seating surface further, Simon and Miguel have set a layer of Zotefoam under the surface of the cork. This is a premium quality foam used industrially in everything from padding in firefighter hats to prosthetics and swimming floats. Doistrinta has positioned this innovative chair firmly in the contract market.

Simon Mount and Miguel Cunha are full of ideas and are eager to apply their fire-retardant and sound-absorbing cork composites to the interior schemes of bars, restaurants, offices and airport lounges, as well as to furniture.

DESIGN EVENTS:
Salone Satellite,
Milan, Italy (Apr 2002)
**Solo Show, St Pancras
Chambers, Kings Cross,
London (Dec 2001)**
One Year On, Islington,
London (July 2001)

UK RETAILERS:
Eat My Handbag Bitch,
London
**Contact Doistrinta
studio for additional
stockists**

FOUNDATION 33

DESIGN EVENTS:
Hidden Art Interior
Showcase, Shoreditch,
London (Sept 2002)
**Salone Satellite,
Milan Furniture
Fair, Milan, Italy
(Apr 2000, 2001 & 2002)**
Hidden Art, 100%
Design, Earls Court,
London (Sept 2001)
**Designersblock,
Bermondsey,
London (Sept 2001)**
Design Now
London, Design
Museum, London
(June – Sept 2001)
**Pentagram Gallery,
Notting Hill, London
(Nov 2000 – Jan 2001)**

UK RETAILERS:
**Applied Arts
Agency, London**
Selfridges, London
**Contact Foundation 33
studio for additional
stockists**

Foundation 33
www.foundation33.com

The term multidisciplinary studio tends to be used rather loosely by designers, but Sam Solhaug and Daniel Eatock's business, formed in March 2000, fully fits the criteria. Based in London's East End, the Foundation 33 studio is always buzzing with the creative energy you would expect from a team working on both commercial and self-generated interiors, graphics, and architectural and furniture design projects.

Bolton-born graphic designer Dan Eatock met architecturally trained Sam Solhaug from the US at the Walker Art Center in Minneapolis in 1999. The duo quickly became friends and identified a similar approach to design. They chose to collaborate on a furniture design that they saw as the happy medium between architecture and graphics. In the workshops of the Walker Art Center, they began work on the Multi-Ply table series. Taking a standard sheet of 18mm 4' x 8' plywood, they started exploring ways of producing a piece of furniture using every part of the board without any waste. This series exemplifies their highly systematic design approach – the ensuing form embodying strict notions of precision, efficiency and rationality. The conceptual sequences gave rise to the structural elements, which led to the final form. The only waste from the plywood sheet was sawdust. This was collected, weighed in pounds and conceptually returned to each table as the numerical designation in the title, for example, 10.2 Multi-Ply Coffee Table.

The investigation of context and situation forms a crucial part of the Foundation 33 approach. The designers will take a brief and circulate ideas for days on end before undertaking any mock-ups or production, in order to pinpoint an almost scientific system that then logically generates the form. Much of the beauty in their work can be appreciated only by delving into the extraordinary intellectual and sometimes playful thought processes behind it.

The Timecapstool (pictured), published exclusively in *Design UK 2*, illustrates a light-hearted approach in Foundation 33's portfolio. Constructed from a strong internal wood structure, the stool/side table is clad in thin sheet ply with a slit cut into the top. The slit invites you to post miscellaneous artefacts into the storage void, although you can't retrieve the items unless you destroy the stool.

A huge proportion of Foundation 33's work is graphic. The studio snapped up the contract from Channel 4 to design the identity for the TV show *Big Brother*. This, in turn, has led to more commissions from Channel 4, not to mention a string of other clients.

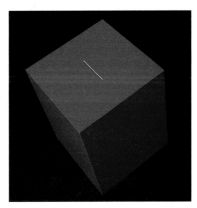

AWARDS:
Best Product Design
Award, Top Drawer
(Spring & Autumn 2002)
**Best Stand Award,
Mode (2001)**
Coram Design
Award (2000)
**Pergo Design
Award (1999)**

DESIGN EVENTS:
**East London Design
Show, London
(Dec 2001 & 2002)**
100% Design,
Earls Court,
London (Sept 2002)
**Top Drawer,
Earls Court, London
(Jan, May, Dec 2002)**
Autumn Fair, NEC,
Birmingham (Sept 2002)
**100% Fusion,
South Bank,
London (Sept 2001)**
Design UK
Designer Showcase,
Designersblock,
London (Sept 2001)
**Mode, Islington,
London (May 2001)**
Contemporary
Decorative Arts,
Sotheby's, London
(Feb 2001)

UK RETAILERS:
Applied Arts Agency,
London
**Back 2 My Place,
Cardiff**
Indish, London
**Inhouse,
Edinburgh & Glasgow**
Mojoe, Brighton
**Purves & Purves,
London**
Right Angle, London
Selfridges, London
Contact Fusion for
additional stockists

Fusion
www.studiofusion.co.uk

Fusion, the act of combining two or more styles, functions, sounds or ingredients, is nothing new. When we get dressed, we combine garments to create our own unique appearance, while in music we marry independent sounds into melody. Adopting this simple formula for product design, Antonio Arevalo and Byron Miller have based their entire design process and philosophy around fusing functions together and creating new objects. This has resulted in a range of exciting products launched from the Fusion studio since it began in June 2001.

After meeting as degree students at Ravensbourne College of Design and Communication, the duo went their separate ways for a few years before working together, initially as a three-strong team with Joshua Simandjuntak, at the Royal College of Art's degree show in summer 2000. Sharing enthusiasm for the fusion concept, the trio merged their skills and rapidly formed a company.

Showing at many exhibitions in the latter half of 2000 provided a massive learning base on which to build the foundations of the Fusion studio. The company was officially showcased at Mode, the design show at London's Business Design Centre, in June 2001, with a handful of quirky products. Reactions from the public, industry and press were hugely positive: Fusion had managed to incorporate a sense of humour and common language in the clever combination of various functions within its designs. 'Why didn't I think of that?' is a common response to many

of them. Antonio Arevalo and Byron Miller have since coined the slogan 'Ideas that make you smile' for their work.

In principle, the Fusion concept is simple, but the reality of applying it to commercial products is much more difficult. The usual issues of material selection, ease of manufacture and production volumes must be manipulated to make sure that final prices are realistic and sufficient sales achieved. This is constantly being reassessed in Fusion's growing collection, which is tailored to achieve wider market appeal. A bestselling design is the Mittscarf (pictured), a fleece scarf with mittens sown into the ends, so that you will never lose your gloves again. Available in various colours and sizes, it has proved a hit across the world.

The designers find their inspiration by looking carefully at how people create new ways to use everyday objects. The Chopfork (pictured), designed for Fusion by Jun Takagi, is a version of standard bamboo chopsticks for Westerners who aren't always adept with chopsticks. It can be used as a fork or as a chopstick if you snap it down the middle.

HANNAH DIPPER

Hannah Dipper
www.hannahdipper.com

When Hannah Dipper decided to study ceramics, a friend exclaimed, 'That's great! People will always need plates', and this has become her strap-line.

Hannah Dipper has always been fascinated by the way things are made, and this prompted her to embark on a degree in 3-D Design: Ceramics at Bath College of Higher Education. Graduating in 1997, she worked part-time in Stoke-on-Trent for three years, learning the technicalities of ceramic design for production while undertaking an MA in Ceramics & Glass at the Royal College of Art, which she completed in 2000. Since then, she has been designing in the UK's declining ceramics industry. The question on many ceramic designers' minds, including Hannah Dipper's, is: Why doesn't the industry use local companies to manufacture their designs instead of sending them to countries where labour is cheap but quality low?

Still, this situation hasn't stopped Hannah Dipper developing new ideas. At the RCA, she created white, porcelain, egg-shaped, hanging Lunar lanterns (pictured), which emit a warm gentle glow from the tea-light concealed inside. She also enjoys working with glass, wood and metal, as illustrated in her diverse portfolio of tableware, vases, lighting and cookware for the likes of Thomas, Rosenthal, Atlântis Crystal, and Queensbury Hunt.

Although her designs are primarily functional, Hannah Dipper is not afraid to introduce more whimsical elements, but she never allows production or material quality to slip in importance. Her eye is finely tuned to the aesthetic appeal of objects and often applies geometry to determine final forms from her initial ideas. She draws her inspiration from a variety of sources, from 1960s urban concrete towerblocks and modernist architectural theory to wide-open natural spaces like the sea, mountains and moors. These influences are evident in all of her pieces, through the combination of flowing organic shapes and varying textures juxtaposed with regular or asymmetric linear manmade forms.

In 2002, Hannah Dipper shifted her attention to metal and designed the Marie Antoinette candelabra made from bent sheet steel and handblown glass for the Laurent-Perrier Design Challenge. She developed this design into an elegant contemporary chandelier for *Design UK 2* (pictured) by laser cutting and bending the steel to form the arms for the individually blown glass candleholders.

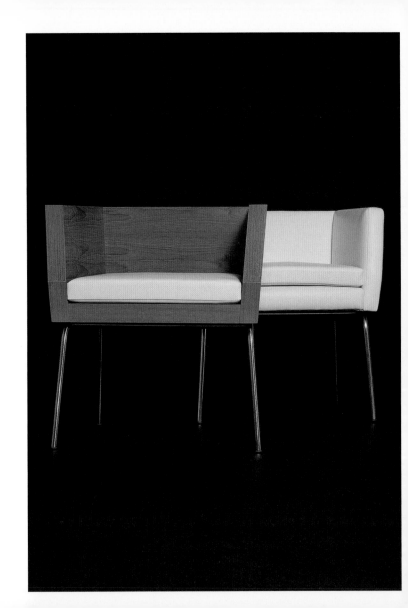

AWARDS:
Winner of Laurent Perrier Design Challenge (2002)
Furniture Makers Jubilee Award finalist (2002)
Design Week Award Finalist (2001)
Worshipful Company of Furniture Makers Jubilee Award joint finalist (2001)
Laurent Perrier Design Challenge finalist (2001)
100% Blueprint Award finalist (2000)
Winner of Panta Nature Award (1997)

DESIGN EVENTS:
100% Design, Earls Court, London (Sept 2002)
Milan Furniture Fair, Milan, Italy (Apr 2002)
100% Design, Earls Court, London (Sept 2001)
Maison et Objet, Paris, France (Sept 2001)
Ambiente, Frankfurt, Germany (Feb 2001)
International Gift Fair, New York, USA (Jan 2001)
The Lighting Show, NEC, Birmingham (Jan 2001)
ICFF, New York, USA (May 2000)
Ambiente, Frankfurt, Germany (Feb 2000)

UK RETAILERS:
The Conran Shop, London
Purves & Purves, London
Viaduct, London
Contact Hugo Eccles for additional stockists

Hugo Eccles
www.hugoeccles.com

Hugo Eccles has worked in the design industry for longer than most of the designers featured in this section, but it was only in 1998 that he founded his own studio, Baionik. With a degree in Product and Furniture Design from Kingston University, and an MA in industrial design from the Royal College of Art, he had attractive credentials for prospective employers. He worked as a staff designer on corporate technology-driven projects for IDEO Product Development until 1997, when he joined Ross Lovegrove's Studio X as project manager and senior designer on a whole host of designs for the likes of Driade, Frighetto, Herman Miller, Guzzini, Mandarina Duck and Acco Rexel.

His involvement with major international brands and the prolific designer Ross Lovegrove gave Hugo Eccles valuable experience before he began working independently. He has a good understanding of the subtleties of the design industry, managing to sustain a regular flow of commissioned work and self-initiated projects. He also has a solid grounding in design management, making him an attractive package to potential manufacturers such as Nike, Pallucco, Honda and Laurent Perrier.

Concerned by the amount of self-indulgent, in-your-face designs being produced, Hugo Eccles focuses on making functional furniture and products, not domestic sculpture. For him, good design is about elegance of manufacture and streamlined quality. He strives to design the most out of the least, applying his solid understanding of material

capabilities. Taking hard-nosed clean shapes, he refines these simple forms by carefully cutting away until he has pinpointed the design solution. Identifying the right material and process is an integral part of the design and something to which he pays a great deal of attention.

Hugo Eccles claims that much of his inspiration comes from an interest in science and technology. He admits to designing almost through the eyes of a child to create a sense of magic, wonder and excitement, while retaining the practical mind of an engineer.

In many of his creations, he experiments with tension by combining natural materials with artificial or geometric shapes, while managing to sustain a tactile and organic appeal for the end user. The Natalia chair (pictured left) was designed exclusively for publication in *Design UK 2*, and is for sale through the contract market. This extremely light armchair, internally constructed from strong honeycomb board, is available fully upholstered or with wooden sides. Its clean lines and unobtrusive design are ideal for the demands of commercial interiors and adheres to all of Hugo Eccles's design principles.

Jonathan Woolley
www.jonathan-woolley.com

Jonathan Woolley became a new face on the British design scene in 2001, when he graduated from Manchester Metropolitan University with a handful of impressively slick furniture creations. Not the sort to wave his arms around and shout, he has instead edged himself quietly into the design world, absorbing the realities of the industry as he goes.

Brought up in Preston and now based in Manchester, Jonathan Woolley is a quiet designer who seems to work best on his own, when he can focus his full attention and energy on new pieces. He has chosen to work with furniture, and his most inspired moments come when manipulating new forms to satisfy his perfectionist design aesthetic.

Intrigued and stimulated by the cleanliness of architectural forms, he sets his own design briefs, experimenting with a beautiful uncluttered arrangement of parts. While exploring the endless configuration of shapes, he always maintains an understanding of common design sensibilities, practicalities and restrictions that accompany the need for functionalism.

Jonathan Woolley's designs are inherently practical and well proportioned, and also easy to manufacture as he uses new forms in existing production techniques. Designing with a slick clean aesthetic, Jonathan Woolley is keen to add beauty to grey sombre interiors without introducing attention-seeking self-indulgent centrepieces that are more sculptural than functional. He believes that design should be used and admired

without taking centre stage – that is, you should be able to live in its presence. Aware that people use objects in the most unexpected ways, Jonathan Woolley concerns himself with the durability of his furniture, while also designing pieces that maintain their good looks from whichever angle they are viewed. He doesn't admire the complicated or frivolous features in a design – in his eyes, this merely adds unnecessary and limited novelty factor. Inspiration for this talented designer comes from companies like Cappellini, who continually introduce stunning new additions from carefully selected talents around the world and the UK.

Currently, Jonathan Woolley is focusing on the growth of his own range of designs suitable for use in domestic and contract markets. His sofa design for furniture manufacturers Ferrious (p 90) was launched at Designersblock in September 2002. Choosing to adopt a simpler production process for his creation for *Design UK 2* (pictured), he has created a cost-effective yet visually alluring chair formed from cutting and folding sheet steel. His design is cleverly tailored to maximize the use of the material; he manages to produce five chairs from one sheet with minimum wastage. The thin curvaceous elegance of this chair breaks with some of his more angular pieces and further illustrates his love of material forming.

Although he is deterred by the immense tooling costs involved with working with plastics, Jonathan Woolley is still keen to experiment with the moulding process, where he can truly realize ideas that have been temporarily waiting on the backburner.

DESIGN EVENTS:
Make Me 3,
Manchester (Oct 2002)
**Designersblock,
South Bank,
London (Sept 2001
& 2002)**
100% Design,
London (Sept 2001
& 2002)
**Make Me 2,
Manchester (Oct 2001)**
New Designers,
Islington,
London (July 2001)

UK RETAILERS:
Ferrious @ Home,
Manchester
Lowe Interiors, London
Contact Jonathan
Woolley for
additional stockists

KAYA HOANG

AWARDS:
100% Design
Foundation Award
(2002)
**Shell Live Entrepreneur
of the year Award
for South Thames
London (2002)**
Goldsmiths Design
Award (2002)
Evening Standard
**Interior Product
Award, Chelsea
Crafts Fair (2001)**
Sir John Cass
Award (1997)
**Habitat Design
Award (1996)**
Jerwood 1st Prize for
Silversmithing (1996)

DESIGN EVENTS:
Dazzle,
Royal National
Theatre, London
(Nov – Jan 2003)
**100% Design,
Earls Court,
London (Sept 2002)**
Talente 2002, Munich,
Germany (Mar 2002)
**Goldsmiths Design
Award, Goldsmith Hall,
London (Feb – Mar 2002)**
Chelsea Crafts Fair,
Chelsea Town Hall,
London (Oct 2001)
**One Year On,
Business Design
Centre, London
(July 2001)**
Abstract Extracts
solo exhibition,
Unit 2 Gallery,
London (Mar 2001)

UK RETAILERS:
Lowe Interiors, London
Mint, London
RHA Furniture, London
**Contact Kaya Hoang
studio for additional
stockists**

Kaya Hoang
www.kayahoang.com

Kaya Hoang was born and raised in Vietnam but moved to the UK where in 1992 she studied first at Central St Martins before gaining her degree in Jewellery and Silversmithing at Sir John Cass School of Arts (now Metropolitan University). During her time there, she refined the high-precision craft of fine metalworking and subsequently spent a few years working on jewellery before embarking on the final leg of her education at the Royal College of Art in 1998. Her two-year MA course, formally titled Goldsmithing, Silversmithing, Metalwork, and Jewellery, became a liberal period for the designer as she explored radical new ideas. After such an intensely creative period, Kaya worked as an artist in residence for a year at London Guildhall University, where she built up a strategy for the commercial application of her ideas in the market place. Keen to translate her skills to the design of platters and vessels, she began a pewter collection that could be produced by outhouse manufacturers. By the time she exhibited at the Chelsea Crafts Fair in October 2001, Kaya had confidence in both her range and her business. The increased interest in her work proved she was right.

There is significant contrast between Kaya's college work and her current collections as she has made a conscious move toward more functional designs. The minimal, visual clarity of form in Kaya's work lends her pieces a sculptural quality that could easily equip them as 21st century ornaments. Working in the semi-precious material pewter, the curvaceous and bulbous forms of her vessels are combined with a highly polished finish (pictured here as her exclusive designs for *Design UK 2*). Her refined forms are derived from the beauty and purity of nature, namely fruits and flora. The seductively shaped openings of her containers mimic the moment when the shell of a seed breaks and starts to sprout providing a subtle reminder of nature's influence in the formation of her metalwork.

Kaya begins her design with freehand sketches of fluid shapes that are inspired by the manipulation and dissection of seeds, nuts, and flowers. From there, she simplifies and abstracts the forms whilst applying necessary functional elements before producing the first prototype.

The polished or brushed final treatment of Kaya's designs stem from her belief that ornate patterns confuse the purity of an object. Indeed, this purity does not lend itself to human fingerprints and proper maintenance can be problematic with her metalwork, especially in retail environments. As all of her pieces are individually handmade and quality-checked by Kaya, they tend to veer towards the expensive so more recently she has toyed with the idea of introducing more obviously functional and affordable pieces in ceramic or glass.

Ultimately, Kaya would like her own shop/gallery space in which to showcase her work alongside that of like-minded artists and designers. Until such time, she gauges their reactions at a variety of exhibitions and fairs and it would seem that the public's response remains consistently positive.

Marko Polo Designs
www.marko-polo.co.uk

Mark Duckworth is the face behind Marko Polo Designs. He set up in the design world after the tremendous response to the concrete stools he showed at the New Designers graduates exhibition in 2001.

After a grounding in textiles, fine art, engineering and sculpture, Mark Duckworth took a BA course in 3-D Design at Manchester Metropolitan University. He spent three years exploring a variety of manufacturing processes in the university's workshops. Keen on the hands-on approach, he spent time constructing new creations that he had dreamt up the night before. This taught him a number of production techniques that he later applied to his no-frills design aesthetic.

Mark Duckworth has always been passionate about the outdoors. On a trip to Greece, he was inspired to work in concrete while exploring the parched, barren landscape. He wanted to mimic rock formations and turn them into unobtrusive yet recognizable functional forms through casting concrete. Back at university, he developed his stool (pictured) over six months, ironing out any production difficulties. Satisfied with the clean sculptural form, he quickly identified its commercial potential and began trawling concrete casting yards in Lancashire from his base in Preston. He was able to present his original casting with that of a manufacturer's in various finishes, as well as a bench version he had also developed, in time for his degree show. Unlike most graduates, Mark Duckworth took the commercial initiative and was able to start trading directly with

his designs. He earned immediate trade and press interest, especially as the stools featured in the garden of Channel 4's third *Big Brother* house.

His straightforward casting procedure lends itself perfectly to mass-production for major retailers, helping to reduce costs significantly. He has not chosen the designer-label route where he would have to carefully tailor his appearance to remain on the cutting edge. Instead, Mark Duckworth leaves any ego at home and concerns himself primarily with the efficient function of his products for the end user. Once positioned, the weighty concrete castings are unlikely to be moved and he is keen that they become a permanent fixture in outdoor environments, so that the material ages graciously in natural surroundings.

He would like to see his furniture in public community areas, such as parks and promenades, and he chose to design a complementary barbecue (pictured) in his signature material as his exclusive product for *Design UK 2*. Suitable for public and private gardens or parks, it features a monumental sculptural base that serves as a communal cooking forum for cheap disposable barbecues. A simple solution inspired by communal barbecues that are a familiar sight in Australia, the form of Mark Duckworth's design was based on an extended inversion of his stool. It further establishes his subtle design aesthetic and emphasizes his total commitment to its end use.

Mark Duckworth is an enterprising and methodical designer who is aware that he could quickly become associated exclusively with concrete, so he is keen to diversify into cast iron and timber.

DESIGN EVENTS:
Make me 3,
Manchester (Oct 2002)
**Designers Block,
Shoreditch Stables,
London (Sept 2002)**
Hardcore, RIBA
Gallery, London
(Mar–May 2002)
**The Rockface
Corporate Gallery,
Birmingham
(Nov 2001–Feb 2002)**
New Creators,
Preston Museum,
Preston (autumn 2001)
**Design UK
Designer Showcase,
Designersblock,
London (Sept 2001)**
100% Design,
Earls Court,
London (Sept 2001)
**New Designers,
Islington, London
(July 2001)**

UK RETAILERS:
**Contact Marko Polo
Designs for stockists**

MARTINO GAMPER

DESIGN EVENTS:
Book Corner touring
exhibition, curated
by the British Council
(Apr 2002–2003)
**Woodlands installation,
Bloomberg
Headquarters,
London (2002)**
Coming Home
light installation,
Design Museum,
London (2002)
**Village Fête, Pirelli
Garden, V&A, London
(Aug 2001 & 2002)**
Two Corner Projects,
Aram, London (2002)
**Bricolage installation,
MAK, Vienna (2001)**
Designersblock 2001,
Bermondsey,
London (Sept 2001)
**Ex-position,
Cité des Arts,
Paris, France (2001)**
Lost and Found
touring exhibition,
curated by the British
Council (2001)
**Spectrum,
Commonwealth Centre,
London (May 2000)**
Corner installation,
Salone del Mobile,
Milan, Italy (Apr 1999)

UK RETAILERS:
Aram, London
**Contact Martino
Gamper studio for
additional stockists**

Martino Gamper
www.gampermartino.com

Martino Gamper is a quiet, modest and rather mysterious designer – a secret people like to keep to themselves. His approach to design is unique, and he often creates space-specific objects that challenge our preconceptions of function and sculpture. Of course, this crisis of identity is Martino Gamper's endearing quality, which might stem from his diverse path of education. Brought up in northern Italy with a background in cabinet-making, he moved to Vienna to study sculpture before joining Matteo Thun's studio in Milan. There he worked for two years as senior product developer on mass-produced household items like cutlery and coffee machines. However, he began craving the freedom of self-initiated experimentation and so began an MA in Design Products at London's Royal College of Art in 1998.

Graduating with a significant body of work and consciously deciding on the self-employment route, he realized that he had to make his designs commercially viable if he were to gain any market interest. That said, Martino Gamper doesn't have an overwhelming desire to mass-produce his designs – in his eyes, the creations illustrate a blend of sculptural beauty with subtle functional applications that perhaps aren't obvious enough for the buying public.

Martino Gamper treads the ambiguous ground between fine art and functional design and, in some instances, pushing structural feasibility to the limits, as with his Booksnake and Totem shelving. He has grown used to conservative UK manufacturers, who tell him that his designs won't work, so he proves them wrong by making the prototypes himself. Once he is satisfied with the result, he may choose to produce the designs in limited editions. Reputable individuals within the industry like Zeev Aram and David Gill, and groups such as the Design Museum, British Council and Bloomberg have tapped into Martino Gamper's talent, but this modest designer has to be pushed before he will volunteer information on such successes.

While studying for his MA, Martino Gamper became obsessed by the corner. This has culminated in a diverse repertoire of designs for this often neglected space, including shelving, benches, tables, neon lighting, even a curvaceous speaker, which provided the inspiration for his exclusive light design for *Design UK 2* (pictured). Interested in the ease of manufacture of the generic paper lampshade, he constructed his own wire framework over which he stretched fabric. The light bulb nests tightly in the three axes that form the corner, emitting a gentle glow. The light is not restricted to use in a corner, and it is as effective free-standing or hung as a pendant. It can be made using any coloured fabric and to any size.

Martino Gamper enjoys using new materials and production techniques, as well as applying traditional craftsmanship to his designs. His approach consistently pays close attention to concept, structure, form and aesthetics.

PHÖRM

AWARDS:
Clerkenwell Green
Award (2002)

DESIGN EVENTS:
East London Design
Show, London
(Dec 2001 & 2002)
Mile End Park Design
Show, Mile End,
London (Nov 2002)
Top Drawer,
Earls Court,
London (Jan 2002)
Designersblock,
Bermondsey,
London (Sept 2001)
Design UK
Designer Showcase,
Designersblock,
London (Sept 2001)
One Year On, Islington,
London (July 2001)

UK RETAILERS:
Lowe Interiors, London
Contact Phörm studio
for additional stockists

Phörm
www.phorm.org

Over the past ten years, the design industry's view of ceramics as fusty and parochial has been turned on its head. This tactile material has enjoyed considerable reapplication within the contemporary design world as more designers apply a modern aesthetic to its capabilities. One new designer to do this is Samantha Dickenson, the talent behind Phörm.

She completed both a foundation course and degree in ceramic design at Central St Martins College of Art & Design, graduating in 2000. The challenge was how, as a new graduate, to establish a suitable working structure. Without the college's workshops, Samantha Dickenson needed access to a kiln. Fortunately, she was offered the use of her ex-tutor's own home kiln in exchange for some babysitting. This gave her the crucial opportunity to experiment and develop new ideas. It allowed her to show her fluid teardrop-inspired Dangle chandelier at the One Year On space at New Designers exhibition in 2001. The twelve-piece chandelier, which she produced by hand, earned considerable industry attention. It was a costly process, however, so inevitably she turned her attention to smaller items of tableware. She also expanded operations to a dedicated studio for ceramics in London's East End in November 2001.

Samantha Dickenson implements an instinctive hands-on approach to her designs, sidestepping computer-aided design. She always carries a sketchbook with her, the pages of which hold the core of her design experimentation. Sitting on a bus, waiting for friends or daydreaming with a cup of tea, she makes the most of spare moments to record her inspirations, thoughts, plans and ideas before realizing them in three dimensions in the studio. Even then, the design process remains fluid as she continues creating, using the unique qualities of plaster until the desired form is achieved. She doesn't pretend that her shapes are born from deep intellectual references but recognizes that the style is brought about by an inquisitive desire for sheer beauty of form. She is drawn towards simple objects and steers clear of unnecessary ornament.

Nature provides a lot of the inspiration for her clean, minimal and ethereal collection – the organic shapes are often arrived at by exploiting the flexible qualities of rubber balloons during the casting stage. Her salt and pepper set (pictured), designed exclusively for *Design UK 2*, slightly offsets yet mimics the curvaceous beauty of balloons and captures a moment in time using porcelain. The two bulbous forms are unique stand-alone pieces elegantly positioned on a wooden base to provide textural contrast. Their relationship to each other is strangely awkward, making the negative space surrounding the salt and pepper holders intriguingly irregular in contrast to the rectangular base. The successfully eye-pleasing proportions of Samantha Dickenson's pieces are brought about almost by default as she encourages the relationship created by pouring plaster into balloons. Few people can fault the sheer beauty of this talented designer's work, and few can resist picking up and touching her pieces.

Procter:Rihl
www.procter-rihl.com

Procter:Rihl is the most established design company featured in this section of the book. Christopher Procter and Fernando Rihl founded an architectural practice in 1995 after they met when studying at the Architectural Association.

The duo embraced furniture design on an early project for a Soho penthouse in 1995, when a client asked them to design some furniture to complement their architectural and interior scheme. AA training stresses the importance of making models, and acrylic was the duo's favourite material for this. The Soho commission proved to be a fascinating task, working with the different scales and functional purpose of architecture and furniture. Following on, they dedicated more time to develop a range of furniture creations by exploring the effects of cutting and layering different coloured sheets of live-edge acrylic, to exploit the material's transparent and optical qualities. Their pioneering designs achieved strong trade and press interest, but the company was quickly pigeon-holed by the industry because of their extensive use of acrylic. They soon saw the importance of switching to another material.

Plywood became their next choice, despite its established widespread use in furniture design. The designers resisted any temptation to bend, twist or fold the wood into unusual new shapes, opting instead to work with the material in sheet form using uncomplicated industrial cutting processes. The result was a variety of different self-assembly shelving systems that challenged the two-dimensional appearance of traditional bookcases. Made from planes of precision-cut plywood, the shelving systems come flat-packed and can be simply slotted together in a variety of configurations. They are strong modular structures without the need for fixings, making production straightforward and, in turn, keeping prices down. Canadian manufacturer Pure Design put the Topo shelving into production in 2000.

The years 2000 and 2001 saw an increase in architectural commissions, resulting in the architects feeling distanced from the world of furniture design. More recently they have channelled time into their furniture range using both plywood and acrylic. They have always been fascinated by new machinery processes and constantly strive to exploit the potential of techniques such as laser-cutting. The designers have introduced laser-etched patterns onto Perspex coffee tables and magazine racks, opening up the possibility of endless, one-off commissioned patterns, or even branded furniture in various colours or material finishes. They are keen to push technological boundaries but they never try to mask the design structure or processes employed, which gives their work a level of design honesty.

Using plywood once more, Procter:Rihl has designed the Yoga shelving system (pictured) for *Design UK 2*. A mobile and compact storage facility for CDs, the design uses a precision-cut yet straightforward slotting construction with minimal additional fixings. Freestanding or leaning against a wall, this commercial and graphic-inspired piece celebrates its easy, no-nonsense assembly.

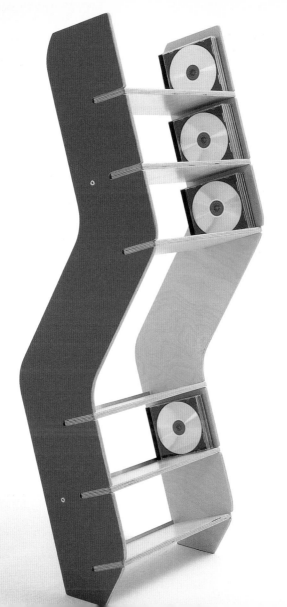

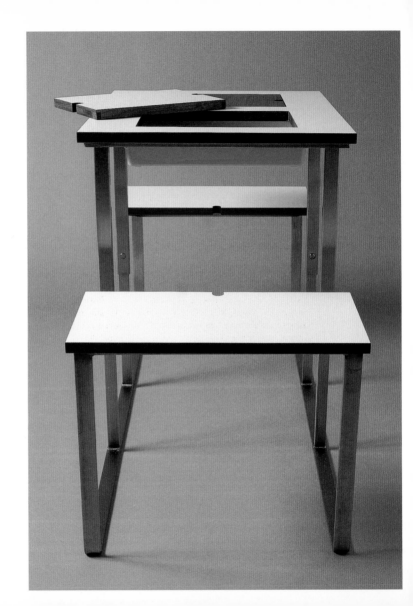

DESIGN EVENTS:
PROTOTYPE UK,
Designersblock,
London (Sept 2002)
**New Designers,
Business Design
Centre, London
(July 2002)**
Milan In A Van,
V&A museum, London
(Apr – June 2002)
**Big William, Salone
Satellite, Milan
Furniture Fair, Milan,
Italy (Apr 2002)**

UK RETAILERS:
**Contact Rose
Cobb studio for
stockists**

Rose Cobb
www.designbyrose.co.uk

One of the newest designers to be featured in *Design UK 2*, Rose Cobb has made an encouraging start to her career. After gaining a degree in architecture in 1996, this Manchester-raised designer began to see her chosen field as a pretentious and difficult industry to penetrate. So, she turned her love of detailing to furniture design and began a master's course in Furniture Design and Technology at Buckinghamshire Chilterns University in 2000.

Although now based in London's Bethnal Green, Rose Cobb is constantly moving homes. Noticing that this is a trait of many of her contemporaries, too, she has designed various well-received products to cope with a nomadic lifestyle. Wishing to find innovative solutions to everyday problems, this quietly ambitious designer always manages to add an element of humour to her creations.

Take the dilemma of moving heavy books to a new home. In most cases, it's a question of emptying pre-fixed shelving units and loading the books into boxes. Books-To-Go combats this problem by combining modular shelving with skateboard wheels. Stack them up for use as a bookshelf and the wheels allow you to reposition them in various rooms. When moving home, simply wheel them away to your new address.

Similarly, her Modular Chest of Drawers fuses furniture and luggage. Sitting on a base unit are three drawers that can be separated into suitcases and instantly taken away for holidays or to a new home with no need to pack.

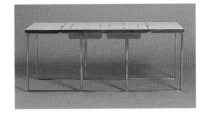

While possessing an outwardly serious aesthetic, this design benefits from an unmistakable element of quirkiness and wit. Addressing issues of space-saving with speed and ease of transportation, all of Rose Cobb's designs invoke a smile and the reaction 'Why didn't I think of that?' The designer, however, is primarily interested in fusing functions. She uses certain recognizable prefabricated components that make subtle references to alternative existing applications.

Rose Cobb is always looking for suitable manufacturers for her designs. She is acutely aware of production capabilities, and favours metals, woods and laminates for ease of manufacture. Taking an industrial viewpoint on design steers her away from the world of one-offs and craft. Not interested in simply re-styling existing objects, her architectural training very much influences her form-follows-function approach. The various functions explored in each piece inform the appearance, as illustrated in Turn Table (pictured), her exclusive design for *Design UK 2*, which begins as a coffee table and can be transformed into a dining table for two. Trays below the surface are intended for storage – their lids flip over to become place mats when the middle table section is raised to form the dining table.

STUDIO PLATFORM

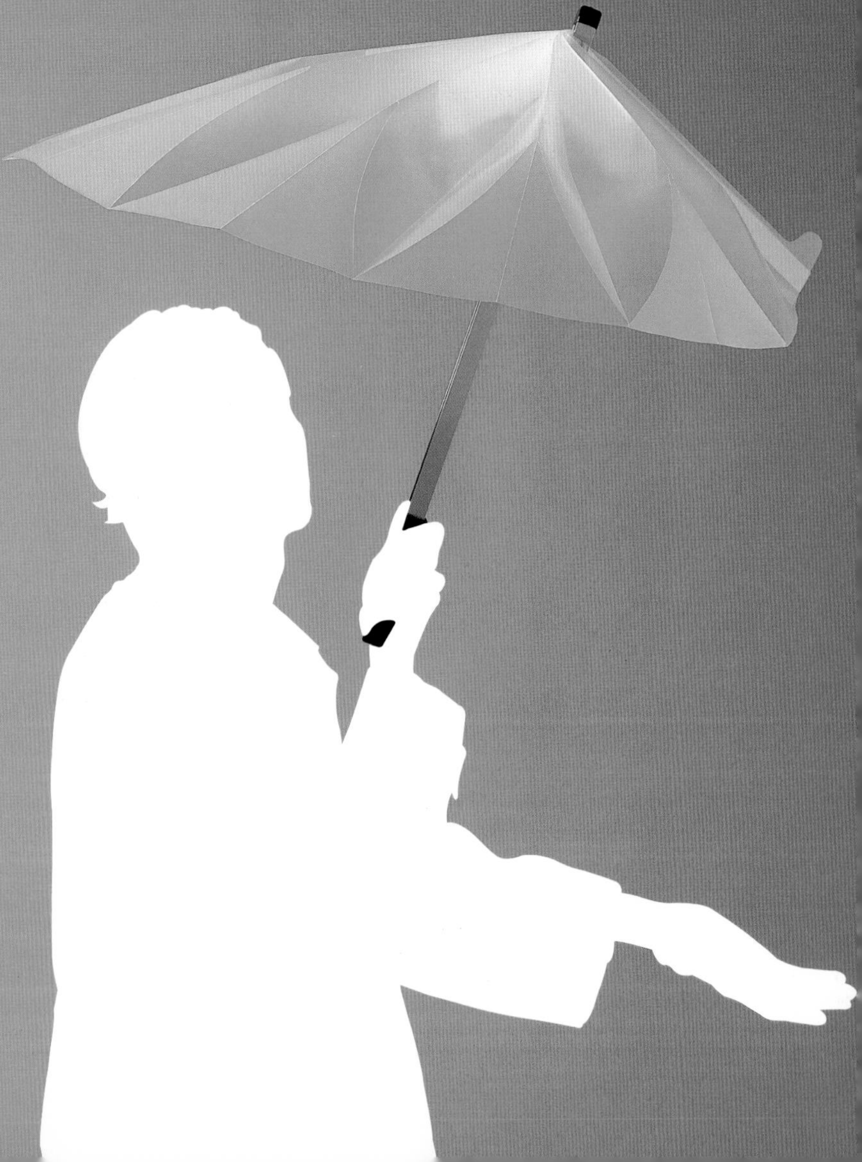

AWARDS:

Winners of Katha
Award (2002)

**Winners of Muji
International Design
Competition (2001)**

Winners of Kukuyo
Innovative Furniture
Design Award (2001)

**Silver prize, Pergo
International Flooring
Award (2001)**

Winners of Opus
International Eyewear
Design Competition
(2000)

**Winners of Sapporo
International Design
Competition (2000)**

Winners of Dalsouple
100% Design
Competition (2000)

**Winners of Corian
Design Award (1999)**

DESIGN EVENTS:

**Manila Fame
International, Manila,
Philippines (Oct 2002)**

Spot On, Salon Haute
Definition, Paris,
France (May 2002)

**Contemporary
Decorative Arts,
Sotheby's,
London (Feb 2002)**

Design UK Designer
Showcase,
Designersblock,
London (Sept 2001)

**The Show, Royal
College of Arts,
London (July 2001)**

Work In Progress,
Royal College of Arts,
London
(Apr 2000 & 2001)

UK RETAILERS:

Inflate, London

**Contact Studio Platform
for additional stockists**

Studio Platform
www.studioplatform.co.uk

The two talented designers who make up Studio Platform are Nick Jinkinson and Nick Paterson. They formed the business in 2001 after several successful project liaisons during their two-year course at London's Royal College of Art. There, the duo developed a mutual understanding of each other's design approach and were determined to explore a variety of creative processes that they could apply to commercial products with unique selling points. The result was the show-stopping chaise longue (pictured), chair and footstool collection made from flocked polypropylene that has been scored and folded to form a strong and comfortable seat, held together on a simple tubular steel structure. The genius of this piece lies in the calculated origami-like folding of a sheet material into a curvaceous and comfortable three-dimensional surface.

Inspiration for the duo comes from the world around them. They thrive on human error and turn restricting or annoying problems into opportunities for design solutions. Typical of this approach is their Bag Bin, which deals with the re-use of plastic carrier bags as refuse sacks. Studio Platform devised an elegant and cost-effective folded polypropylene bin with discreet wire supports to hold the bag, thus getting round the problem of how to keep the bag open without hooking it over a cupboard or door handle.

Attracting the attention of global retailing brand Muji, Studio Platform was asked to come up with a design for an umbrella. The solution (pictured), and published exclusively in *Design UK 2*, questions and reinvents the effectiveness of a normal umbrella. The awkward central positioning of your arm generally prevents you using the full circumference of the umbrella, resulting in a wet shoulder or back. Studio Platform's solution is to offset the positioning of the arm to allow a greater area of uninterrupted cover, at the same time avoiding the use of a wire support structure plus fabric. Polypropylene has been scored so that it folds away and can be opened out into a strong leaf-like umbrella structure.

Both designers insist that they are not stylists. Their approach is reminiscent of the founding principles of Modernism – form follows function – and they strive continually to achieve most from least, which, of course, has economic advantages that attract clients. Every design they introduce to the market must possess new function, otherwise they can't justify its existence in a world swamped with whimsical frivolities. Appearances are important in a product, but these designers work on the premise that good design results in good style.

Suck UK
www.suck.uk.com

The presence of the Suck UK brand continues to grow; since launching in June 1999, Sam and Jude's business has expanded beyond recognition. The owners, who never reveal their surnames, met when studying Product Design at Central St Martins but went their separate ways after graduation in 1996. Working as freelance designers, they rapidly became frustrated by mediocre projects and, meeting in the pub one day, decided to produce their own commercial products.

Suck UK was trialled at the Mode exhibition at the Business Design Centre in Islington, London, where the East End duo showcased a variety of prototypes to gauge the response from the public and trade buyers. Initial orders were positive and helped to bankroll production of Suck UK's most popular pieces.

The company established itself with a graphically strong brand identity stamped across all of its products, packaging, dispatch notes and promotional material. A confident outward image and attractive affordable contemporary products quickly earned the trust of buyers around the world. Increased production meant that UK manufacturing became more cost-effective. Sam and Jude quickly became swamped with administration and logistics. Now they employ three full-time staff and up to five more when busy.

So what is it about the company that attracts people? Is it the provocative name? Does its presence in numerous shops and endless design shows give added confidence to the consumer?

Do the reasonable prices attract customers? Even if the answers are all yes, it must still be the products. Sam and Jude are all too aware of the design industry's snobby reputation, and have always designed products that remain non-exclusive and accessible, due to sensible and realistic pricing as well as consistent and clear packaging.

Using elements of humour without resorting to kitsch or parody, their products always manage to grab your attention. The Slide Light and Illuminating Coffee Table (pictured) were responsible for Suck UK's initial wave of good press and still sell well. As the company continues to grow, so does its knowledge of manufacturing processes, allowing for a diversity of products and material usage seen across the collection. More recently, the duo have embraced the use of polished sheet stainless steel, which they have pressed for the Bulb wall light and the Bottle Opener Fridge Magnet. As part of this series, and as an exclusive design for *Design UK 2*, the duo have created a polished steel floor light (pictured), which emits a reflective glow from the top, with a touch of red reflected off the barely visible back panel through a thin slit running down the front section.

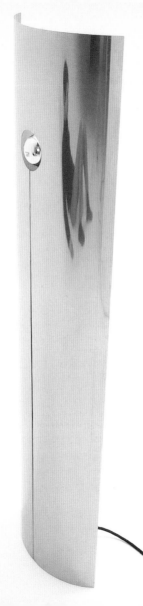

DESIGN EVENTS:
PROTOTYPE UK,
Designersblock,
London (Sept 2002)
100% Design,
Earls Court,
London (Sept 2002)
Tendence, Frankfurt,
Germany (Aug 2002)
Salone del Mobile,
Milan Furniture Fair,
Italy (April 2002)
Future Map 01,
London Institute
Gallery, London
(Nov 2001)
Happy Hour, Mint,
London (Oct 2001)
New Designers,
Business Design
Centre, London
(July 2001)

UK RETAILERS:
Aria, London
Purves & Purves,
London
Viaduct, London
Contact two create
studio for additional
stockists

two create
www.twocreate.co.uk

Lucy Nunn and Tobie Snowdowne formed two create, a multidisciplinary design partnership, not long after graduating from Central St Martins in 2001. The couple first met when interviewed for the foundation course, but it wasn't until their second year of a degree course in Product Design that they identified their shared enthusiasm for design and an ability to work together efficiently on the various elements of a project.

In the months following their success at the New Designers exhibition at London's Business Design Centre in July 2001, two create were approached about a variety of projects. Tobie Snowdowne's final-year project was the Surface Chair (pictured), made from an uncomplicated yet cleverly cut and wrapped aluminium structure covered in carpet. The design was snapped up by MDF Italia, which put it into production as part of its '10 projects for the future' collection, launched in Milan in April 2002. Lucy Nunn's playful stationery collection Office Playtime, which deals with the boredom, frustrations and stress threshold of working in an office, caught the attentions of Worldwide Co. They added it to their range the same year.

The appeal of these designers is their ability to redefine function with the invention of new forms, while considering realistic production capabilities and commercial implications. They concern themselves with the misuse of existing objects and aim to create new functions to which everyday consumers can relate. Their designs have a quirky appeal and

a beauty that suit a gallery environment as well as an interior setting. The designs fall somewhere between experimental and commercial. This is illustrated by the Polished Concept mirror (pictured), designed for *Design UK 2*, that fits perfectly into the existing range of products while furthering two create's exploration of processes, materials and functions. The mirror is created using highly polished, mirrored, stainless-steel sheet from Avestapolarit. This has been laser-cut, folded and lacquered to create a lightweight, multifunctional object. When not in use, the mirror stands alone as an object of beauty.

Two create's collection deals with the manipulation of flat sheet or rod material into tantalizing three-dimensional objects. This approach isn't new, but somehow the duo manage to strike new ground with it every time.

Learning the harsh realities of trying to succeed as designers in the UK, two create are determined to infiltrate the industry at varying levels: by working on their own collections and those for other manufacturers, trend prediction, consultancy work, material development, and interior and graphic work.

In the first edition of *Design UK*, the following designers were featured in the Designers chapter. Since then, they have gone on to tackle a considerable amount of interesting new projects and this section summarises those ongoing business progressions.

Amy Cushing

Amy continues to add more vibrant flat kiln-formed glasswork to her collection as well as new designs for the Mosquito Murano collection. She secures an increasing number of commissions for interiors, including glass tiles, partitions, wall pieces, and window installations. In 2002, she launched the Isabelle Starling collection of jewellery in collaboration with Ben Day using bespoke pieces of glass set with precious metals and gemstones. In the same year, she was commissioned by Wedgwood to design and produce a collection of glassware.

Anthony Dickens
www.anthonydickens.com

Anthony's proactive nature and energetic imagination has resulted in a variety of projects developing product concepts for Audi, Blockbuster, and Rizla, whilst working on lighting commissions for Purves & Purves, Slug & Lettuce, Elbow Rooms, Powergen, and a range of office accessories and kids toys for AKTA. While continuing his on-going private interior work, Anthony's latest project was the design of AKTA's first retail premises in the O2 Centre on London's Finchley Road.

Bodo Sperlein
www.bodosperlein.com

'The modern master of bone china' (*Independent on Sunday*), Bodo Sperlein continues to develop his own-label ranges with the introduction of The Red Berry Collection that incorporates abstract pattern to his signature white bone china tableware. Recently, Bodo has begun designing in pewter, which has resulted in a collaboration with Mulberry on a pewter and leather gift collection. Nahm, the award-winning Michelin-starred Thai restaurant at the Halkin Hotel now serves its immaculate dishes on Bodo's refined tableware. He has also designed a fireplace for CVO Firevault (p 66).

Carl Clerkin

Over the last two years Carl has worked with Gitta Gschwendtner on various products for Habitat. His work with William Warren of WW.Modcons produced clever, humorous items including a bathroom cabinet, mailbox, and house number plates. Commissioned by the Design Council, the duo also designed future school furniture. Carl's work continues to appear in international exhibitions.

Caterina Fadda
www.caterinafadda.com

Caterina maintains her shop/studio space in London's OXO Tower (p 172), where she works on designs for her collection together with new colours in her ceramic ranges. As well as taking part in several international design competitions and exhibitions, Caterina has increased the consultancy side of her business while continuing with her own label production.

Ella Doran
www.elladoran.co.uk

Ella Doran has built up an enviable brand reputation since first launching her design tablemats in 1996. International demand has continually grown over the years so

Ella has secured a worldwide distributor to deal with orders so that she can focus her attention on new design work. Whilst expanding her own range, she has developed a range of tableware and accessories for Portmeirion Potteries and a range of gift products exclusively for Tate Enterprises. She is currently working on bathroom and bedding projects.

El Ultimo Grito

El Ultimo Grito, comprising Roberto Feo and Rosario Hurtado, have continued to grow from strength to strength. The duo manages a healthy balance between 'real world' and self-initiated projects coupled with numerous international exhibitions. Their unique and humorous approach to problem solving has resulted in a variety of projects for Trico, Hidden, Mathmos, Anura, Bloomberg, Moroso, and Lavazza.

Fiona Davidson

Fiona continues to flourish as a freelance designer working on products, exhibition design, and interiors. Her conceptual approach has proved a strong match with that of Gitta Gschwendtner and the two have worked together on a variety of projects such as material-led liaisons with DuPont Corian in 2000 and the European Council of Vinyl Manufacturers in 2001. They also designed the interior of advertising agency Wieden + Kennedy's new offices.

Georg Baldele

The last two years has seen Georg Baldele's reputation grow considerably. His attention has turned towards the marvels of crystal resulting in various projects with Swarovski, including window installations in their new Brompton Road store. His glamorous contemporary crystal chandeliers have been installed in many private and commercial environments including SoHo House in New York and The Geffrye Museum in London. His Niagara Light made from Crystal fabric was installed in The Design Museum (p 76), and his papier mâché Caveman furniture has been exhibited internationally with Japanese group Sputnik.

Geraldine McGloin
www.geraldinemcgloin.com

Geraldine McGloin continues to design and produce handmade ceramic designs in her new studio in London's East End. Always striving for quality over quantity, she has brought her work to a wider audience through various international exhibitions whilst working on commissions for presentation pieces. Her network of retailers continues to grow despite her decision to avoid the mass-production of her high quality ceramic tableware.

Gitta Gschwendtner

Gitta's reputation has continued to grow since the first edition of *Design UK*, as more companies and institutions have chosen to employ the rather quirky yet commercial skills of this German-born designer. Working on self-initiated projects, exhibitions, and collaborations, Gitta has also worked on new products for the likes of Mathmos, Purves & Purves, and Innermost. In addition, her talent for exhibition design has been called upon by the Crafts Council, the Victoria & Albert Museum, and the Science Museum.

Happell
www.happell.co.uk

Dene Happell's business has certainly witnessed an increase in the number of contract and domestic interior projects over the last few years. Mainly working on projects in Glasgow and Edinburgh, 2002 namely saw Dene redesigning and developing the brand identity of the Small Business Gateway offices in Scotland. His collection of 3D tiles were launched in 2001 and received noticeable acclaim in London, Milan, and New York in 2002, resulting in their manufacture and distribution by Canadian company Lolah.

Hive
www.hivespace.com

Hive's well-known range of furniture and accessories has had several new successful additions, such as the Circulation and Cityscape felt rugs (winner of the Textile Category at the OXO Peugeot Design Awards 2002); the Orbit chair with pelleted felt upholstery; and the Meta collection of stainless steel accessories. Owners Monika Piatkowski and Mark Dyson have launched Hive:Enclosure as a separate interior design consultancy, and the couple have worked on several commissions including a fire accessory range for CVO Fire (p 66).

Hub
www.hub-design.co.uk

Anna Thomson and Andrew Tanner's business reputation has rocketed over the last two years and so too has their collection of contemporary ceramic products. Continually adding to the Hub in-house collection, the duo has increased their client list to incorporate interior designers, restaurants, and international retail outlets in the likes of New York, Hong Kong, Paris, and Copenhagen. Clients include Ted Baker, Alexander McQueen, DKNY, Virgin Atlantic, and Fitch Architects. 2003 sees Anna and Andrew concentrating on more research-based projects working closely with architects, specifiers, and retail outlets.

Lynne Wilson
www.lynnewilson.co.uk

Lynne Wilson's passion for designing has been identified by several companies over the last few years resulting in a number of freelance projects involving exhibition and stand design as well as furniture designs for Purves & Purves and Volume Furniture. She has continued to develop her own design ideas such as the Modern Heroes clock collection whilst undertaking a part time accessory design and making course at the London College of Fashion.

Maké Design
www.limarhaban.com

Make Design, now trading as Li Marhaban Design Ltd, has turned it's focus away from pure product design by moving into the realm of interior commission work. Working on a number of private installations, Li Marhaban has collaborated with architects in Amsterdam on a steady stream of both domestic and commercial restorations in the capital's conservation areas. Still operating from his London workshop, Li has introduced a new coat hook design to his range as well as coat hangers for a Japanese boutique owned by Comme des Garcons.

Marc Boase
www.marcboase.com

While adding more stunning ceramic tableware designs to his well known collection, Marc has spent the last few years working on domestic and commercial furniture and interior commissions: these include a salon in Shoreditch, a tailor in Brighton, and interiors for Mark Williams and Steve Coogan. He has set up a design consultancy with architect Stan Jones called Bones Partnership that covers the design spectrum from graphics to architecture.

Max Shepherd

In 2001, Max Shepherd's career direction changed when he opened Goodge, a bar on London's Goodge Street. With his business partners, he has transformed the premises into a popular drinking venue. This venture has temporarily pulled him away from his design roots, but he plans to make a comeback on the design scene in 2003 with his own collection of furniture.

Nelson
www.julienelson.co.uk

In early 2002, Julie Nelson developed her ceramic interior lighting for use as outdoor sculptures placed over floor-mounted garden lights. Incorporating more texture and larger dimensions, the range has been well received, much like her interior work. Julie has also been working with manufacturers on other accessory designs. Her biggest project was the design of the interior and exterior of a magnificent beach house in East Sussex, complete in summer 2003.

One Foot Taller
www.onefoottaller.com

Katarina Barac now runs One Foot Taller independently, since her partner decided to pursue a career working for Dyson. It was always their intention to operate as a design consultancy, which has resulted in a diversity of projects such as recycling containers for K2 Products; an innovative clipping devise for lorry advertising; design of loft apartment interiors in collaboration with Timorous Beasties; further development of The Arches complex in Glasgow; and a bar and noodle kitchen called Soba. For OFT's own range, Katarina has developed the Ethal range of lights and a new plastic outdoor bench, as well as some new products for Habitat's Pop range in 2003.

Tom Kirk
www.tomkirk.com

Tom Kirk has redirected his focus from product-orientated designs for retail towards a more commission-based approach. Working with architects, interior designers and specifiers, Tom has undertaken a number of high-impact bespoke lighting installations over the last two years for both commercial and domestic interiors. His chandelier has proved a big hit and has been installed in some of the stores of Gina Shoes Ltd, Hudson Shoes, and Oasis. He has undertaken some branding work for Carling, as well as working with Fox Linton Associates and Site Specific Ltd on private houses.

WW.Modcons

William Warren's work continues to epitomize the renowned wit and irony of British design. The Japanese distributor Trico has courted his approach resulting in a collection in 2001. He was involved in a project to promote pine for the Scandinavian group Wood for Good at Purves & Purves in 2002 whilst also working on a design program for BBC2. His attitude towards design is similar to that of Carl Clerkin and the two designers have worked collaboratively on various projects – both were awarded a grant by the Design Council to develop furniture for secondary schools.

APPLIED ARTS AGENCY BABY
NOEL HENNESSY FURNITURE
BOOM! INTERIORS CRAFTS CO
ARAM COLSTON + CO DAVID
LIGNE ROSET CAZ SYSTEMS
FORM ABODE INTERIORS MA
OGGETTI AREA SQUARED DE
RAISBECK & REASON SELFRID
CONCRETE BUTTERFLY POLIF
THE LONDON LIGHTING CO.
MOMENTUM RJM FURNITURE
PURVES & PURVES MINT UN
DE LA ESPADA FERRIOUS@H

INFLATE LEIGH BUCKLAND
OMUS TWO COLUMBIA ROAD
NCIL GALLERY SHOP WHIPPET
LLOR THEMES & VARIATIONS
BURBIA INDISH KEY LONDON
ONETTE PLACES AND SPACES
GN EAT MY HANDBAG BITCH
ES CHARLES PAGE THE HOME
M ONE PONTCANNA STREET
SSEL **DIRECTORY** BOWWOW
OMANE INTERIORS CENTURY
THIS LAST DESIGNERS GUILD
E HABITAT BACK 2 MY PLACE

LONDON CENTRAL

Alessi 22 Brook Street, London W1K 5DF 020 7518 9091 www.alessi.com

Alma 8 Vigo Street, London W1S 3HJ 020 7439 0925 www.almahome.co.uk

Aram 110 Drury Lane, London WC2B 5SG 020 7557 7557 www.aram.co.uk

Artemide 90–92 Great Portland Street, London W1W 7JY 020 7631 5200 www.artemide.com

Century 68 Marylebone High Street, London W1U 5JH 020 7487 5100 www.centuryd.com

Chaplins 17–18 Berners Street, London W1T 3LN 020 7323 6552 www.chaplins.co.uk

The Conran Shop 55 Marylebone High Street, London W1U 5HS 020 7723 2223 www.conran.com
12 Conduit Street, London W1S 2XQ 020 7399 0710

CVO Firevault 36 Great Titchfield Street, London W1W 8BQ 020 7580 5333 www.cvofirevault.co.uk

Habitat 196 Tottenham Court Road, London W1T 7LG 020 7631 3880 www.habitat.net

Heal's 196 Tottenham Court Road, London W1T 7LQ 020 7636 1666 www.heals.co.uk

Key London 92 Wimpole Street, London W1G 0EG 020 7499 9461 www.key-london.com

Ligne Roset 23–25 Mortimer Street, London W1N 7RJ 020 7323 1248 www.lrwestend.co.uk
For nationwide stores 0870 77 77 202 www.ligne-roset.co.uk

Mint 70 Wigmore Street, London W1U 2SF 020 7224 4406

Noel Hennessy Furniture 6 Cavendish Square, London W1G 0PD 020 7323 3360 www.noelhennessy.com

Purves & Purves 222 Tottenham Court Road, London W1T 7QE 020 7580 8223 www.purves.co.uk

Selfridges 400 Oxford Street, London W1A 1AB 08708 377 377 www.selfridges.co.uk

Skandium 72 Wigmore Street, London W1U 2SG 020 7935 2077 www.skandium.com

Tom Tom 42 New Compton Street, London WC2H 8DA 020 7240 7909 www.tomtomshop.co.uk

LONDON NORTH AND NORTH WEST

Area Squared Design 9 Camden Passage, London N1 8EA 020 7704 2734

Aria 295–297 Upper Street, London N1 2TU 020 7704 1999 www.ariashop.co.uk
133 Upper Street, London N1 1QP 020 7226 1021

BOOM! Interiors 115–117 Regents Park Road, London NW1 8UR 020 7722 6622 www.boominteriors.com

Charles Page 61 Fairfax Road, London NW6 4EE 020 7328 9851 www.charlespage.co.uk

Crafts Council Gallery Shop 44a Pentonville Road, London N1 9BY 020 7806 2559
www.craftscouncil.org.uk

Fandango 50 Cross Street, London N1 2BA 020 7226 1777 www.fandango.uk.com

Geoffrey Drayton 85 Hampstead Road, London NW1 2PL 020 7387 5840 www.geoffrey-drayton.co.uk

Indish 13 & 16 Broadway Parade, London N8 9DE 020 8342 9496 www.indish.co.uk

Living Space 36 Cross Street, London N1 2BG 020 7359 3950 www.intospace.co.uk

Maisonette 79 Chamberlayne Road, London NW10 3ND 020 8964 8444 www.maisonette.uk.com

Planet Bazaar 149 Drummond Street, London NW1 2PB 020 7387 8326 www.planetbazaar.co.uk

RJM Furniture 203 Kentish Town Road, London NW5 2JU 020 7428 9761 www.rjmfurniture.com
Gainsborough Studios, 1 Poole Street, London N1 5EA

Twentytwentyone 274 Upper Street, London N1 2UA 020 7288 1996 www.twentytwentyone.com

LONDON WEST

Bowles and Linares 32 Hereford Road, London W2 5AJ 020 7229 9886 www.bowlesandlinares.co.uk

BOWWOW 70 Princedale Road, London W11 4NL 020 7792 8532 www.bowwow.co.uk

Flow 1–5 Needham Road, London W11 2RP 020 7243 0782 www.flowgallery.co.uk

14 Holland Street 14 Holland Street, London W8 4LT 020 7938 2244

Isokon Plus Turnham Green Terrace Mews, Chiswick, London W4 1QU 020 8994 0636
www.isokonplus.com

Mission 45 Hereford Road, London W2 5AH 020 7792 4633 www.intomission.com

Themes & Variations 231 Westbourne Grove, London W11 2SE 020 7727 5531
www.themesandvariations.co.uk

Vessel 114 Kensington Park Road, London W11 2PW 020 7727 8001 www.vesselgallery.com

LONDON SOUTH AND SOUTH WEST

B&B Italia 250 Brompton Road, London SW3 2AS 020 7591 8111 www.bebitalia.it

Babylon 301 Fulham Road, London SW10 9QH 020 7376 7255 www.babylonlondon.com

Chaplins 118–120 Brompton Road, London SW3 1JJ 020 7589 7897 www.chaplins.co.uk

Christopher Farr 6 Burnsall Street, London SW3 3ZJ 020 7349 0888 www.cfarr.co.uk

The Conran Shop Michelin House, 81 Fulham Road, London SW3 6RD 020 7589 7401 www.conran.com

Conran 2 350 King's Road, London SW3 5UU 020 7559 1140 www.conran.com

Crafts Council Shop at the V&A Victoria & Albert Museum, South Kensington, London SW7 2RL
020 7589 5070 www.craftscouncil.org.uk

David Mellor 4 Sloane Square, London SW1 8EE 020 7730 4259 www.davidmellordesign.com

De La Espada 60 Sloane Avenue, London SW3 3DD 020 7581 4474 www.delaespada.com

Designers Guild 267–271 & 275–277 King's Road, London SW3 5EN 020 7351 5775
www.designersguild.com

Design Museum Shop 28 Shad Thames, London SE1 2YD 020 7940 8773 www.designmuseum.org

Leigh Buckland 40–42 Old Town, London SW4 0LB 020 7720 5353 www.leighbuckland.com

The London Lighting Co. 135 Fulham Road, London SW3 6RT 020 7589 3612

Oggetti 143 Fulham Road, London SW3 6SD 020 7581 8088

OXO Tower Wharf Bargehouse Street, South Bank, London SE1 9PH 020 7401 2255 www.oxotower.co.uk

Places and Spaces 30 Old Town, London SW4 0LB 020 7498 0998 www.placesandspaces.com

Poliform 278 King's Road, London SW3 5AW 020 7368 7600 www.poliform.it

POP UK 278 Upper Richmond Road, Putney, London SW15 6TQ 020 8788 8811 www.popuk.com
17 High Street, Wimbledon Village, London SW19 5DX 020 8946 1122

Rabih Hage 69–71 Sloane Avenue, London SW3 3DH 020 7823 8288 www.rabih-hage.com

Right Angle 34 Tranquil Vale, London SE3 0AX 020 8852 8857

Sarf 99 St John's Hill, London SW11 1SY 020 7228 0005 www.sarf.co.uk

Whippet 190 Upper Richmond Road West, London SW14 8AN 020 8878 3141

LONDON EAST

Applied Arts Agency 30 Exmouth Market, London EC1R 4QE 020 7837 2632 www.appliedartsagency.co.uk

Budge & Coward 67 Roman Road, London E2 0QN 020 8980 8837 www.budgeandcoward.com

Eat My Handbag Bitch 6 Dray Walk, The Old Truman Brewery, 91–95 Brick Lane, London E1 6QL
020 7375 3100 www.eatmyhandbagbitch.co.uk

Flin Flon 138 St John Street, London EC1V 4UA 020 7253 8849 www.flinflon.co.uk

Her House 30d Great Sutton Street, London EC1V 0DU 020 7689 0606 www.herhouse.uk.com

Inflate 28 Exmouth Market, London EC1R 4QE 020 7713 9096 www.inflate.co.uk

Ligne Roset 37–39 Commercial Road, London E1 1LF (no telephone number at time of going to press)

Lowe Interiors 18 Exmouth Market, London EC1R 4QE 020 7278 1140 www.loweinteriors.co.uk

Mac London 142 Clerkenwell Road, London EC1R 5DL 020 7713 1234 www.mac-london.com

Morris & Co 387 The Arches, Geffrye Street, London E2 8HZ 020 7739 8539 www.morrisandco.co.uk

Overdose on Design 182 Brick Lane, London E1 6SA 020 7613 1266 www.overdoseondesign.com

Purves & Purves Unit 4, Canada Place, Canary Wharf, London E14 5AH 020 7719 1169 www.purves.co.uk

SCP 135–139 Curtain Road, London EC2A 3BX 020 7739 1869 www.scp.co.uk

Twentytwentyone 274 Upper Street, London EC1R 1XN 020 7288 1996 www.twentytwentyone.com

Two Columbia Road 2 Columbia Road, London E2 7NN 020 7729 9933 www.twocolumbiaroad.com

Unto This Last 230 Brick Lane, London E2 7EB www.untothislast.co.uk

Viaduct 1–10 Summer's Street, London EC1R 5BD 020 7278 8456 www.viaduct.co.uk

Vitra 30 Clerkenwell Road, London EC1M 5PQ 020 7608 6200 www.vitra.com

SOUTH EAST ENGLAND

Caz Systems 17–19 Church Street, Brighton BN1 1RB 01273 326 471 www.cazsystems.com

Central 33–35 Little Clarendon Street, Oxford OX1 2HU 01865 311 141 www.central-furniture.co.uk

Chaplins 477–507 Uxbridge Road, Hatch End, Pinner, Middlesex HA5 4JS 020 8421 1779
        www.chaplins.co.uk

Geoffrey Drayton 104 High Street, Epping, Essex CM16 4AF 01992 573 929 www.geoffrey-drayton.co.uk

Mojoe 24 Church Street, Brighton BN1 1RB 01273 208 708 www.mojoe.co.uk

RHA Furniture 133–135 Kew Road, Richmond, Surrey TW9 2PN 020 8332 8715 www.rhafurniture.com

Roost 26 Kensington Gardens, Brighton BN1 4AL 01273 625 223

Schiang 58 Holywell Hill, St Albans, Hertfordshire AL1 1BX 08702 202 055 www.schiang.com

SOUTH WEST AND WALES

Back 2 my Place 5 Ivor House, Bridge Street, Cardiff CF10 2EE 029 2040 0800 www.b2mp.com

Mart 8 Jacobs Wells Road, Hotwells, Bristol BS8 1EA 0117 904 3245

Momentum 31 Charles Street, Cardiff CF10 2GA 029 2023 6266 www.momentumcardiff.com

One Pontcanna Street 1 Pontcanna Street, Cardiff CF11 9HQ 02920 388 499
        www.onepontcannastreet.com

Seduti 8–10 High Street Arcade, Cardiff CF1 1BB 029 2037 2523 www.seduti.com

Suburbia 17 Regent Street, Clifton, Bristol BS8 4HW 0117 974 3880

The Wedge 9 Catherine Hill, Frome BA11 1BY 01373 472 077

MIDLANDS

Abode Interiors 7–9 Market Place, Leicester LE1 5GG 0116 262 9909 www.abode-interiors.co.uk

Atomic Interiors Furniture Showroom, Plumptre Square, Nottingham NG1 1JF 0115 941 5577
www.atomicinteriors.co.uk
Accessories & Gifts, 14 Exchange Arcade, Nottingham NG1 2DD

Capsule 126 Charles Street, Leicester LE1 1LB 0116 262 6932 www.capsulefurniture.co.uk

Fusion 30 Church Street, Birmingham B3 2NP 0121 236 1020 www.fusionlifestyle.co.uk

Mooch 321 Bradford Street, Birmingham B5 6ET 0121 622 0390 www.mooch.eu.com

Raisbeck & Reason 29 Regent Street, Leamington Spa, Warwickshire CV32 5EJ 01926 889 879
www.raisbeckandreason.co.uk

Shannon 68 Walcot Street, Bath BA1 5BD 01225 424 222 www.shannon-uk.com

XU 55 Cornwall Street, Birmingham B3 2DH 0121 236 6060 www.xux.co.uk

NORTH ENGLAND

David Mellor The Round Building, Hathersage, Sheffield S32 1BA 01433 650 220
www.davidmellordesign.com

Domane Interiors Union House, 5 Bridge Street, Leeds LS2 7RF 0113 245 0701 www.domaneinteriors.co

Domus Constance House, 117 High Street, Norton, Stockton-on-Tees TS20 1AA 01642 649 411

Ferrious @ Home Arch 61 Whitworth Street West, Manchester M1 5WQ 0161 228 6880
www.ferrious.co.uk

Form 6 The Plaza, West One, 8 Fitzwilliam Street, Sheffield S1 4JB 01142 758700 www.formliving.com

The Home Salts Mill, Victoria Road, Saltaire, Bradford BD18 3LB 01274 530 770
www.saltsmill.org.uk/thehome

The Humble Abode 7 Garden Street, Sheffield S1 4BJ 0114 272 8999 www.thehumbleabode.co.uk

Innerform 24 Hulme Street, Manchester M1 5BW 0161 238 8558 www.innerform.com

Lloyd Davies 14 John Dalton Street, Manchester M2 6JR 0161 832 3700 www.lloyddavies.co.uk

Loft 24–28 Dock Street, Leeds LS10 1JF 0113 305 1515 www.loftonline.net

Mason 70 North Street, Leeds LS2 7PN 0113 242 2434 www.masonfurniture.com

Mooch 321 Bradford Street, Birmingham B5 6ET 0121 622 0390 www.mooch.eu.com

Prego No 7 The Plaza, West One, 8 Fitzwilliam Street, Sheffield S1 4JB 0114 275 5512

The Room Store Grand Hall, Albert Dock, Liverpool L3 4AA 0151 708 0000 www.theroomstore.co.uk

Selfridges 1 Exchange Square, Manchester M3 1BD 08708 377 377 www.selfridges.co.uk
No 1 The Dome, The Trafford Centre, Manchester M17 8DA

Snowhome 38 Gillygate, York YO31 7EQ 01904 671 155 www.snow-home.co.uk

Tempter 12a Nelson Street, Newcastle upon Tyne, NE1 5AW 0191 230 2251 www.tempterinteriors.com

Unique Interiors 252–256 Whitegate Drive, Blackpool FY3 9JW 01253 698 989 www.uniqueinteriors.co.uk

Utility 85 Bold Street, Liverpool L1 4HF 0151 707 9919 www.utilityretail.co.uk
86 Bold Street, Liverpool L1 4HY 0151 708 4192

SCOTLAND

Concrete Butterfly 317–319 Cowgate, Old Town, Edinburgh EH1 1NA 0131 558 7130
www.concretebutterfly.com

Dallas + Dallas 18 Montrose Street, Glasgow G1 1RE 0141 552 2939 www.dallasanddallas.com

Designshop 116 Causewayside, Edinburgh EH9 1PU 0131 667 7078 www.designshop.eu.com

Form First Floor, The Lighthouse, 11 Mitchell Lane, Glasgow G1 3LX 0141 225 8422
www.thelighthouse.co.uk

Inhouse Edinburgh 28 Howe Street, Edinburgh EH3 6TG 0131 225 2888 www.inhousenet.co.uk

Inhouse Glasgow 24–26 Wilson Street, Glasgow G1 1SS 0141 552 5902 www.inhousenet.co.uk

Tangram 33–37 Jeffrey Street, Edinburgh EH1 1DH 0131 556 6551 www.tangramfurnishers.co.uk

Tony Walker Interiors Whitehall Court, 14 Telford Road, Edinburgh EH4 2BD 0131 343 6151
www.tonywalkerinteriors.com
70 Ingram Street, Glasgow G1 1EX 0141 574 1340

NORTHERN IRELAND

Batik Metthr-Hoose Raa, The GasWorks, Belfast, BT7 2JA 028 9024 9311 www.batikonline.co.uk

Equinox 32 Howard Street, Belfast BT1 6PF 028 9023 0089 www.e-equinox.co.uk

Lounge 13 Wellington Place, Belfast BT1 6GB 028 9024 4474

CHANNEL ISLANDS

Colston + Co 4 West Centre, St Helier, Jersey JE2 4ST, Channel Islands 01534 510 300
www.colstonandco.co.uk

ACKNOWLEDGEMENTS

Author's Acknowledgments

The author would like to thank all of the shop owners and their staff, designers, manufacturers, photographers, PR agencies, and advisors who gave their time to this book. More specifically, he would like to thank: his agent and friend, Alexei Orlov; the Conran Octopus team, specifically Katey Day, Lorraine Dickey, Chi Lam, and Liz Boyd; Michael Johnson, Kath Tudball, and Julia Woollams at johnson banks; and the numerous friends and family for their encouragement and support.

Publisher's Acknowledgments

Conran Octopus would like to thank all contributing shops, designers and the following manufacturers and photographers for their kind permissions to reproduce their images in this book.

2 Ingo Maurer; 10–11 Cuckooland; 12 Alessi; 13 Modus Publicity; 14 David Couple; 20 Fabian Ferrari; 22 Simon Howard; 26–27 Simon Siegel; 28–29 B&B Italia/Camron PR; 35 Zanotta; 40–41 Chris Tubbs; 42–43 Paul Kennerley; 45 Simon Siegel; 46–47 Foscarini/Ergo PR; 48 Hitch Mylius Ltd.; 51 Pure Design, Canada; 52–53 Cappellini/ Victoria Murray PR; 56–57 Christopher Farr Ltd; 62–63 The Conran Shop; 64 Samantha Sweet; 65 Crafts Council; 70 David Mellor Design; 71 Architects: Sir Michael Hopkins & Partners; 74–75 Designers Guild; 76 Jefferson Smith; 78–79 Gus Campbell Photography; 81 Domane Interiors; 82 Unique Interieur; 83 Nikolas Barrera; 84–85 Chris Tubbs; 86–87 twenty two over seven architects; 88 Jonathan Ellis; 91 Studio 2 Photography Ltd; 92 Marianna Wahlsten; 95 Barry Griffiths; 96–97 F Mccourt 2002; 98–99 iittala; 100–101Mark Humphrey Design Ltd; 102–103 Tuomas Jaaskelainen; 104–105 Guy Drayton; 106–107 Habitat; 108–109 Heal's; 110–111 Studio Myerscough; 112–113 Justin Slee/ Salts Estates Ltd.; 120 Driade; 122–123 Jan Chlebik; 130 Ligne Roset; 134–135 David Burrow 136–137 Loft; 138–139 Elizabeth Brown 140–141 Magis; 146–147 Maisonette; 150 Tagliabue/Bian Furniture; 152 Uli Schade; 154–155 Jens Marott (Misha Stefan Architects); 162 Ian Scigiuzzi; 164–165 Paul Ellis; 166–167 Elizabeth Brown; 170–171 chairs designed by Eames, 1953 (fibreglass, metal and wood) by Charles Eames (1907–80) and Ray (1912–88), Private Collection/ Bonhams, London, UK / Bridgeman Art Library; 172 Timothy Soar; 173 Peter Durant/Arcblue; 174 Nick Hannam; 178–179 Poliform/Phyllis Walters PR; 180 D.D'urbino & P.Lomazzi; 181 Po UK 182 Artifort; 184–185 Purves & Purves press 186–187 Camron PR; 189 Pianca; 191 Pierantoni Bonacina; 196–197 The Room Store; 200–201 Steve Brown; 204 James Merrell; 208–209 Selfridges; 210–211 Paul O'Connor/The Walcot Studio; 212–213 Skandium Press; 214–215 Cloud Nine; 216–217 Magis; 220–221 Kevin Gibson; 222–223 Themes & Variations; 224–225 Graham Mancha; 226–227 Paul Graham; 228 Mark Whitfield; 229 Paul Tyagi; 232 de Sede; 234–235 Sophie Broadbridge; 238–239 Orrefors; 240 MD Italia; 242 Jean Prouvé/Cité chair/Hans Hansen/ Vitra; 243 Matthew Sowerby/The Lighthouse Trust; 244–245 The Wedge; 246–247 Lina Ikse Bergman; p253–266 Tom Stewart/Conran Octopus; 267 Studio Fusion; 268 Tom Stewart/ Conran Octopus; 269 Hannah Dipper; 270 Tom Stewart/Conran Octopus; 273–287 Tom Stewart/Conran Octopus; 287 Studio Platform; 288 Suck UK; 289–290 Tom Stewart/Conran Octopus; 291 MDF Italia/Viaduct

The author has made every effort to ensure that the information contained in this book is correct and up to date at the time of publication He apologizes in advance for any unintentional omissions and would be pleased to include up-dated information in subsequent editions.